U.S.
UNCLE
SAM

written by **STEVE DARNALL**

co-plotted &
illustrated by **ALEX ROSS**

lettered by **TODD KLEIN**

UNCLE SAM
ISBN 1 84023 083 5

Published by Titan Books Ltd., 42-44
Dolben St., London SE1 0UP under licence
from DC Comics.
Cover, introduction and compilation
copyright © 1999 DC Comics.
All Rights Reserved.

Originally published in single magazine
form as UNCLE SAM 1-2. Copyright
© 1997 DC Comics. All Rights Reserved.
All characters, their distinctive likenesses
and related indicia featured in this
publication are trademarks of DC Comics.
The stories, characters, and incidents
featured in this publication are entirely
fictional.

Printed in Canada
10 9 8 7 6 5 4 3 2 1
First Edition: October 1999

Cover illustration by Alex Ross.

To order titles from the backlist page,
please quote reference code US/GN.

Jenette Kahn
President & Editor-in-Chief

Paul Levitz
Executive Vice President & Publisher

Karen Berger
Executive Editor and
Editor-original series

Bob Kahan and Rick Taylor
Editors-collected edition

Joan Hilty
Assistant Editor-original series

Jim Spivey
Associate Editor-collected edition

Georg Brewer
Design Director

Robbin Brosterman
Art Director

Richard Bruning
VP-Creative Director

Patrick Caldon
VP-Finance & Operations

Dorothy Crouch
VP-Licensed Publishing

Terri Cunningham
VP-Managing Editor

Joel Ehrlich
Senior VP-Advertising & Promotions

Lillian Laserson
VP & General Counsel

Bob Rozakis
Executive Director-Production

Bob Wayne
VP-Direct Sales

It's a strangled, tortured cry — the cry of patriotism.

That's the noise UNCLE SAM makes: the language you've heard all your life, from school room to the nightly news, now wrapped around your neck like a rope. Written by Steve Darnall, illustrated and "co-plotted" by Alex Ross, UNCLE SAM, first published in two parts in 1997, says that the country may have betrayed every promise on which it was founded — and that means that the promises remain to be kept. Everything you ever believed in may go up in smoke here ("The dream is under fire," reads one caption, "burning down from the inside"), but in UNCLE SAM that is the air you breathe.

An old man lies crumpled on the sidewalk; he has thin white hair and a long white goatee. He's dressed in a black coat and red-and-white striped trousers. People pass on by. There's a fly on the old man's forehead. His left arm is stretched out, his fingers curled like a beggar's, but he looks you right in the face. His angry eyes say he lies on the pavement not to ask for what you've got but to ask you how you got it. He might be a bum, he might be a judge; as you follow his story, you keep changing your mind.

In the course of his travels, this ranting derelict will tour America's killing fields: the battlefields of the Revolutionary War, the Andersonville concentration camp, the 1832 Illinois massacre of the Blackhawks by Federal troops, a century later the deadly attack on striking auto workers in Dearborn, Michigan. The scenes will leap off the pages; like the old man, you will be sucked in, but you may be able to maintain a distance he is denied. The betrayals he witnesses — of "Equal Justice Under the Law," of "All Men Are Created Equal" — turn his terror into comedy: He thinks he's still in charge!

When you first meet Uncle Sam, you have no idea who he really is. All that comes out of his mouth is babble: presidential sound-bites, our memory of yesterday's political news turning into Uncle Sam's political unconscious. "People have a right to know whether or not their president's a crook," he hears himself saying. "I am not a crook." "I don't care what the facts are!" "I've signed legislation that will outlaw Russia forever." But soon enough, with the old man driven into a dumpster in search of food, he begins to hear words from every source. John Brown pops into his head; "The crimes of the guilty land will never be purged except with blood." In a split-second he finds himself riding in JFK's motorcade in Dallas, and Jackie turns her face to his. "This is not my beautiful wife," Uncle Sam says. Is this his country? Is he the witness or the actor, the victim or the executioner? Can he stand to breathe the country's air one minute more? Can you? Do you have any choice?

The tale ends almost where it began: the old man on the street again, muttering to himself. But then the kindness of strangers puts a bounce in his step. As he moves off, singing — singing "Yankee Doodle" — he passes under a little swinging shop sign; there's a pyramid topped by an eye painted on it. "Novus Ordo Seclorum," it reads: "New Order of the Ages." You might laugh: if you're lucky, you run your fingers over those words every day. Those are the words on the dollar bill. I laughed, but then I felt privileged and happy, as if I'd just been told a secret. That the motto of the country should turn up advertising the sort of occultist shop where you get your fortune read seemed more than perfect.

It's a great history lesson, the journeys Darnall and Ross put the old man through, harrying him across landscapes of racism, fraud, thievery, cruelty, into country junkshops and raising him high above the monuments of Washington, D.C., again and again taking him to the edge of madness, and always with a sense of the absurd, of the impossible — the idea of a nation founded on ideals as shining as those of the U. S. of A. coming to seem, in these pages, more impossible than anything else. But, UNCLE SAM finally says, that's how it was, and that's how it is.

— *Greil Marcus*

Greil Marcus is the author of *MYSTERY TRAIN* and *INVISIBLE REPUBLIC*.
He writes a monthly column for *ESQUIRE*.

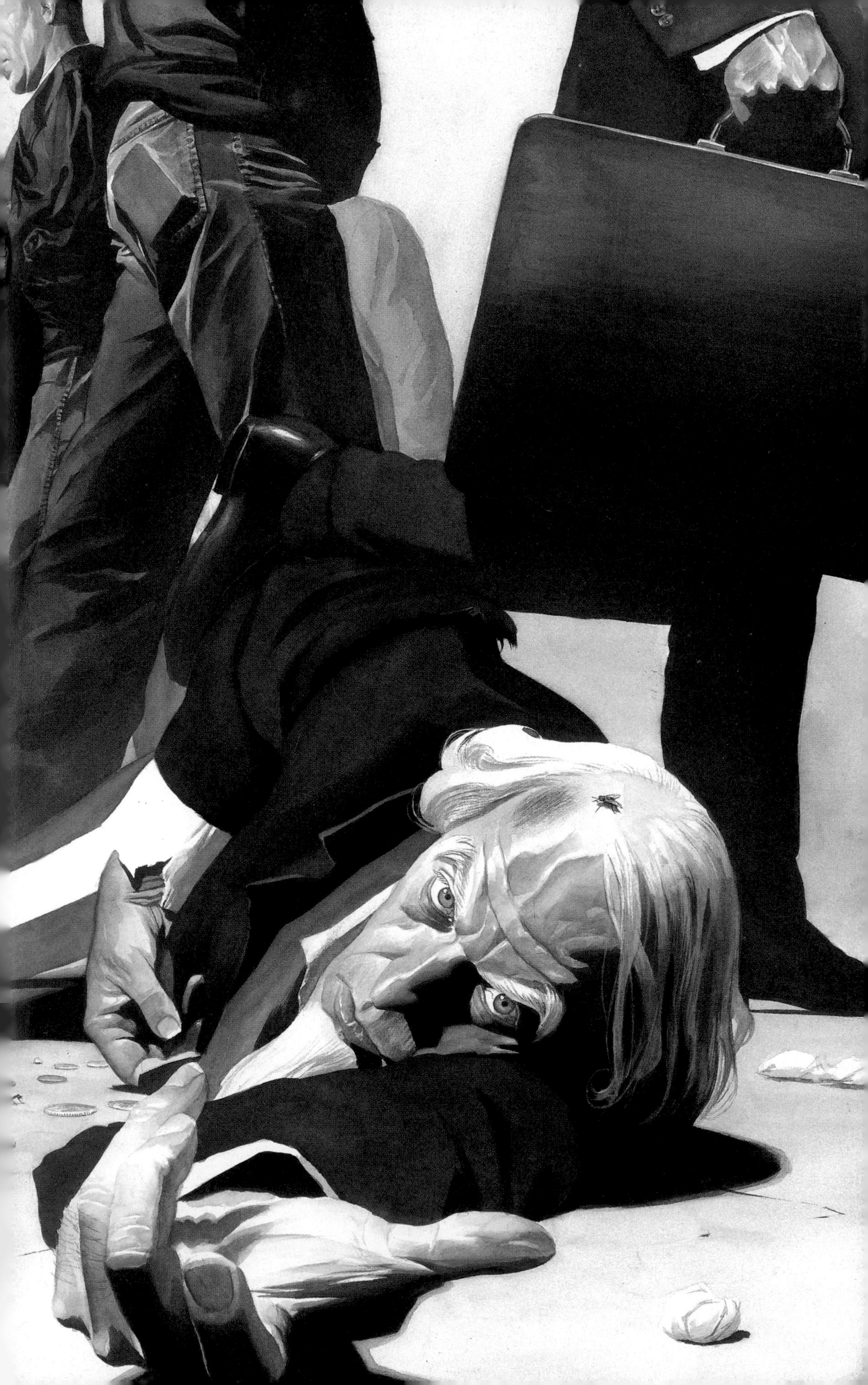

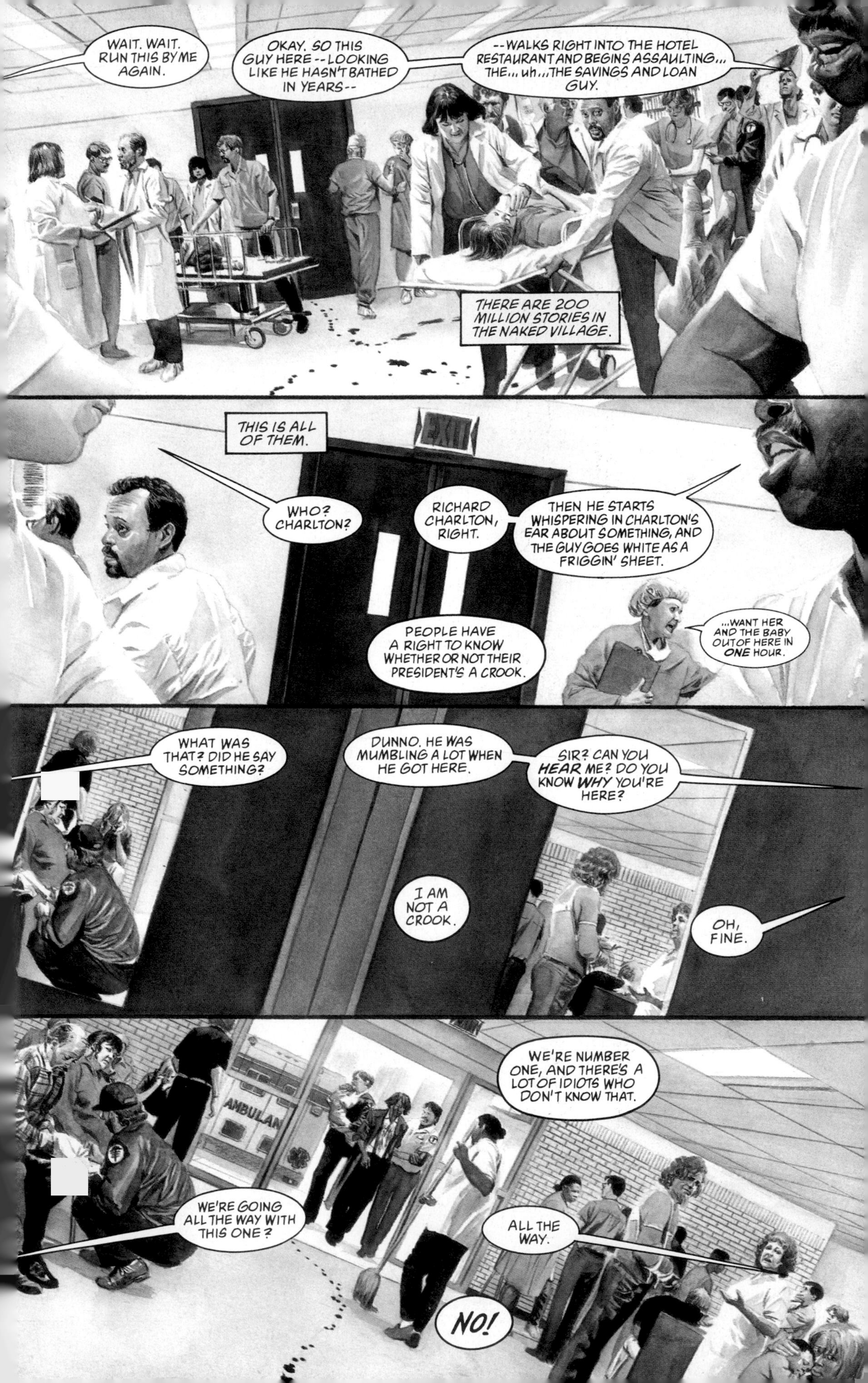

WAIT. WAIT. RUN THIS BY ME AGAIN.
OKAY. SO THIS GUY HERE--LOOKING LIKE HE HASN'T BATHED IN YEARS--
--WALKS RIGHT INTO THE HOTEL RESTAURANT AND BEGINS ASSAULTING... THE... uh... THE SAVINGS AND LOAN GUY.
THERE ARE 200 MILLION STORIES IN THE NAKED VILLAGE.
THIS IS ALL OF THEM.
WHO? CHARLTON?
RICHARD CHARLTON, RIGHT.
THEN HE STARTS WHISPERING IN CHARLTON'S EAR ABOUT SOMETHING, AND THE GUY GOES WHITE AS A FRIGGIN' SHEET.
PEOPLE HAVE A RIGHT TO KNOW WHETHER OR NOT THEIR PRESIDENT'S A CROOK.
...WANT HER AND THE BABY OUT OF HERE IN ONE HOUR.
WHAT WAS THAT? DID HE SAY SOMETHING?
DUNNO. HE WAS MUMBLING A LOT WHEN HE GOT HERE.
SIR? CAN YOU HEAR ME? DO YOU KNOW WHY YOU'RE HERE?
I AM NOT A CROOK.
OH, FINE.
WE'RE NUMBER ONE, AND THERE'S A LOT OF IDIOTS WHO DON'T KNOW THAT.
WE'RE GOING ALL THE WAY WITH THIS ONE?
ALL THE WAY.
NO!

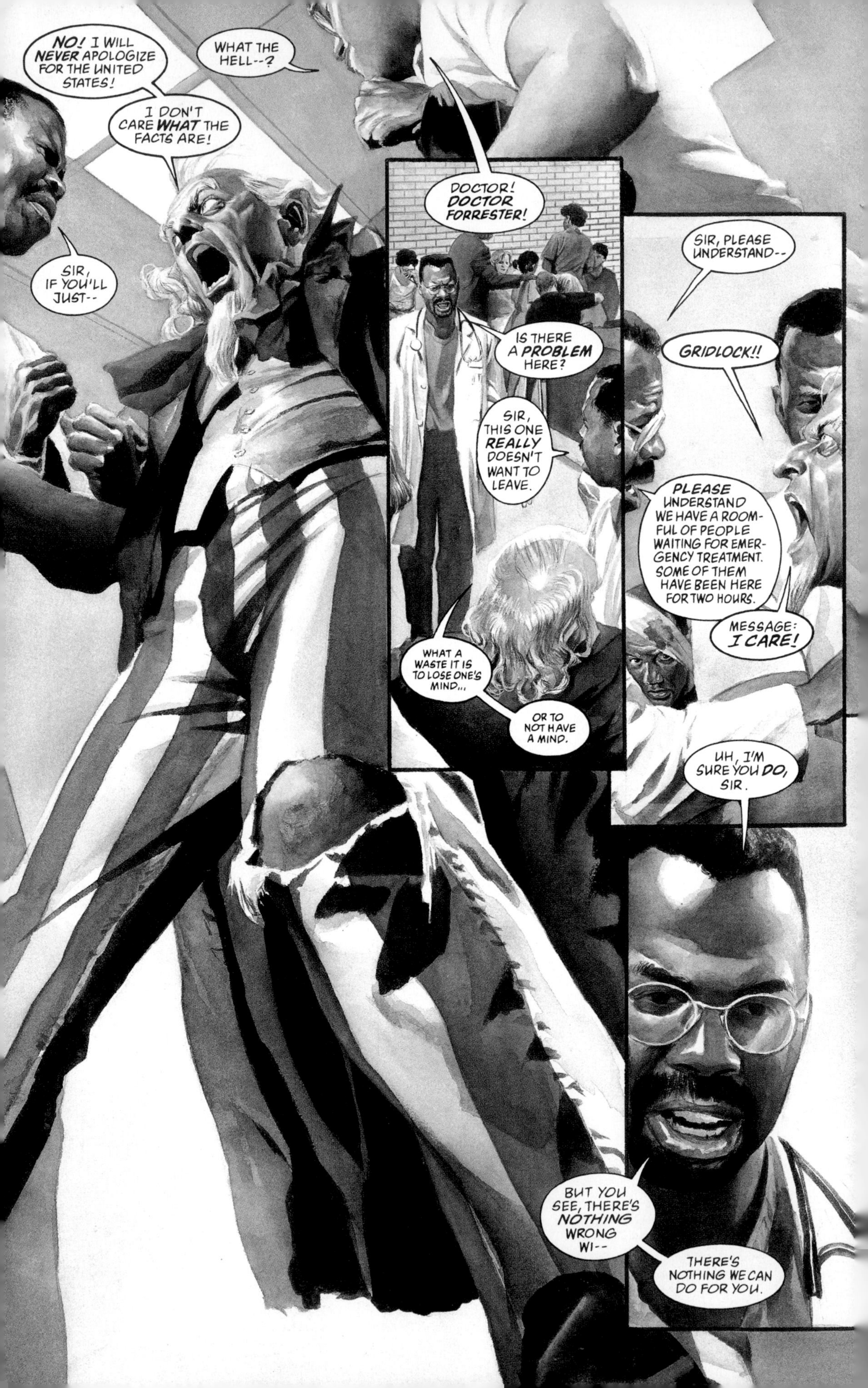
NO! I WILL NEVER APOLOGIZE FOR THE UNITED STATES!
WHAT THE HELL--?
I DON'T CARE WHAT THE FACTS ARE!
SIR, IF YOU'LL JUST--
DOCTOR! DOCTOR FORRESTER!
IS THERE A PROBLEM HERE?
SIR, THIS ONE REALLY DOESN'T WANT TO LEAVE.
WHAT A WASTE IT IS TO LOSE ONE'S MIND...
OR TO NOT HAVE A MIND.
SIR, PLEASE UNDERSTAND--
GRIDLOCK!!
PLEASE UNDERSTAND WE HAVE A ROOMFUL OF PEOPLE WAITING FOR EMERGENCY TREATMENT. SOME OF THEM HAVE BEEN HERE FOR TWO HOURS.
MESSAGE: I CARE!
UH, I'M SURE YOU DO, SIR.
BUT YOU SEE, THERE'S NOTHING WRONG WI--
THERE'S NOTHING WE CAN DO FOR YOU.

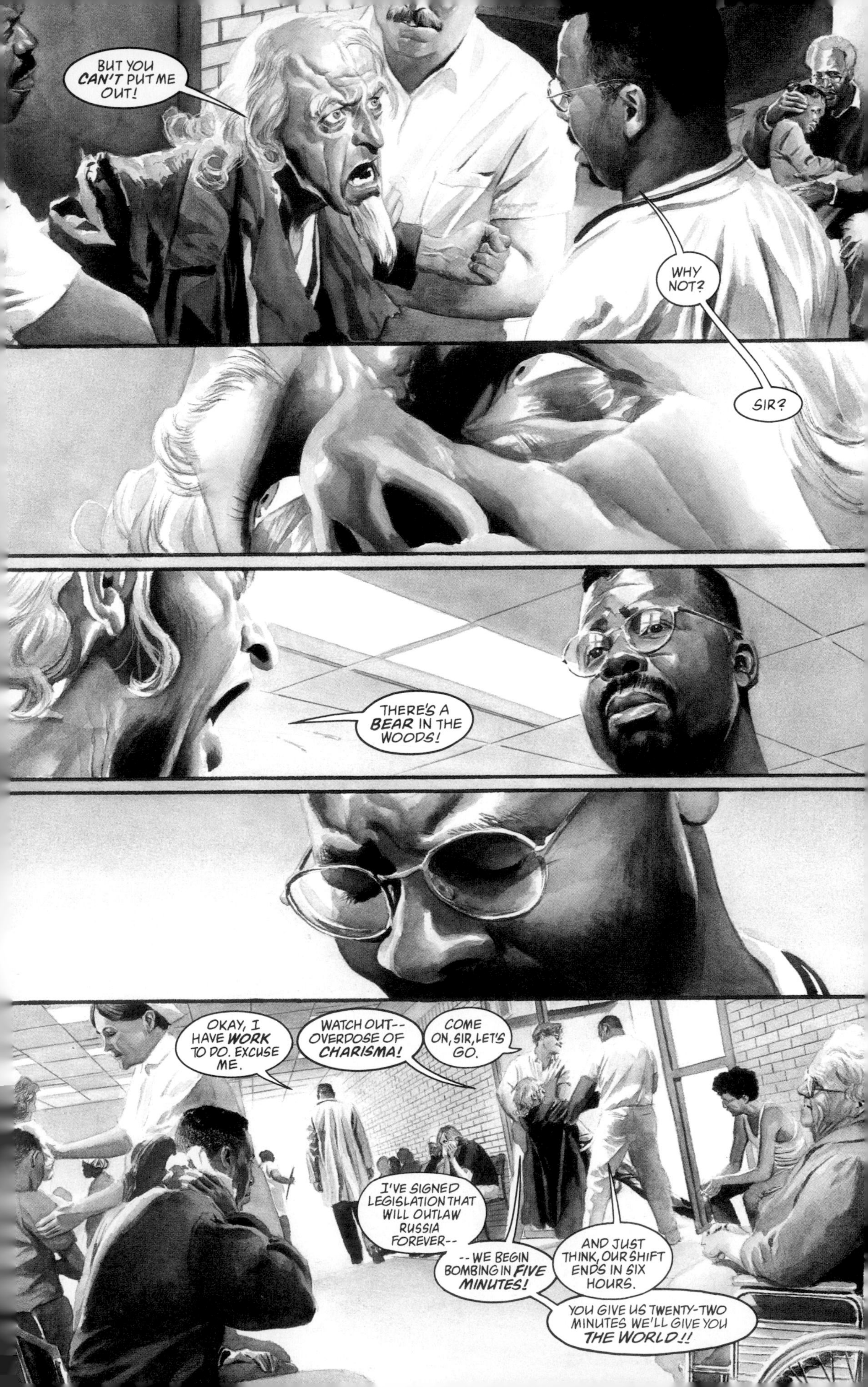
BUT YOU CAN'T PUT ME OUT!
WHY NOT?
SIR?
THERE'S A BEAR IN THE WOODS!
OKAY, I HAVE WORK TO DO. EXCUSE ME.
WATCH OUT-- OVERDOSE OF CHARISMA!
COME ON, SIR, LET'S GO.
I'VE SIGNED LEGISLATION THAT WILL OUTLAW RUSSIA FOREVER--
--WE BEGIN BOMBING IN FIVE MINUTES!
AND JUST THINK, OUR SHIFT ENDS IN SIX HOURS.
YOU GIVE US TWENTY-TWO MINUTES WE'LL GIVE YOU THE WORLD!!

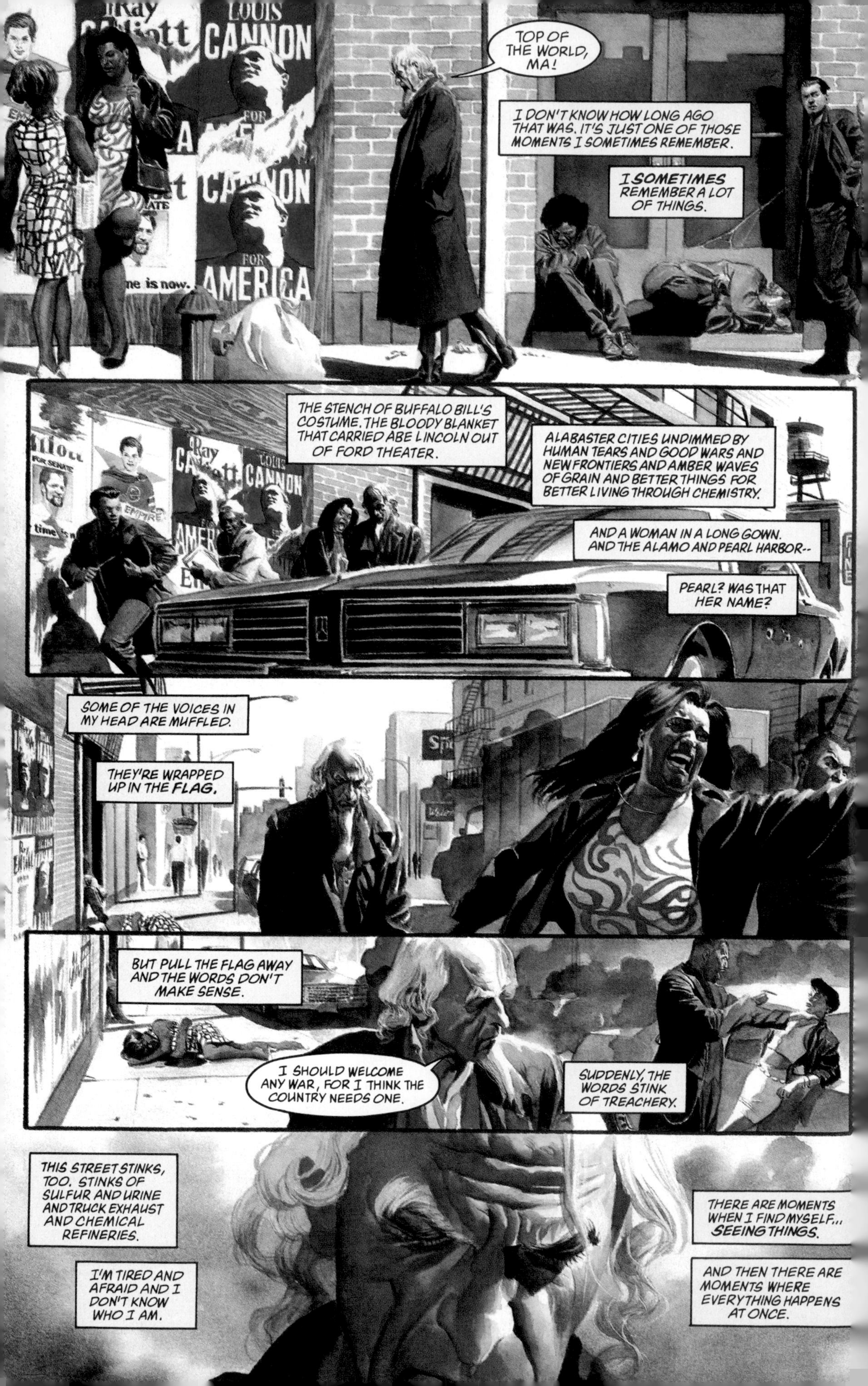

Ray Elliott
LOUIS CANNON
CANNON
FOR
AMERICA
me is now.
TOP OF THE WORLD, MA!
I DON'T KNOW HOW LONG AGO THAT WAS. IT'S JUST ONE OF THOSE MOMENTS I SOMETIMES REMEMBER.
I SOMETIMES REMEMBER A LOT OF THINGS.
THE STENCH OF BUFFALO BILL'S COSTUME. THE BLOODY BLANKET THAT CARRIED ABE LINCOLN OUT OF FORD THEATER.
ALABASTER CITIES UNDIMMED BY HUMAN TEARS AND GOOD WARS AND NEW FRONTIERS AND AMBER WAVES OF GRAIN AND BETTER THINGS FOR BETTER LIVING THROUGH CHEMISTRY.
AND A WOMAN IN A LONG GOWN. AND THE ALAMO AND PEARL HARBOR--
PEARL? WAS THAT HER NAME?
SOME OF THE VOICES IN MY HEAD ARE MUFFLED.
THEY'RE WRAPPED UP IN THE FLAG.
BUT PULL THE FLAG AWAY AND THE WORDS DON'T MAKE SENSE.
I SHOULD WELCOME ANY WAR, FOR I THINK THE COUNTRY NEEDS ONE.
SUDDENLY, THE WORDS STINK OF TREACHERY.
THIS STREET STINKS, TOO. STINKS OF SULFUR AND URINE AND TRUCK EXHAUST AND CHEMICAL REFINERIES.
I'M TIRED AND AFRAID AND I DON'T KNOW WHO I AM.
THERE ARE MOMENTS WHEN I FIND MYSELF... SEEING THINGS.
AND THEN THERE ARE MOMENTS WHERE EVERYTHING HAPPENS AT ONCE.

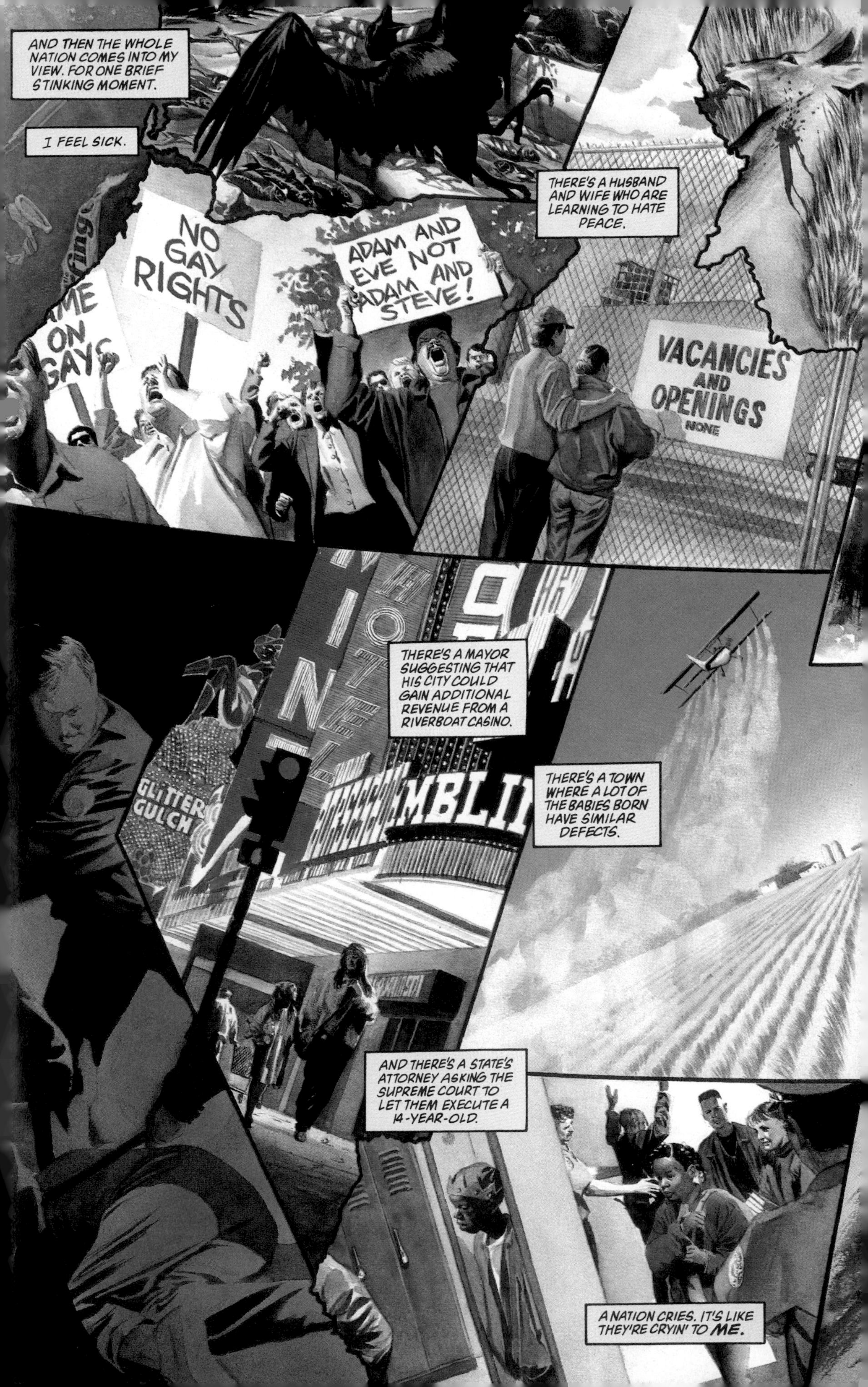
AND THEN THE WHOLE NATION COMES INTO MY VIEW. FOR ONE BRIEF STINKING MOMENT.
I FEEL SICK.
NO GAY RIGHTS
ADAM AND EVE NOT ADAM AND STEVE!
ON GAYS
THERE'S A HUSBAND AND WIFE WHO ARE LEARNING TO HATE PEACE.
VACANCIES AND OPENINGS
NONE
THERE'S A MAYOR SUGGESTING THAT HIS CITY COULD GAIN ADDITIONAL REVENUE FROM A RIVERBOAT CASINO.
GLITTER GULCH
THERE'S A TOWN WHERE A LOT OF THE BABIES BORN HAVE SIMILAR DEFECTS.
AND THERE'S A STATE'S ATTORNEY ASKING THE SUPREME COURT TO LET THEM EXECUTE A 14-YEAR-OLD.
A NATION CRIES. IT'S LIKE THEY'RE CRYIN' TO **ME.**

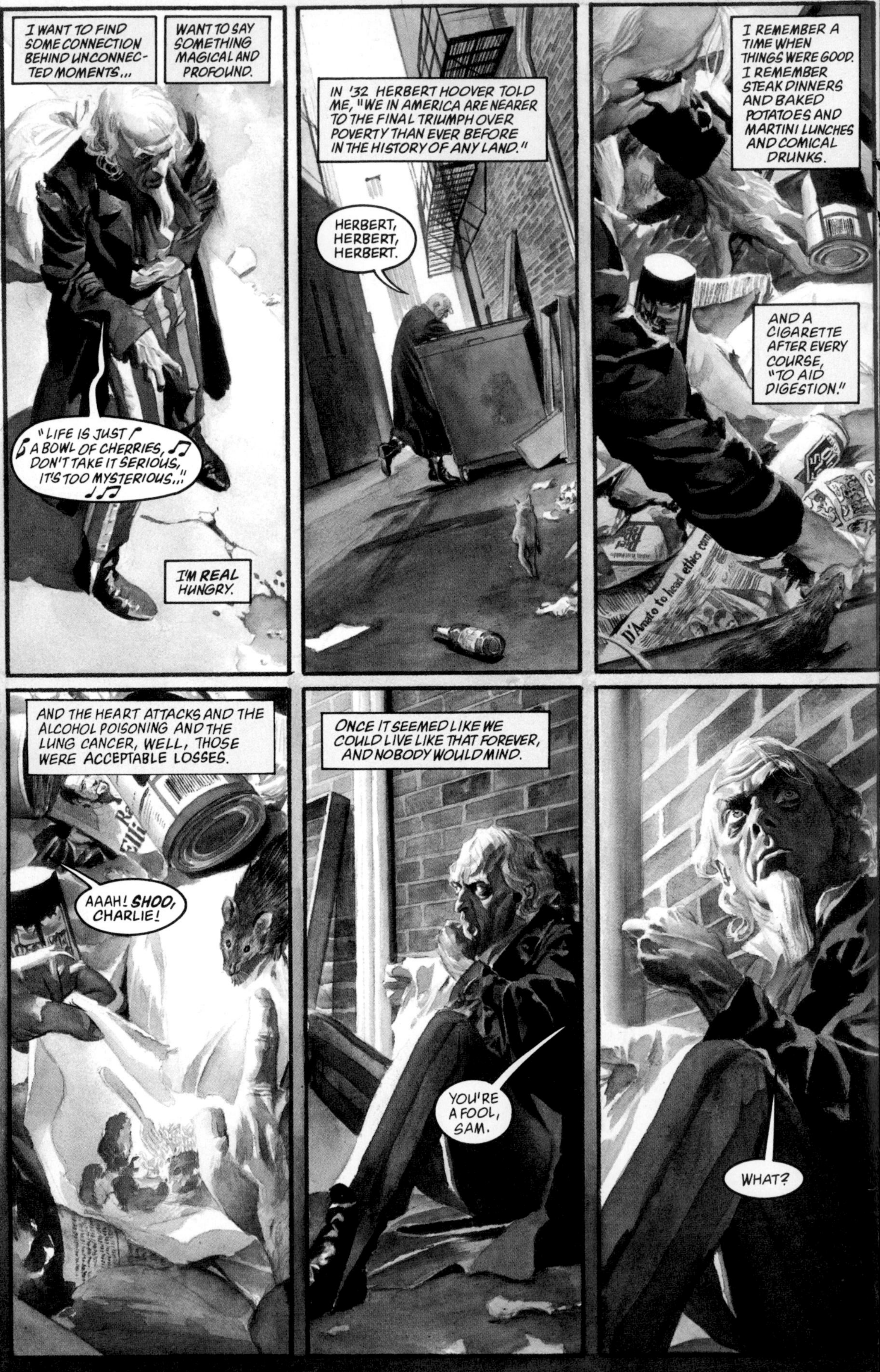
I WANT TO FIND SOME CONNECTION BEHIND UNCONNECTED MOMENTS...
WANT TO SAY SOMETHING MAGICAL AND PROFOUND.
"LIFE IS JUST A BOWL OF CHERRIES, DON'T TAKE IT SERIOUS, IT'S TOO MYSTERIOUS..."
I'M REAL HUNGRY.
IN '32 HERBERT HOOVER TOLD ME, "WE IN AMERICA ARE NEARER TO THE FINAL TRIUMPH OVER POVERTY THAN EVER BEFORE IN THE HISTORY OF ANY LAND."
HERBERT, HERBERT, HERBERT.
I REMEMBER A TIME WHEN THINGS WERE GOOD. I REMEMBER STEAK DINNERS AND BAKED POTATOES AND MARTINI LUNCHES AND COMICAL DRUNKS.
AND A CIGARETTE AFTER EVERY COURSE, "TO AID DIGESTION."
D'Amato to heed ethics
AND THE HEART ATTACKS AND THE ALCOHOL POISONING AND THE LUNG CANCER, WELL, THOSE WERE ACCEPTABLE LOSSES.
AAAH! SHOO, CHARLIE!
ONCE IT SEEMED LIKE WE COULD LIVE LIKE THAT FOREVER, AND NOBODY WOULD MIND.
YOU'RE A FOOL, SAM.
WHAT?

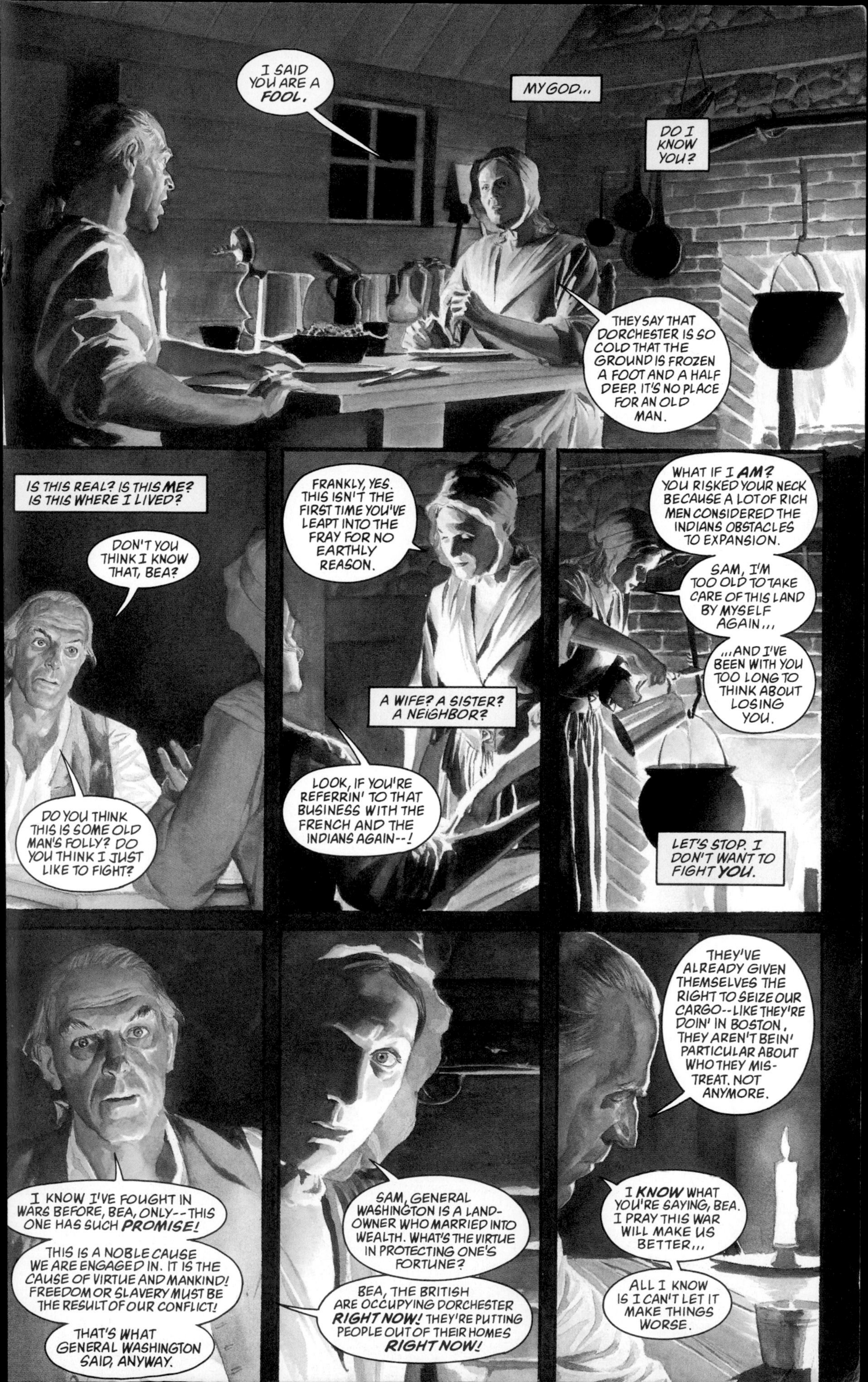
I SAID YOU ARE A FOOL.
MY GOD...
DO I KNOW YOU?
THEY SAY THAT DORCHESTER IS SO COLD THAT THE GROUND IS FROZEN A FOOT AND A HALF DEEP. IT'S NO PLACE FOR AN OLD MAN.
IS THIS REAL? IS THIS ME? IS THIS WHERE I LIVED?
DON'T YOU THINK I KNOW THAT, BEA?
DO YOU THINK THIS IS SOME OLD MAN'S FOLLY? DO YOU THINK I JUST LIKE TO FIGHT?
FRANKLY, YES. THIS ISN'T THE FIRST TIME YOU'VE LEAPT INTO THE FRAY FOR NO EARTHLY REASON.
A WIFE? A SISTER? A NEIGHBOR?
LOOK, IF YOU'RE REFERRIN' TO THAT BUSINESS WITH THE FRENCH AND THE INDIANS AGAIN--!
WHAT IF I AM? YOU RISKED YOUR NECK BECAUSE A LOT OF RICH MEN CONSIDERED THE INDIANS OBSTACLES TO EXPANSION.
SAM, I'M TOO OLD TO TAKE CARE OF THIS LAND BY MYSELF AGAIN...
...AND I'VE BEEN WITH YOU TOO LONG TO THINK ABOUT LOSING YOU.
LET'S STOP. I DON'T WANT TO FIGHT YOU.
I KNOW I'VE FOUGHT IN WARS BEFORE, BEA, ONLY-- THIS ONE HAS SUCH PROMISE!
THIS IS A NOBLE CAUSE WE ARE ENGAGED IN. IT IS THE CAUSE OF VIRTUE AND MANKIND! FREEDOM OR SLAVERY MUST BE THE RESULT OF OUR CONFLICT!
THAT'S WHAT GENERAL WASHINGTON SAID, ANYWAY.
SAM, GENERAL WASHINGTON IS A LAND-OWNER WHO MARRIED INTO WEALTH. WHAT'S THE VIRTUE IN PROTECTING ONE'S FORTUNE?
BEA, THE BRITISH ARE OCCUPYING DORCHESTER RIGHT NOW! THEY'RE PUTTING PEOPLE OUT OF THEIR HOMES RIGHT NOW!
THEY'VE ALREADY GIVEN THEMSELVES THE RIGHT TO SEIZE OUR CARGO--LIKE THEY'RE DOIN' IN BOSTON, THEY AREN'T BEIN' PARTICULAR ABOUT WHO THEY MIS-TREAT. NOT ANYMORE.
I KNOW WHAT YOU'RE SAYING, BEA. I PRAY THIS WAR WILL MAKE US BETTER...
ALL I KNOW IS I CAN'T LET IT MAKE THINGS WORSE.

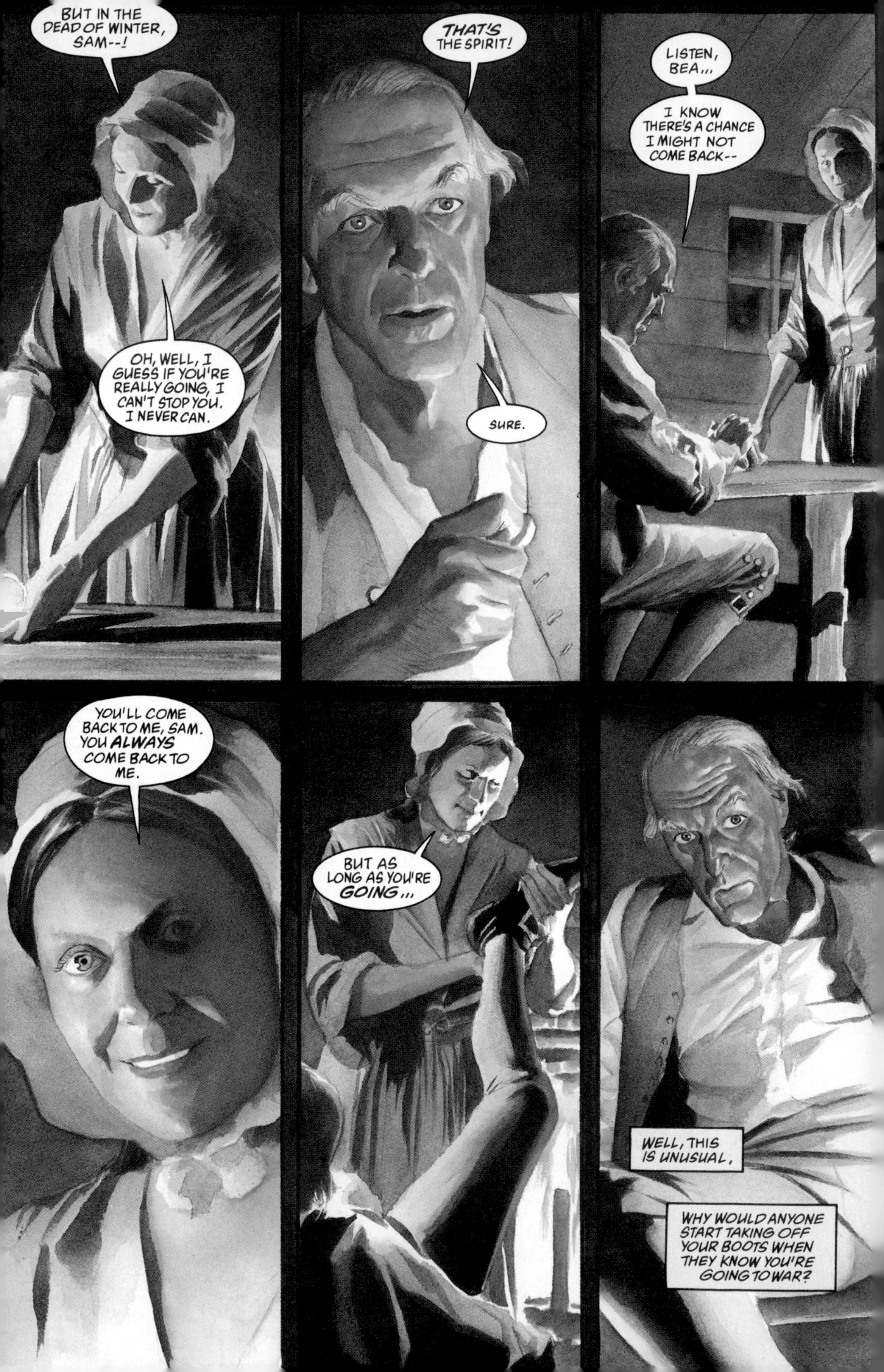
BUT IN THE DEAD OF WINTER, SAM--!
OH, WELL, I GUESS IF YOU'RE REALLY GOING, I CAN'T STOP YOU. I NEVER CAN.
THAT'S THE SPIRIT!
SURE.
LISTEN, BEA...
I KNOW THERE'S A CHANCE I MIGHT NOT COME BACK--
YOU'LL COME BACK TO ME, SAM. YOU ALWAYS COME BACK TO ME.
BUT AS LONG AS YOU'RE GOING...
WELL, THIS IS UNUSUAL.
WHY WOULD ANYONE START TAKING OFF YOUR BOOTS WHEN THEY KNOW YOU'RE GOING TO WAR?

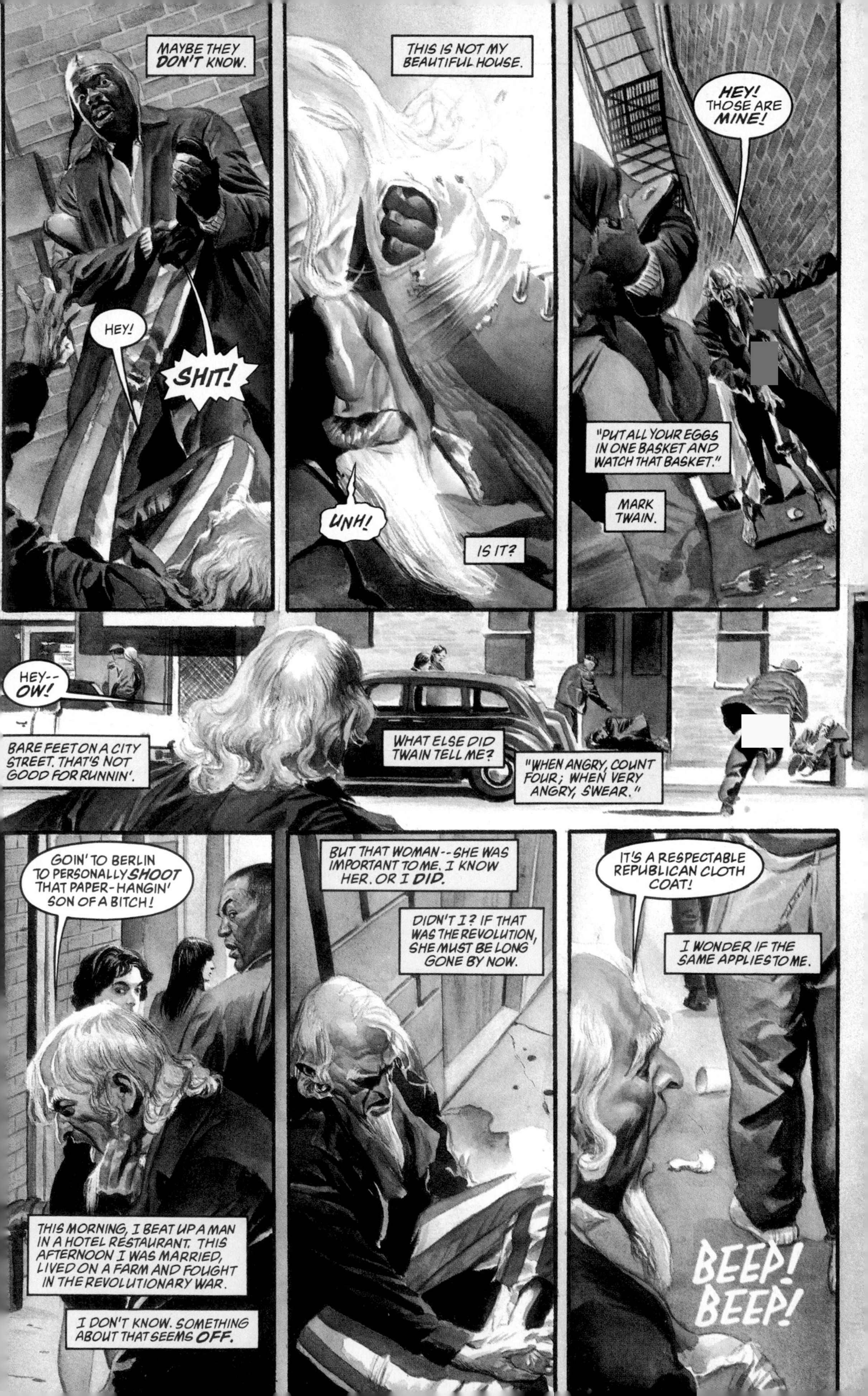
MAYBE THEY DON'T KNOW.
HEY!
SHIT!
THIS IS NOT MY BEAUTIFUL HOUSE.
UNH!
IS IT?
HEY! THOSE ARE MINE!
"PUT ALL YOUR EGGS IN ONE BASKET AND WATCH THAT BASKET."
MARK TWAIN.
HEY-- OW!
BARE FEET ON A CITY STREET. THAT'S NOT GOOD FOR RUNNIN'.
WHAT ELSE DID TWAIN TELL ME?
"WHEN ANGRY, COUNT FOUR; WHEN VERY ANGRY, SWEAR."
GOIN' TO BERLIN TO PERSONALLY SHOOT THAT PAPER-HANGIN' SON OF A BITCH!
THIS MORNING, I BEAT UP A MAN IN A HOTEL RESTAURANT. THIS AFTERNOON I WAS MARRIED, LIVED ON A FARM AND FOUGHT IN THE REVOLUTIONARY WAR.
I DON'T KNOW. SOMETHING ABOUT THAT SEEMS OFF.
BUT THAT WOMAN--SHE WAS IMPORTANT TO ME. I KNOW HER. OR I DID.
DIDN'T I? IF THAT WAS THE REVOLUTION, SHE MUST BE LONG GONE BY NOW.
IT'S A RESPECTABLE REPUBLICAN CLOTH COAT!
I WONDER IF THE SAME APPLIES TO ME.
BEEP! BEEP!

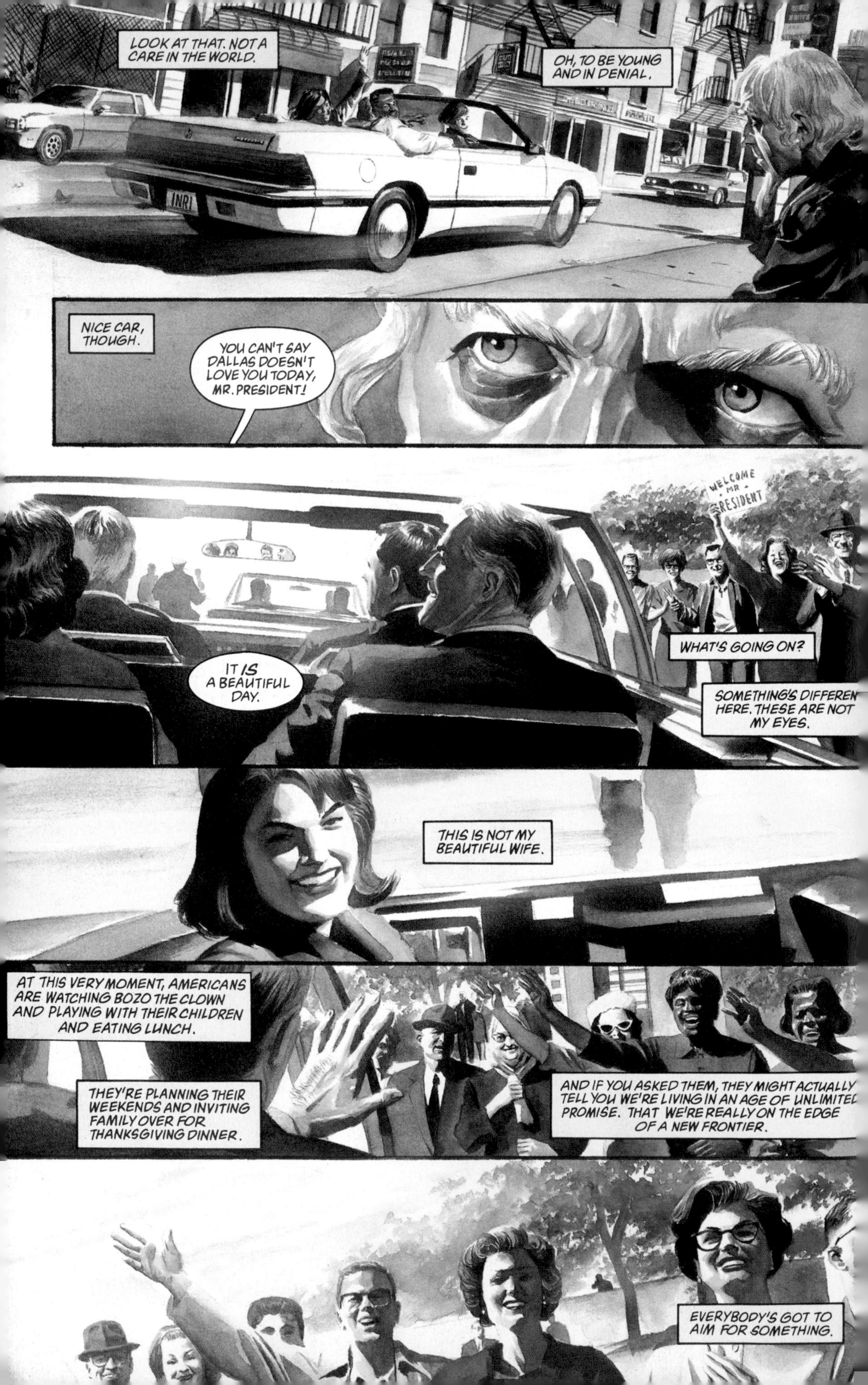
LOOK AT THAT. NOT A CARE IN THE WORLD.
OH, TO BE YOUNG AND IN DENIAL.
INRI
NICE CAR, THOUGH.
YOU CAN'T SAY DALLAS DOESN'T LOVE YOU TODAY, MR. PRESIDENT!
WELCOME MR PRESIDENT
IT IS A BEAUTIFUL DAY.
WHAT'S GOING ON?
SOMETHING'S DIFFEREN HERE. THESE ARE NOT MY EYES.
THIS IS NOT MY BEAUTIFUL WIFE.
AT THIS VERY MOMENT, AMERICANS ARE WATCHING BOZO THE CLOWN AND PLAYING WITH THEIR CHILDREN AND EATING LUNCH.
THEY'RE PLANNING THEIR WEEKENDS AND INVITING FAMILY OVER FOR THANKSGIVING DINNER.
AND IF YOU ASKED THEM, THEY MIGHT ACTUALLY TELL YOU WE'RE LIVING IN AN AGE OF UNLIMITED PROMISE. THAT WE'RE REALLY ON THE EDGE OF A NEW FRONTIER.
EVERYBODY'S GOT TO AIM FOR SOMETHING.

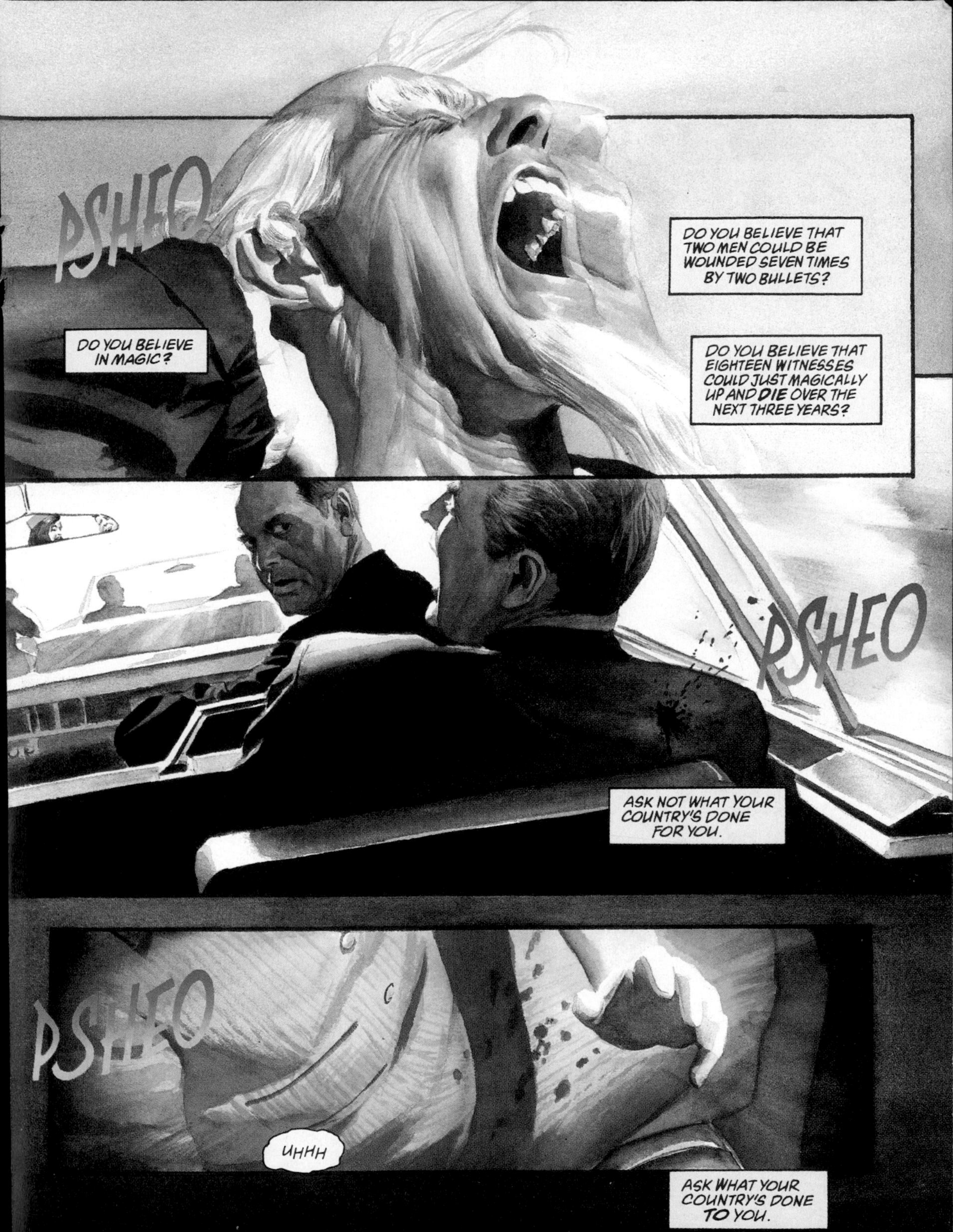
PSHEO
DO YOU BELIEVE IN MAGIC?
DO YOU BELIEVE THAT TWO MEN COULD BE WOUNDED SEVEN TIMES BY TWO BULLETS?
DO YOU BELIEVE THAT EIGHTEEN WITNESSES COULD JUST MAGICALLY UP AND DIE OVER THE NEXT THREE YEARS?
PSHEO
ASK NOT WHAT YOUR COUNTRY'S DONE FOR YOU.
PSHEO
UHHH
ASK WHAT YOUR COUNTRY'S DONE TO YOU.

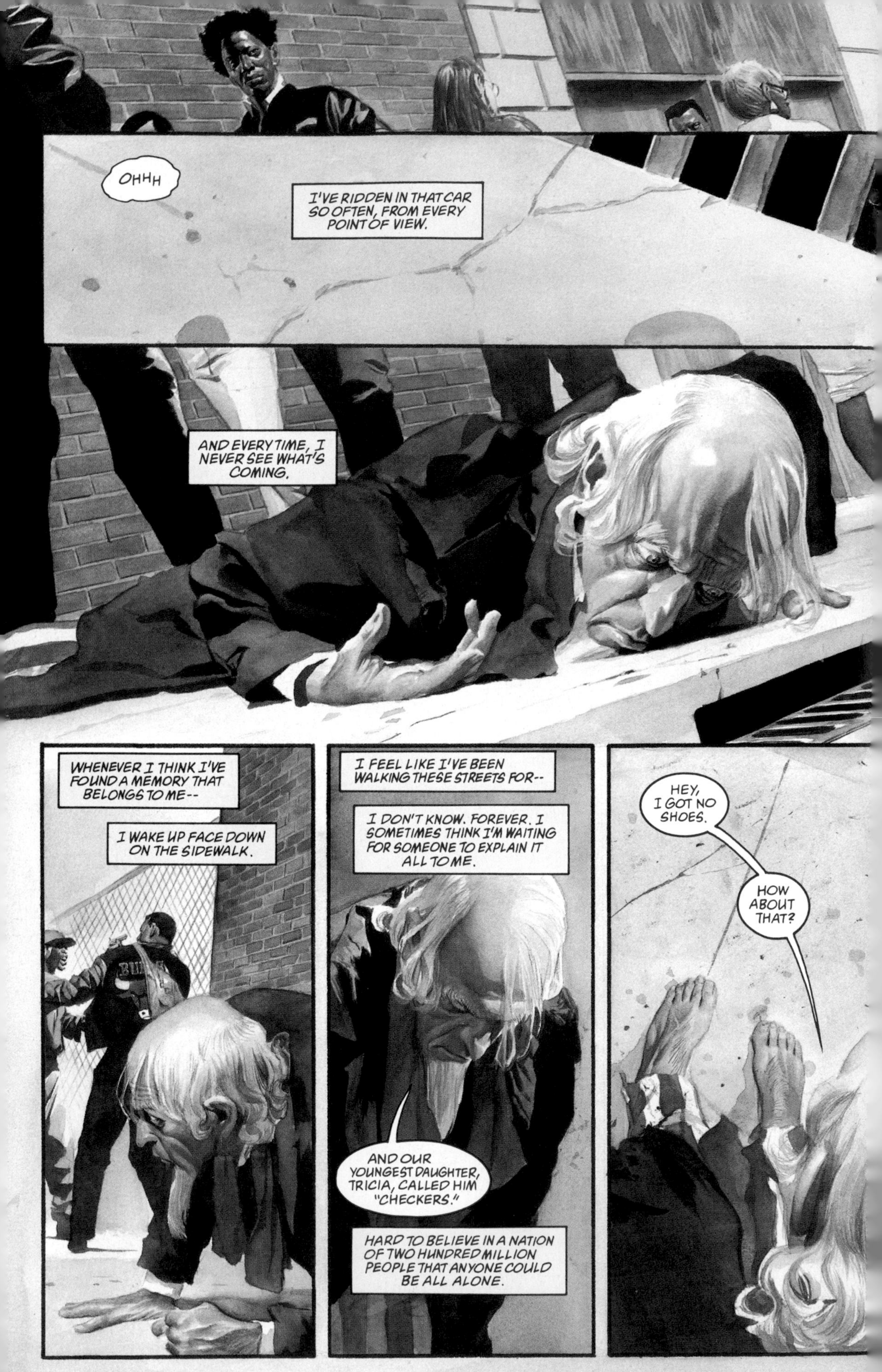
OHHH
I'VE RIDDEN IN THAT CAR SO OFTEN, FROM EVERY POINT OF VIEW.
AND EVERY TIME, I NEVER SEE WHAT'S COMING.
WHENEVER I THINK I'VE FOUND A MEMORY THAT BELONGS TO ME--
I WAKE UP FACE DOWN ON THE SIDEWALK.
I FEEL LIKE I'VE BEEN WALKING THESE STREETS FOR--
I DON'T KNOW. FOREVER. I SOMETIMES THINK I'M WAITING FOR SOMEONE TO EXPLAIN IT ALL TO ME.
AND OUR YOUNGEST DAUGHTER, TRICIA, CALLED HIM "CHECKERS."
HARD TO BELIEVE IN A NATION OF TWO HUNDRED MILLION PEOPLE THAT ANYONE COULD BE ALL ALONE.
HEY, I GOT NO SHOES.
HOW ABOUT THAT?

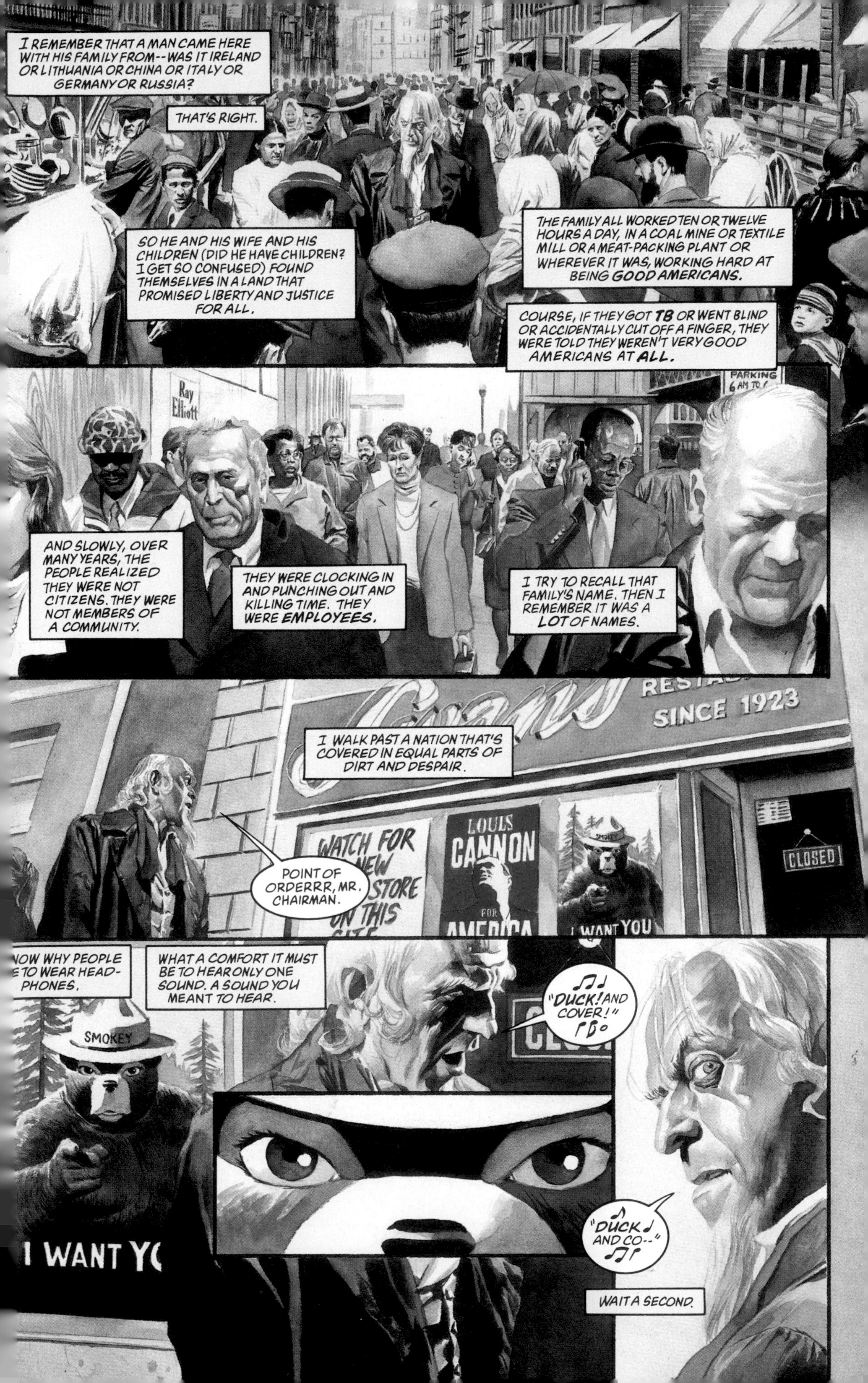
I REMEMBER THAT A MAN CAME HERE WITH HIS FAMILY FROM--WAS IT IRELAND OR LITHUANIA OR CHINA OR ITALY OR GERMANY OR RUSSIA?
THAT'S RIGHT.
SO HE AND HIS WIFE AND HIS CHILDREN (DID HE HAVE CHILDREN? I GET SO CONFUSED) FOUND THEMSELVES IN A LAND THAT PROMISED LIBERTY AND JUSTICE FOR ALL.
THE FAMILY ALL WORKED TEN OR TWELVE HOURS A DAY, IN A COAL MINE OR TEXTILE MILL OR A MEAT-PACKING PLANT OR WHEREVER IT WAS, WORKING HARD AT BEING GOOD AMERICANS.
COURSE, IF THEY GOT TB OR WENT BLIND OR ACCIDENTALLY CUT OFF A FINGER, THEY WERE TOLD THEY WEREN'T VERY GOOD AMERICANS AT ALL.
Ray Elliott
PARKING 6 AM TO
AND SLOWLY, OVER MANY YEARS, THE PEOPLE REALIZED THEY WERE NOT CITIZENS. THEY WERE NOT MEMBERS OF A COMMUNITY.
THEY WERE CLOCKING IN AND PUNCHING OUT AND KILLING TIME. THEY WERE EMPLOYEES.
I TRY TO RECALL THAT FAMILY'S NAME. THEN I REMEMBER IT WAS A LOT OF NAMES.
SINCE 1923
I WALK PAST A NATION THAT'S COVERED IN EQUAL PARTS OF DIRT AND DESPAIR.
POINT OF ORDERRR, MR. CHAIRMAN.
WATCH FOR NEW STORE ON THIS
LOUIS CANNON FOR AMERICA
I WANT YOU
CLOSED
NOW WHY PEOPLE E TO WEAR HEAD-PHONES.
WHAT A COMFORT IT MUST BE TO HEAR ONLY ONE SOUND. A SOUND YOU MEANT TO HEAR.
"DUCK! AND COVER!"
SMOKEY
I WANT YO
"DUCK AND CO--"
WAIT A SECOND.

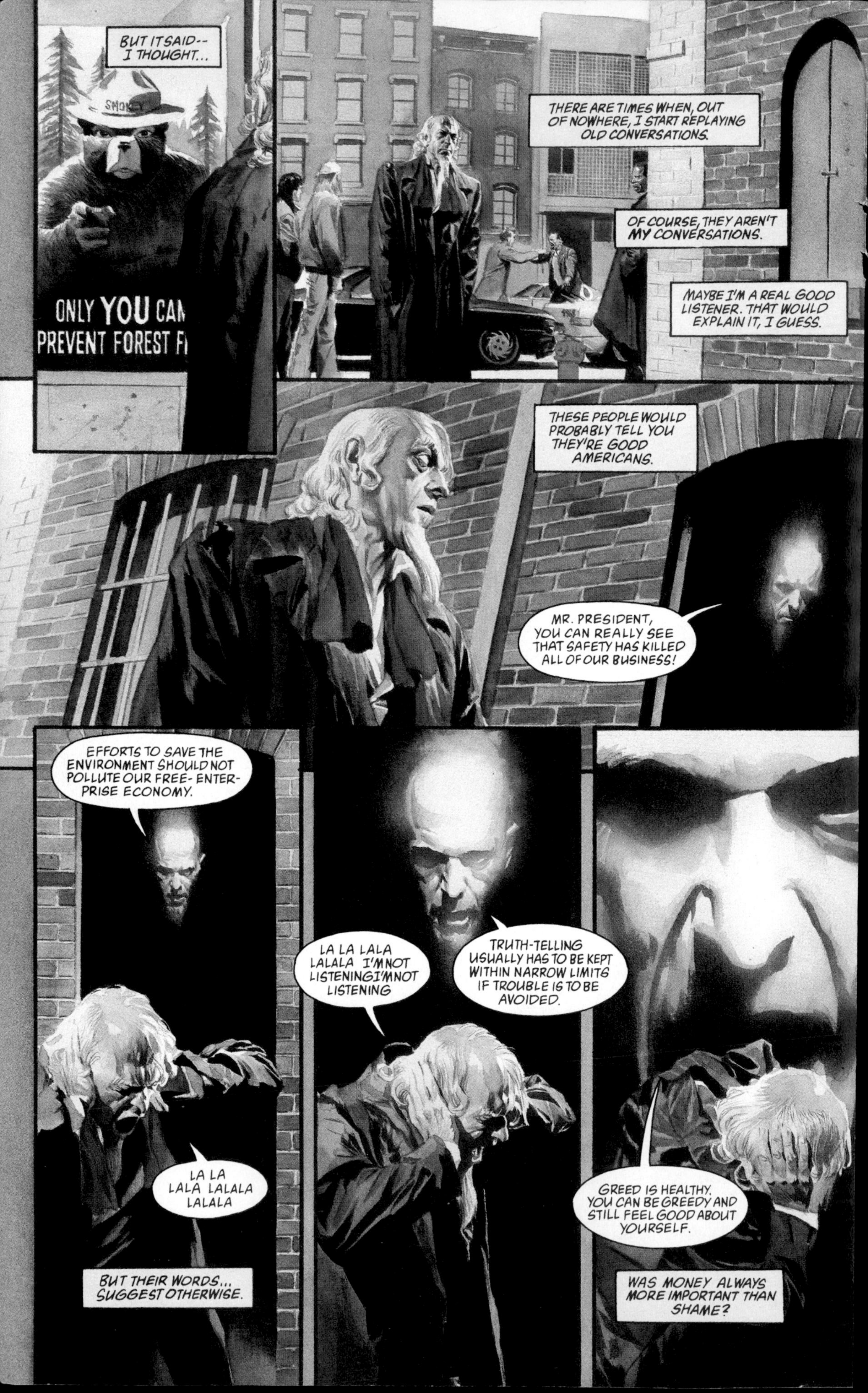
BUT IT SAID-- I THOUGHT...
SMOKEY
ONLY YOU CAN
PREVENT FOREST F
THERE ARE TIMES WHEN, OUT OF NOWHERE, I START REPLAYING OLD CONVERSATIONS.
OF COURSE, THEY AREN'T MY CONVERSATIONS.
MAYBE I'M A REAL GOOD LISTENER. THAT WOULD EXPLAIN IT, I GUESS.
THESE PEOPLE WOULD PROBABLY TELL YOU THEY'RE GOOD AMERICANS.
MR. PRESIDENT, YOU CAN REALLY SEE THAT SAFETY HAS KILLED ALL OF OUR BUSINESS!
EFFORTS TO SAVE THE ENVIRONMENT SHOULD NOT POLLUTE OUR FREE-ENTERPRISE ECONOMY.
LA LA LALA LALALA LALALA
BUT THEIR WORDS... SUGGEST OTHERWISE.
LA LA LALA LALALA I'M NOT LISTENING I'M NOT LISTENING
TRUTH-TELLING USUALLY HAS TO BE KEPT WITHIN NARROW LIMITS IF TROUBLE IS TO BE AVOIDED.
GREED IS HEALTHY. YOU CAN BE GREEDY AND STILL FEEL GOOD ABOUT YOURSELF.
WAS MONEY ALWAYS MORE IMPORTANT THAN SHAME?

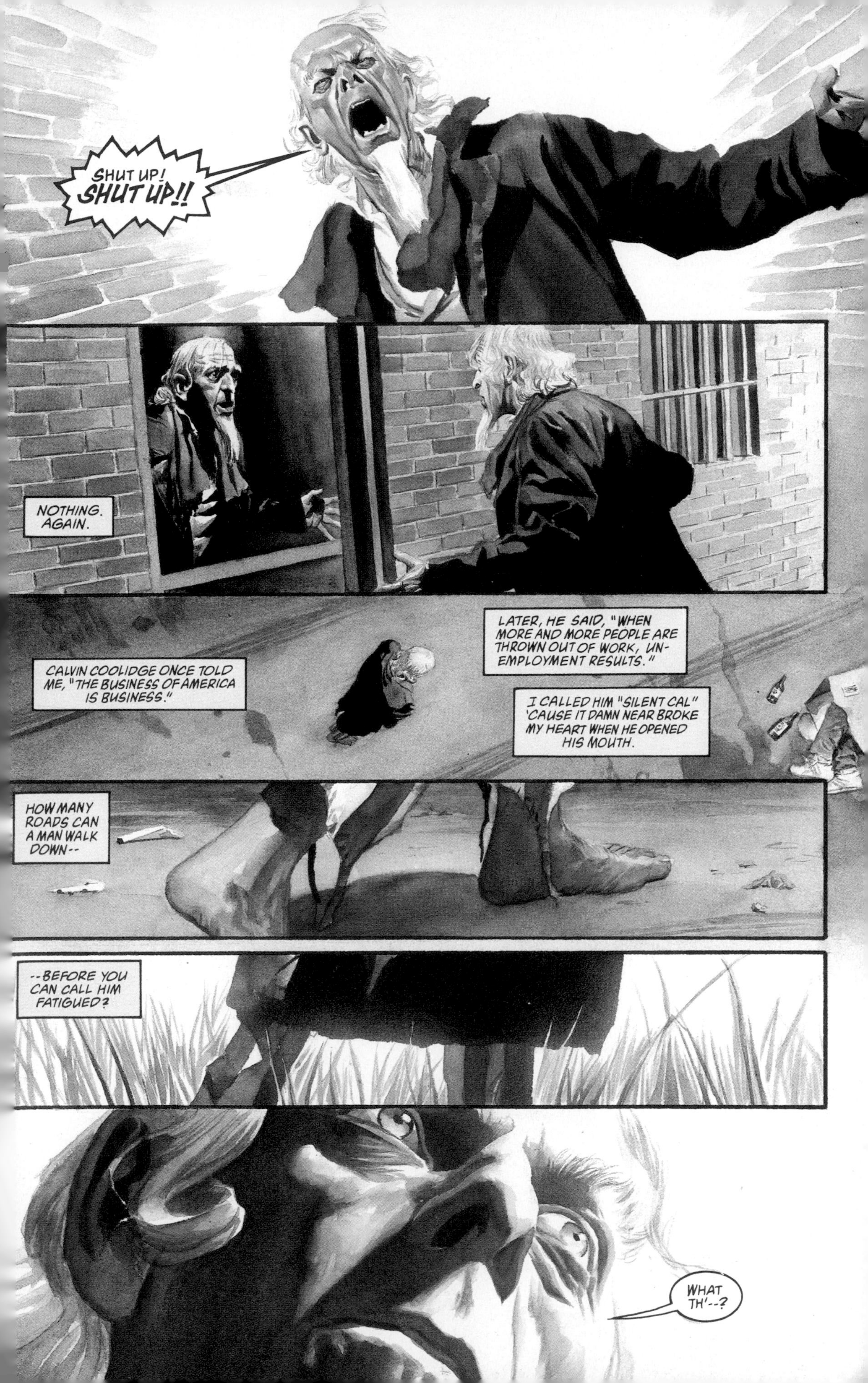
SHUT UP! SHUT UP!!
NOTHING. AGAIN.
CALVIN COOLIDGE ONCE TOLD ME, "THE BUSINESS OF AMERICA IS BUSINESS."
LATER, HE SAID, "WHEN MORE AND MORE PEOPLE ARE THROWN OUT OF WORK, UN-EMPLOYMENT RESULTS."
I CALLED HIM "SILENT CAL" 'CAUSE IT DAMN NEAR BROKE MY HEART WHEN HE OPENED HIS MOUTH.
HOW MANY ROADS CAN A MAN WALK DOWN--
--BEFORE YOU CAN CALL HIM FATIGUED?
WHAT TH'--?

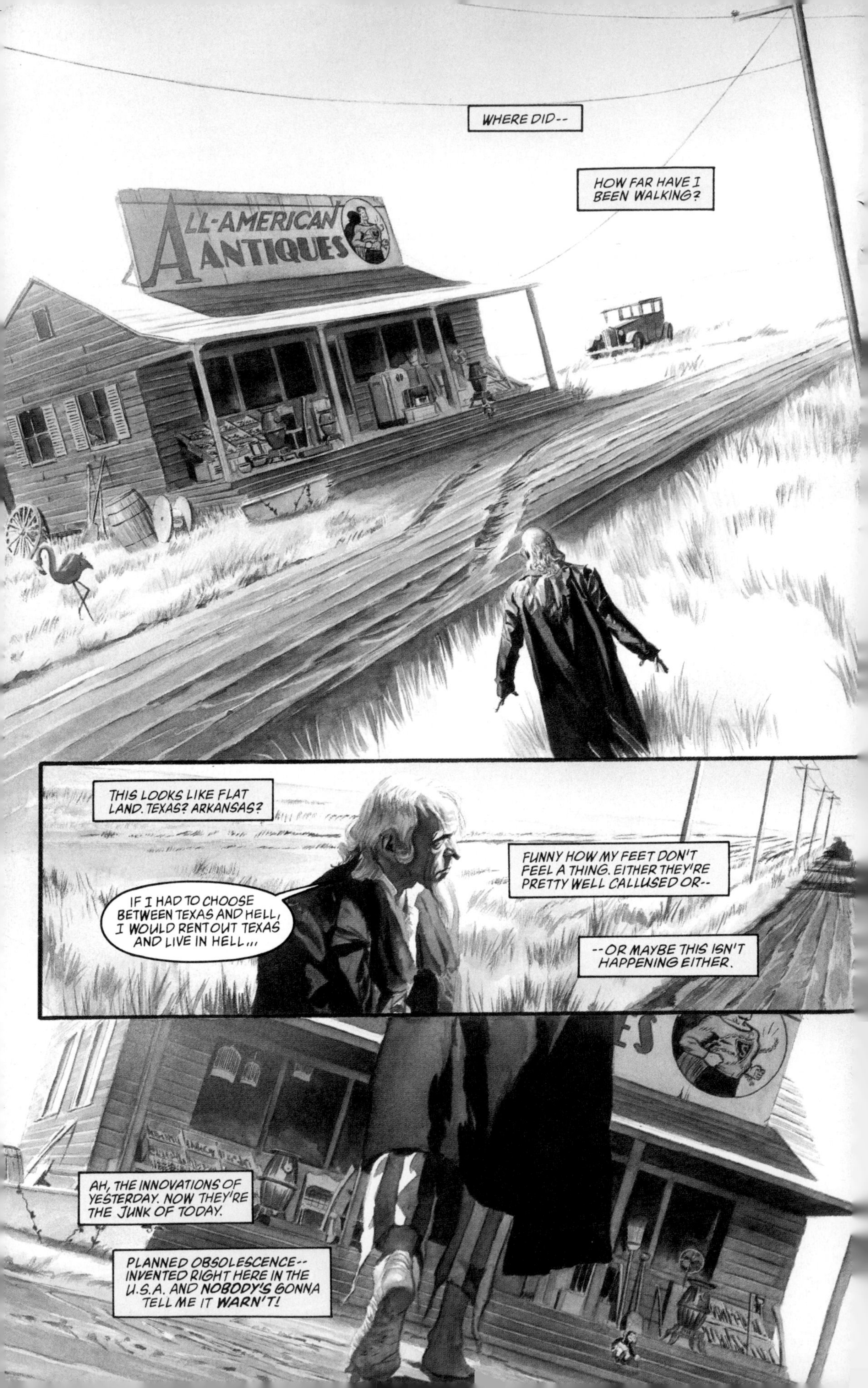
WHERE DID--
HOW FAR HAVE I BEEN WALKING?
ALL-AMERICAN ANTIQUES
THIS LOOKS LIKE FLAT LAND. TEXAS? ARKANSAS?
IF I HAD TO CHOOSE BETWEEN TEXAS AND HELL, I WOULD RENT OUT TEXAS AND LIVE IN HELL...
FUNNY HOW MY FEET DON'T FEEL A THING. EITHER THEY'RE PRETTY WELL CALLUSED OR--
--OR MAYBE THIS ISN'T HAPPENING EITHER.
AH, THE INNOVATIONS OF YESTERDAY. NOW THEY'RE THE JUNK OF TODAY.
PLANNED OBSOLESCENCE-- INVENTED RIGHT HERE IN THE U.S.A. AND NOBODY'S GONNA TELL ME IT WARN'T!

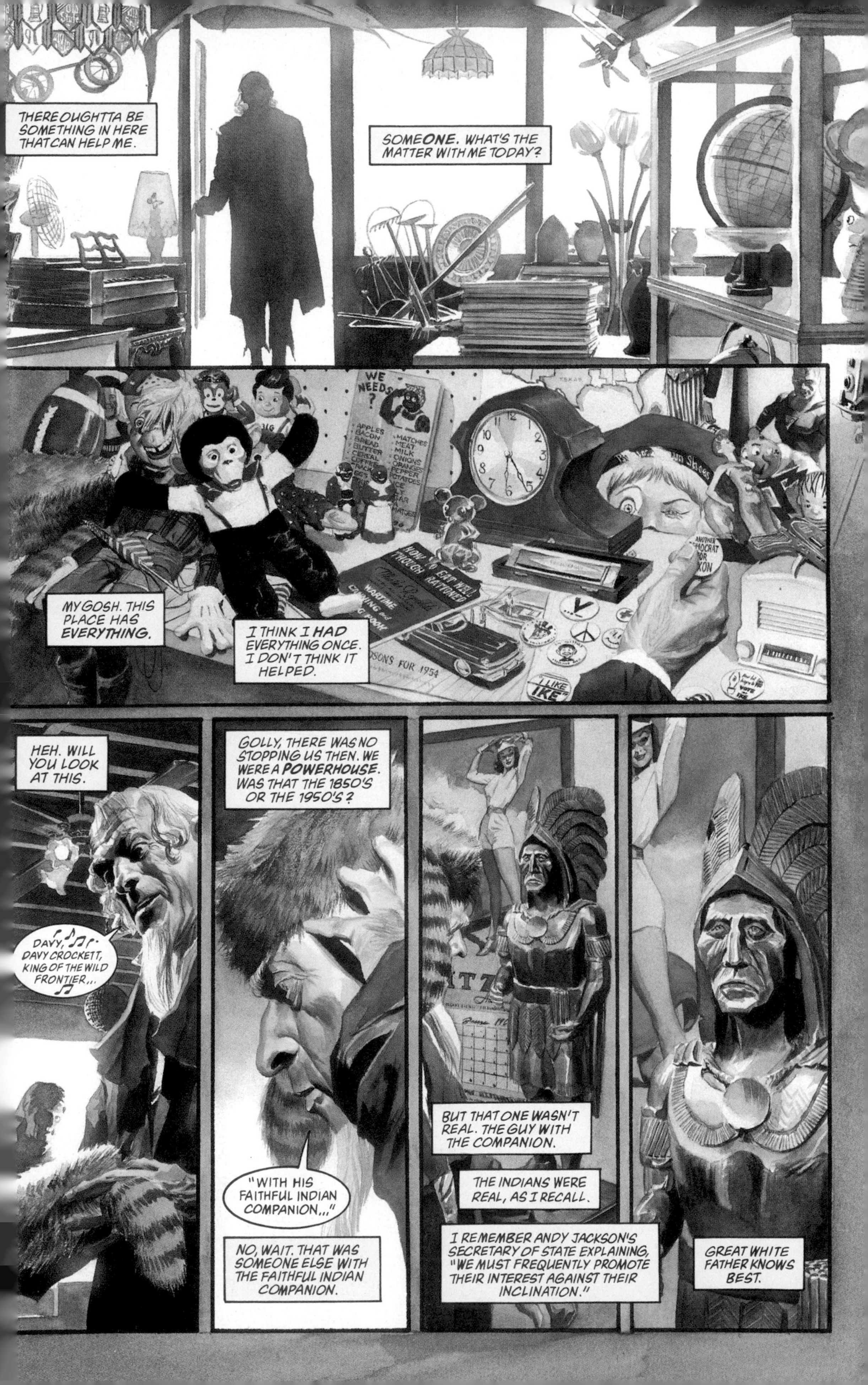
THERE OUGHTTA BE SOMETHING IN HERE THAT CAN HELP ME.
SOMEONE. WHAT'S THE MATTER WITH ME TODAY?
MY GOSH. THIS PLACE HAS EVERYTHING.
I THINK I HAD EVERYTHING ONCE. I DON'T THINK IT HELPED.
HEH. WILL YOU LOOK AT THIS.
DAVY, DAVY CROCKETT, KING OF THE WILD FRONTIER...
GOLLY, THERE WAS NO STOPPING US THEN. WE WERE A POWERHOUSE. WAS THAT THE 1850'S OR THE 1950'S?
"WITH HIS FAITHFUL INDIAN COMPANION..."
NO, WAIT. THAT WAS SOMEONE ELSE WITH THE FAITHFUL INDIAN COMPANION.
BUT THAT ONE WASN'T REAL. THE GUY WITH THE COMPANION.
THE INDIANS WERE REAL, AS I RECALL.
I REMEMBER ANDY JACKSON'S SECRETARY OF STATE EXPLAINING, "WE MUST FREQUENTLY PROMOTE THEIR INTEREST AGAINST THEIR INCLINATION."
GREAT WHITE FATHER KNOWS BEST.

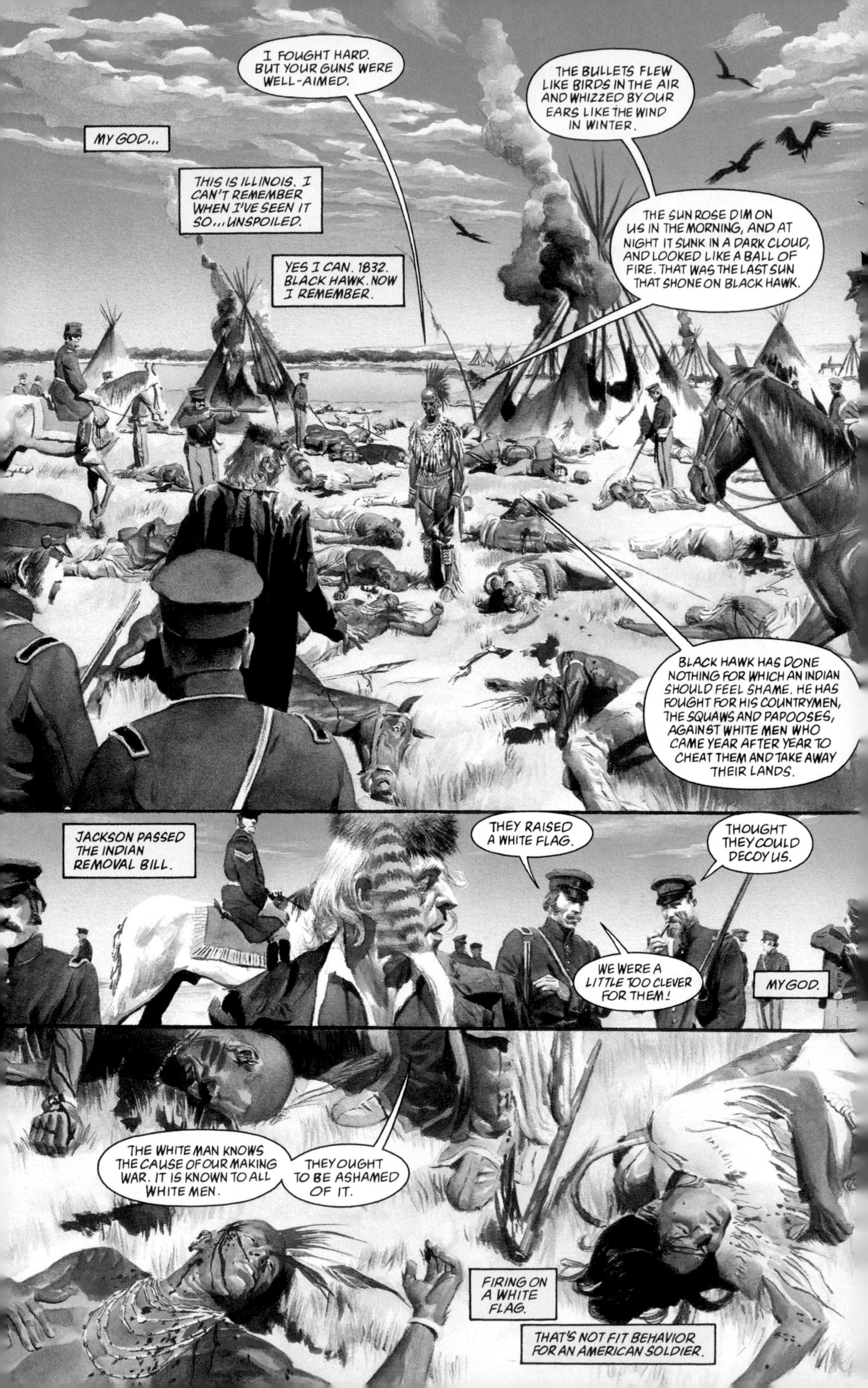
MY GOD...
THIS IS ILLINOIS. I CAN'T REMEMBER WHEN I'VE SEEN IT SO... UNSPOILED.
YES I CAN. 1832. BLACK HAWK. NOW I REMEMBER.
I FOUGHT HARD. BUT YOUR GUNS WERE WELL-AIMED.
THE BULLETS FLEW LIKE BIRDS IN THE AIR AND WHIZZED BY OUR EARS LIKE THE WIND IN WINTER.
THE SUN ROSE DIM ON US IN THE MORNING, AND AT NIGHT IT SUNK IN A DARK CLOUD, AND LOOKED LIKE A BALL OF FIRE. THAT WAS THE LAST SUN THAT SHONE ON BLACK HAWK.
BLACK HAWK HAS DONE NOTHING FOR WHICH AN INDIAN SHOULD FEEL SHAME. HE HAS FOUGHT FOR HIS COUNTRYMEN, THE SQUAWS AND PAPOOSES, AGAINST WHITE MEN WHO CAME YEAR AFTER YEAR TO CHEAT THEM AND TAKE AWAY THEIR LANDS.
JACKSON PASSED THE INDIAN REMOVAL BILL.
THEY RAISED A WHITE FLAG.
THOUGHT THEY COULD DECOY US.
WE WERE A LITTLE TOO CLEVER FOR THEM!
MY GOD.
THE WHITE MAN KNOWS THE CAUSE OF OUR MAKING WAR. IT IS KNOWN TO ALL WHITE MEN.
THEY OUGHT TO BE ASHAMED OF IT.
FIRING ON A WHITE FLAG.
THAT'S NOT FIT BEHAVIOR FOR AN AMERICAN SOLDIER.

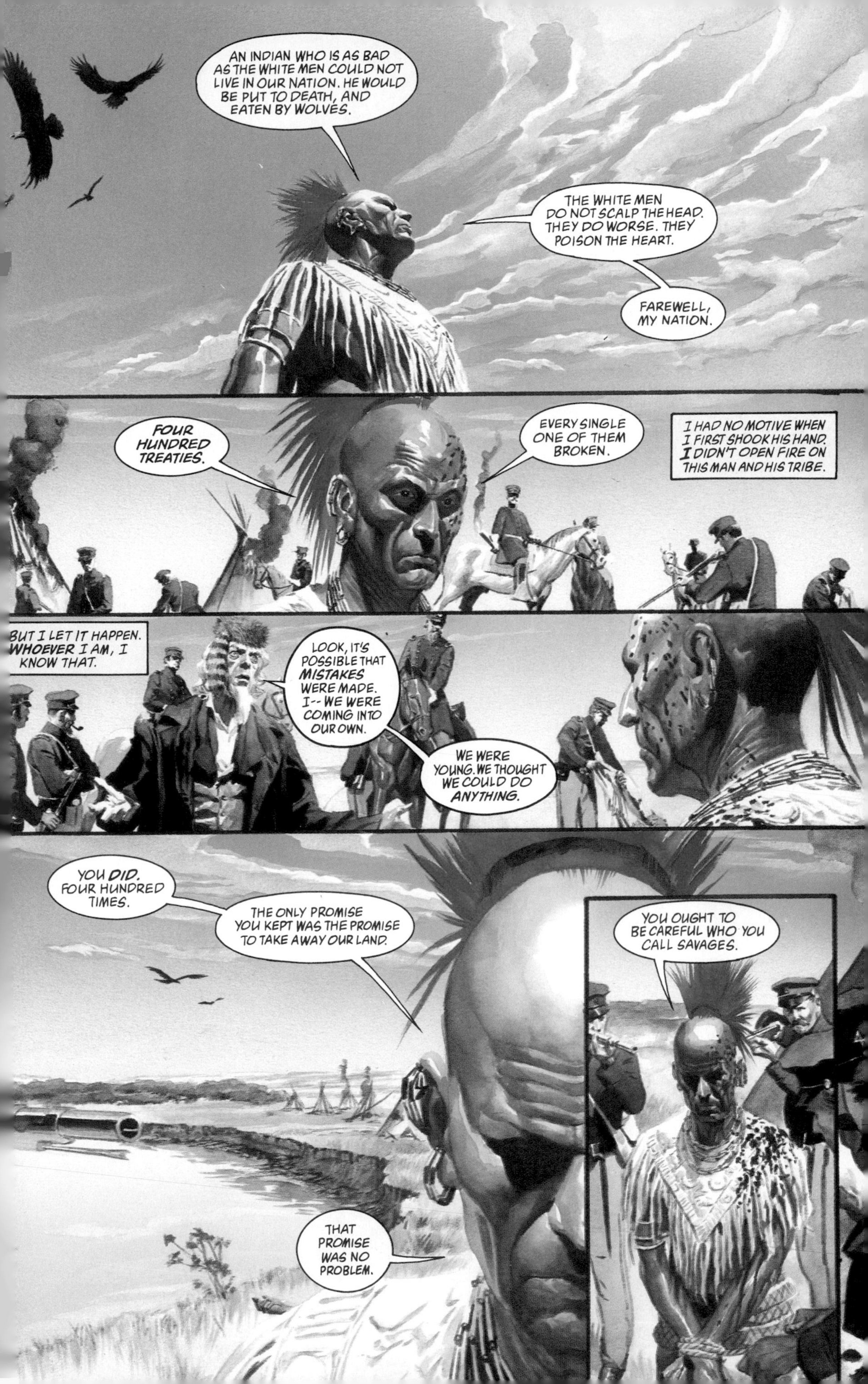
AN INDIAN WHO IS AS BAD AS THE WHITE MEN COULD NOT LIVE IN OUR NATION. HE WOULD BE PUT TO DEATH, AND EATEN BY WOLVES.
THE WHITE MEN DO NOT SCALP THE HEAD. THEY DO WORSE. THEY POISON THE HEART.
FAREWELL, MY NATION.
FOUR HUNDRED TREATIES.
EVERY SINGLE ONE OF THEM BROKEN.
I HAD NO MOTIVE WHEN I FIRST SHOOK HIS HAND. I DIDN'T OPEN FIRE ON THIS MAN AND HIS TRIBE.
BUT I LET IT HAPPEN. WHOEVER I AM, I KNOW THAT.
LOOK, IT'S POSSIBLE THAT MISTAKES WERE MADE. I-- WE WERE COMING INTO OUR OWN.
WE WERE YOUNG. WE THOUGHT WE COULD DO ANYTHING.
YOU DID. FOUR HUNDRED TIMES.
THE ONLY PROMISE YOU KEPT WAS THE PROMISE TO TAKE AWAY OUR LAND.
THAT PROMISE WAS NO PROBLEM.
YOU OUGHT TO BE CAREFUL WHO YOU CALL SAVAGES.

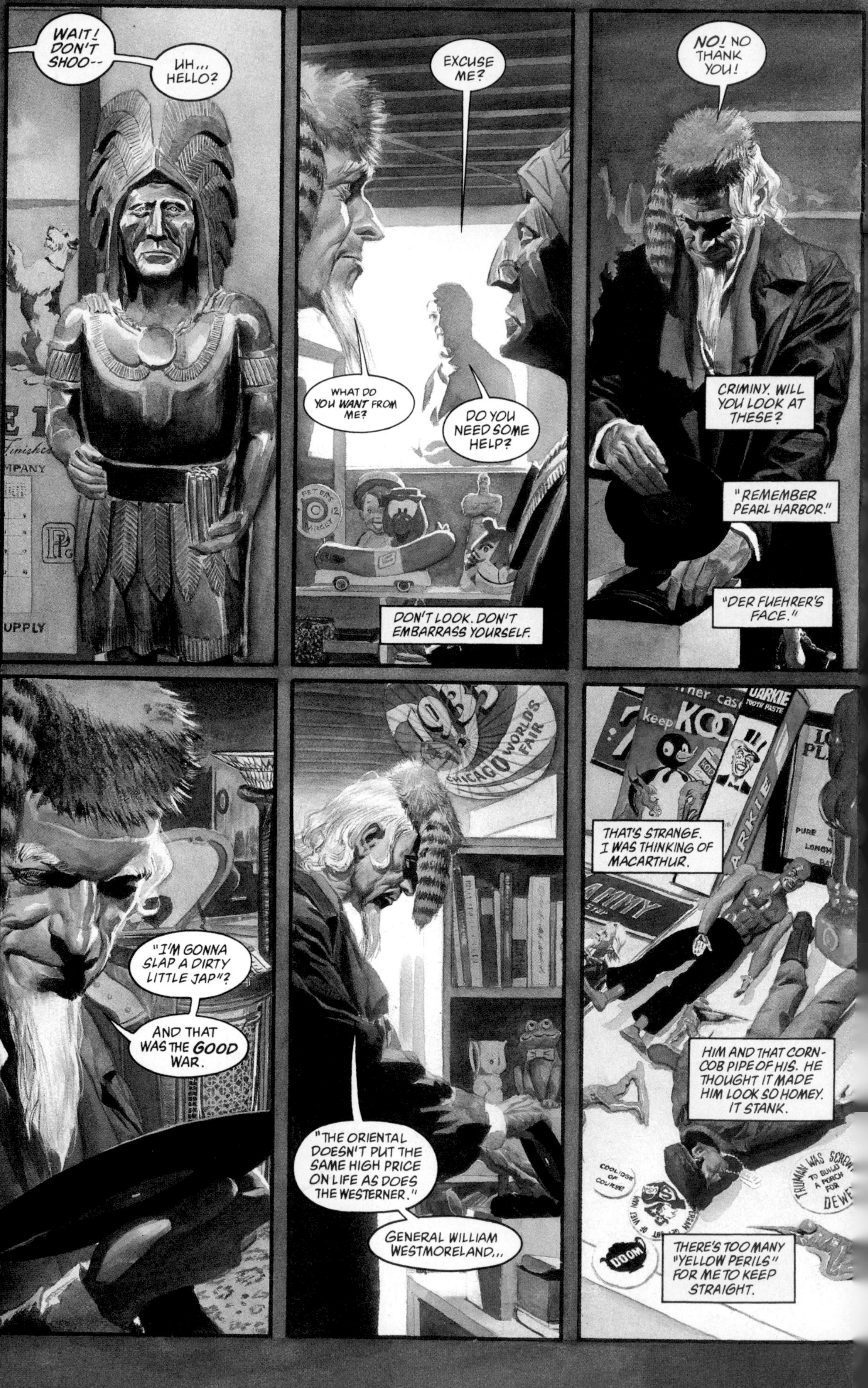

WAIT! DON'T SHOO--
UH... HELLO?
EXCUSE ME?
WHAT DO YOU WANT FROM ME?
DO YOU NEED SOME HELP?
DON'T LOOK. DON'T EMBARRASS YOURSELF.
NO! NO THANK YOU!
CRIMINY. WILL YOU LOOK AT THESE?
"REMEMBER PEARL HARBOR."
"DER FUEHRER'S FACE."
"I'M GONNA SLAP A DIRTY LITTLE JAP"?
AND THAT WAS THE GOOD WAR.
CHICAGO WORLD'S FAIR
"THE ORIENTAL DOESN'T PUT THE SAME HIGH PRICE ON LIFE AS DOES THE WESTERNER."
GENERAL WILLIAM WESTMORELAND...
THAT'S STRANGE. I WAS THINKING OF MACARTHUR.
HIM AND THAT CORN-COB PIPE OF HIS. HE THOUGHT IT MADE HIM LOOK SO HOMEY. IT STANK.
COOLIDGE OF COURSE
DOOM
THERE'S TOO MANY "YELLOW PERILS" FOR ME TO KEEP STRAIGHT.

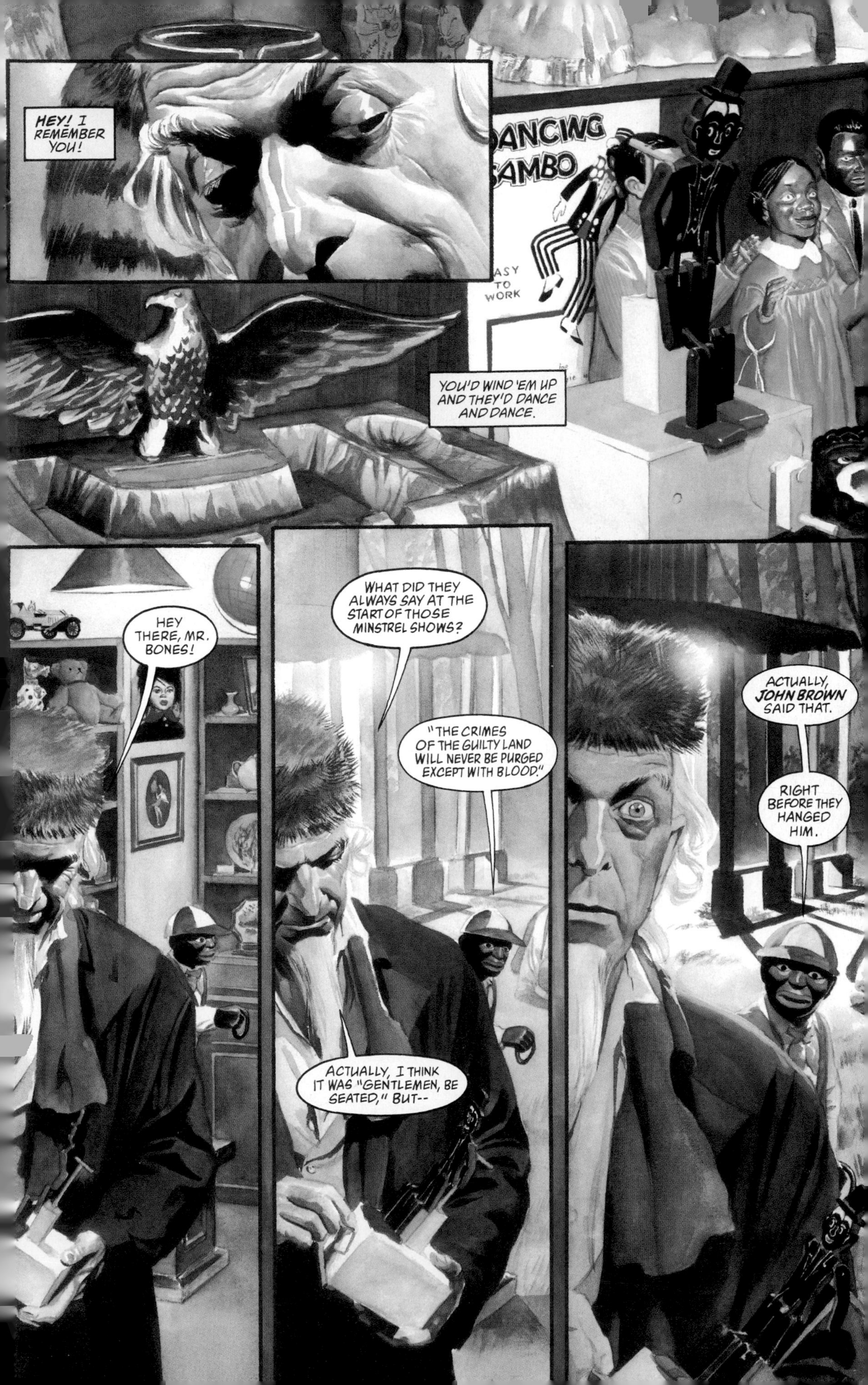
HEY! I REMEMBER YOU!
DANCING SAMBO
EASY TO WORK
YOU'D WIND 'EM UP AND THEY'D DANCE AND DANCE.
HEY THERE, MR. BONES!
WHAT DID THEY ALWAYS SAY AT THE START OF THOSE MINSTREL SHOWS?
"THE CRIMES OF THE GUILTY LAND WILL NEVER BE PURGED EXCEPT WITH BLOOD."
ACTUALLY, I THINK IT WAS "GENTLEMEN, BE SEATED," BUT--
ACTUALLY, JOHN BROWN SAID THAT.
RIGHT BEFORE THEY HANGED HIM.

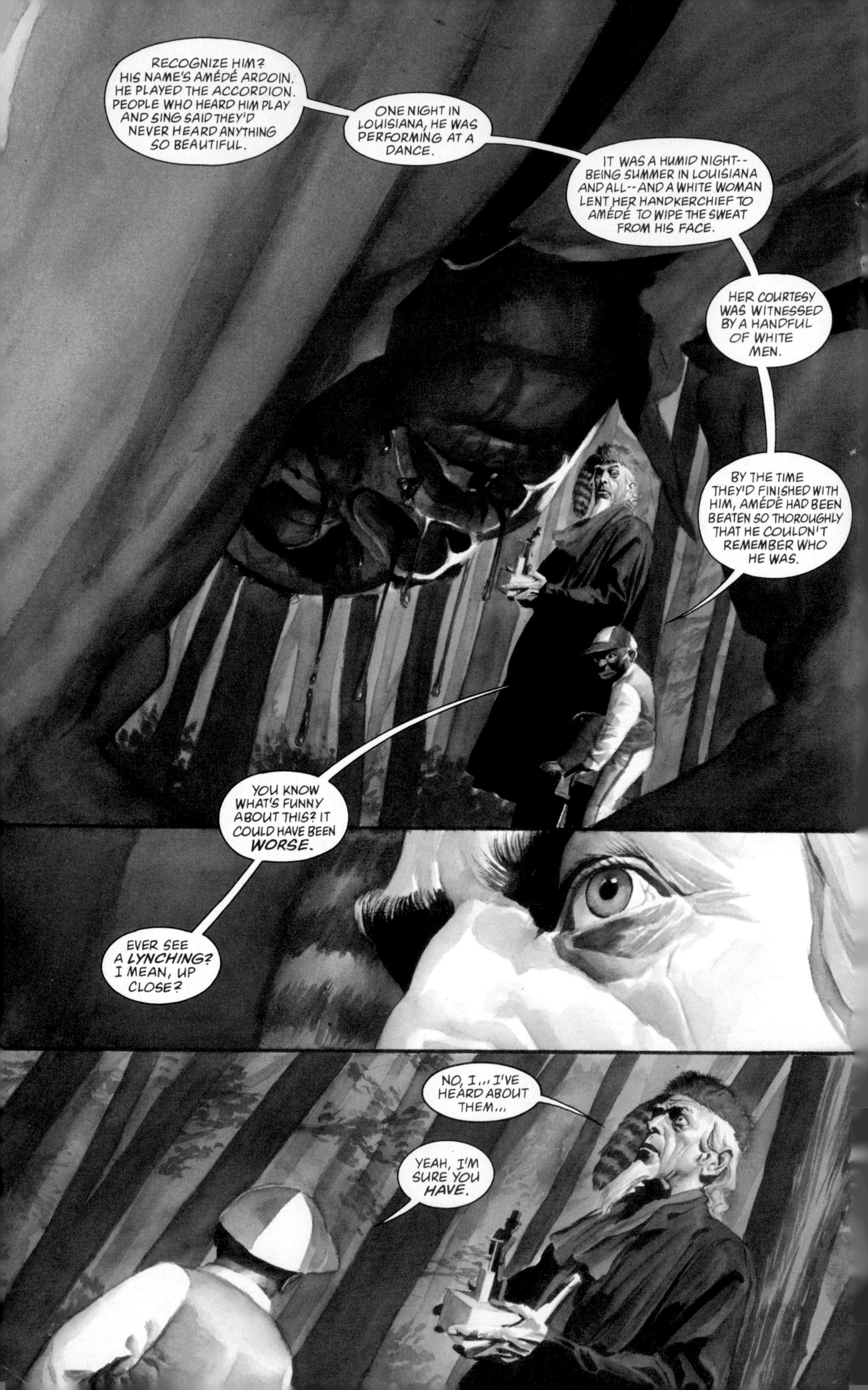
RECOGNIZE HIM? HIS NAME'S AMÉDÉ ARDOIN. HE PLAYED THE ACCORDION. PEOPLE WHO HEARD HIM PLAY AND SING SAID THEY'D NEVER HEARD ANYTHING SO BEAUTIFUL.
ONE NIGHT IN LOUISIANA, HE WAS PERFORMING AT A DANCE.
IT WAS A HUMID NIGHT-- BEING SUMMER IN LOUISIANA AND ALL--AND A WHITE WOMAN LENT HER HANDKERCHIEF TO AMÉDÉ TO WIPE THE SWEAT FROM HIS FACE.
HER COURTESY WAS WITNESSED BY A HANDFUL OF WHITE MEN.
BY THE TIME THEY'D FINISHED WITH HIM, AMÉDÉ HAD BEEN BEATEN SO THOROUGHLY THAT HE COULDN'T REMEMBER WHO HE WAS.
YOU KNOW WHAT'S FUNNY ABOUT THIS? IT COULD HAVE BEEN WORSE.
EVER SEE A LYNCHING? I MEAN, UP CLOSE?
NO, I... I'VE HEARD ABOUT THEM...
YEAH, I'M SURE YOU HAVE.

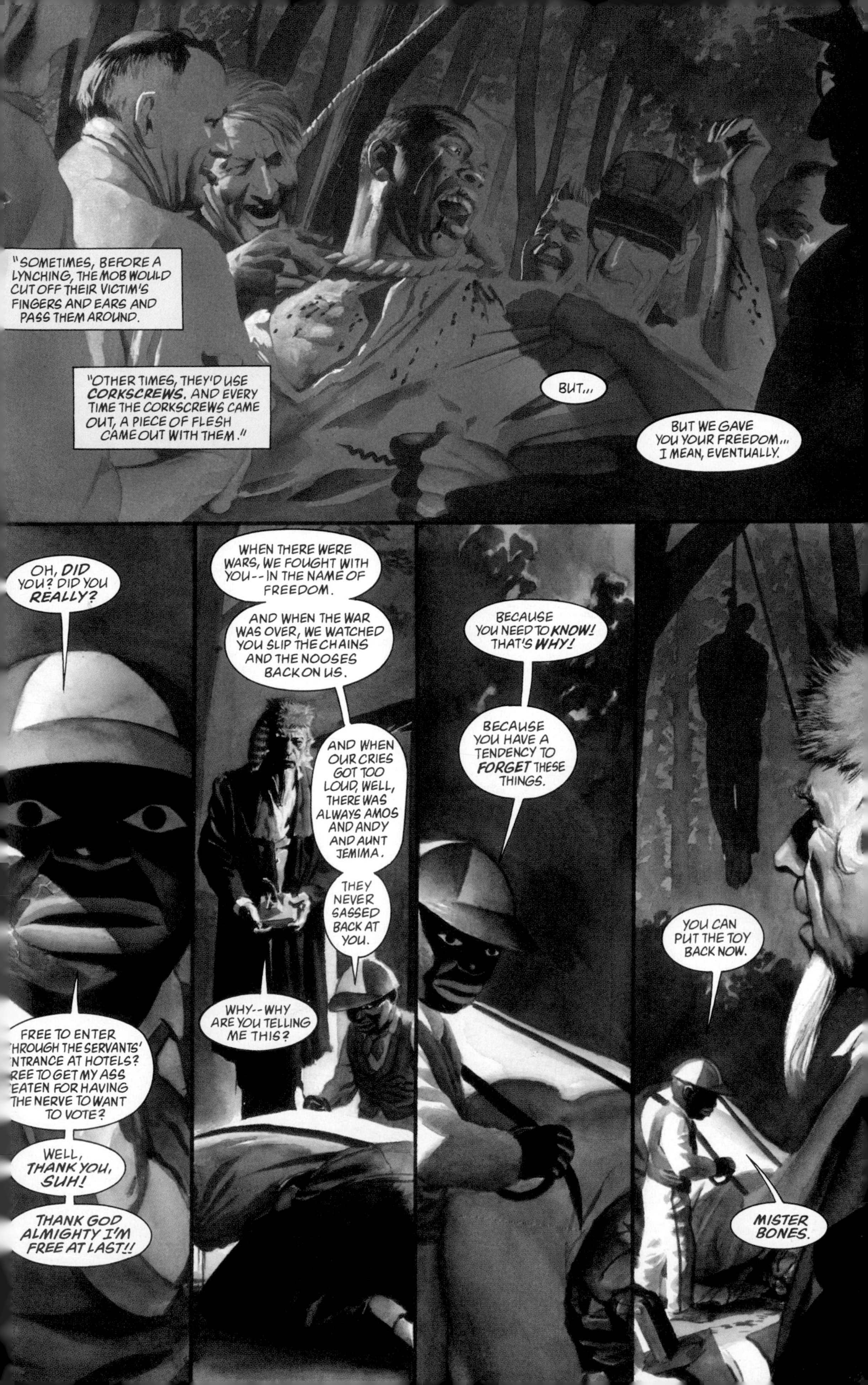
"SOMETIMES, BEFORE A LYNCHING, THE MOB WOULD CUT OFF THEIR VICTIM'S FINGERS AND EARS AND PASS THEM AROUND.
"OTHER TIMES, THEY'D USE **CORKSCREWS**. AND EVERY TIME THE CORKSCREWS CAME OUT, A PIECE OF FLESH CAME OUT WITH THEM."
BUT...
BUT WE GAVE YOU YOUR FREEDOM... I MEAN, EVENTUALLY.
OH, **DID** YOU? DID YOU **REALLY?**
FREE TO ENTER THROUGH THE SERVANTS' ENTRANCE AT HOTELS? FREE TO GET MY ASS BEATEN FOR HAVING THE NERVE TO WANT TO VOTE?
WELL, **THANK YOU, SUH!**
THANK GOD ALMIGHTY I'M FREE AT LAST!!
WHEN THERE WERE WARS, WE FOUGHT WITH YOU--IN THE NAME OF FREEDOM.
AND WHEN THE WAR WAS OVER, WE WATCHED YOU SLIP THE CHAINS AND THE NOOSES BACK ON US.
AND WHEN OUR CRIES GOT TOO LOUD, WELL, THERE WAS ALWAYS AMOS AND ANDY AND AUNT JEMIMA.
THEY NEVER SASSED BACK AT YOU.
WHY--WHY ARE YOU TELLING ME THIS?
BECAUSE YOU NEED TO **KNOW!** THAT'S **WHY!**
BECAUSE YOU HAVE A TENDENCY TO **FORGET** THESE THINGS.
YOU CAN PUT THE TOY BACK NOW.
MISTER BONES.

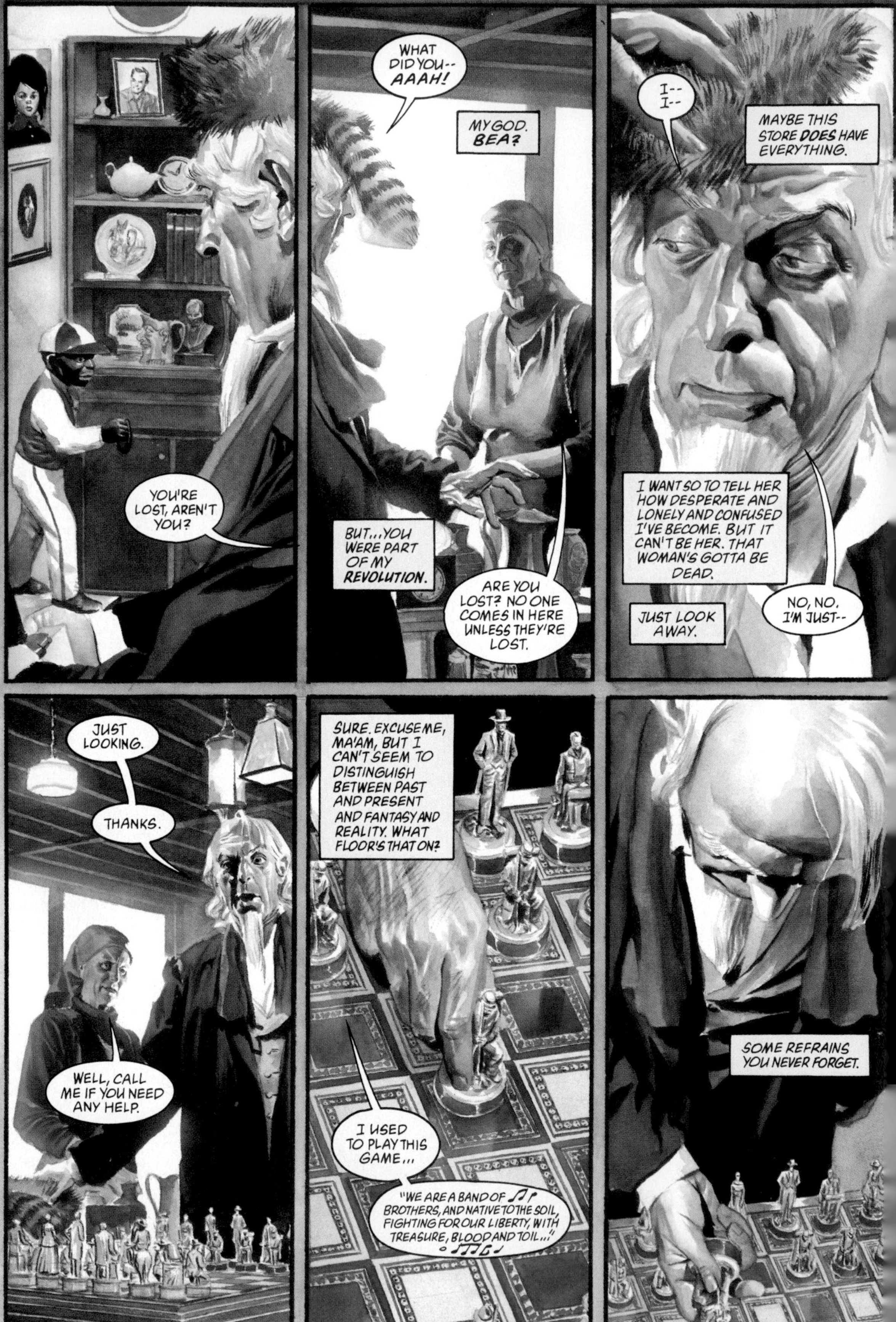
YOU'RE LOST, AREN'T YOU?
WHAT DID YOU-- AAAH!
MY GOD. BEA?
BUT... YOU WERE PART OF MY REVOLUTION.
ARE YOU LOST? NO ONE COMES IN HERE UNLESS THEY'RE LOST.
I-- I--
MAYBE THIS STORE DOES HAVE EVERYTHING.
I WANT SO TO TELL HER HOW DESPERATE AND LONELY AND CONFUSED I'VE BECOME. BUT IT CAN'T BE HER. THAT WOMAN'S GOTTA BE DEAD.
JUST LOOK AWAY.
NO, NO. I'M JUST--
JUST LOOKING.
THANKS.
WELL, CALL ME IF YOU NEED ANY HELP.
SURE. EXCUSE ME, MA'AM, BUT I CAN'T SEEM TO DISTINGUISH BETWEEN PAST AND PRESENT AND FANTASY AND REALITY. WHAT FLOOR'S THAT ON?
I USED TO PLAY THIS GAME...
"WE ARE A BAND OF BROTHERS, AND NATIVE TO THE SOIL, FIGHTING FOR OUR LIBERTY, WITH TREASURE, BLOOD AND TOIL..."
SOME REFRAINS YOU NEVER FORGET.

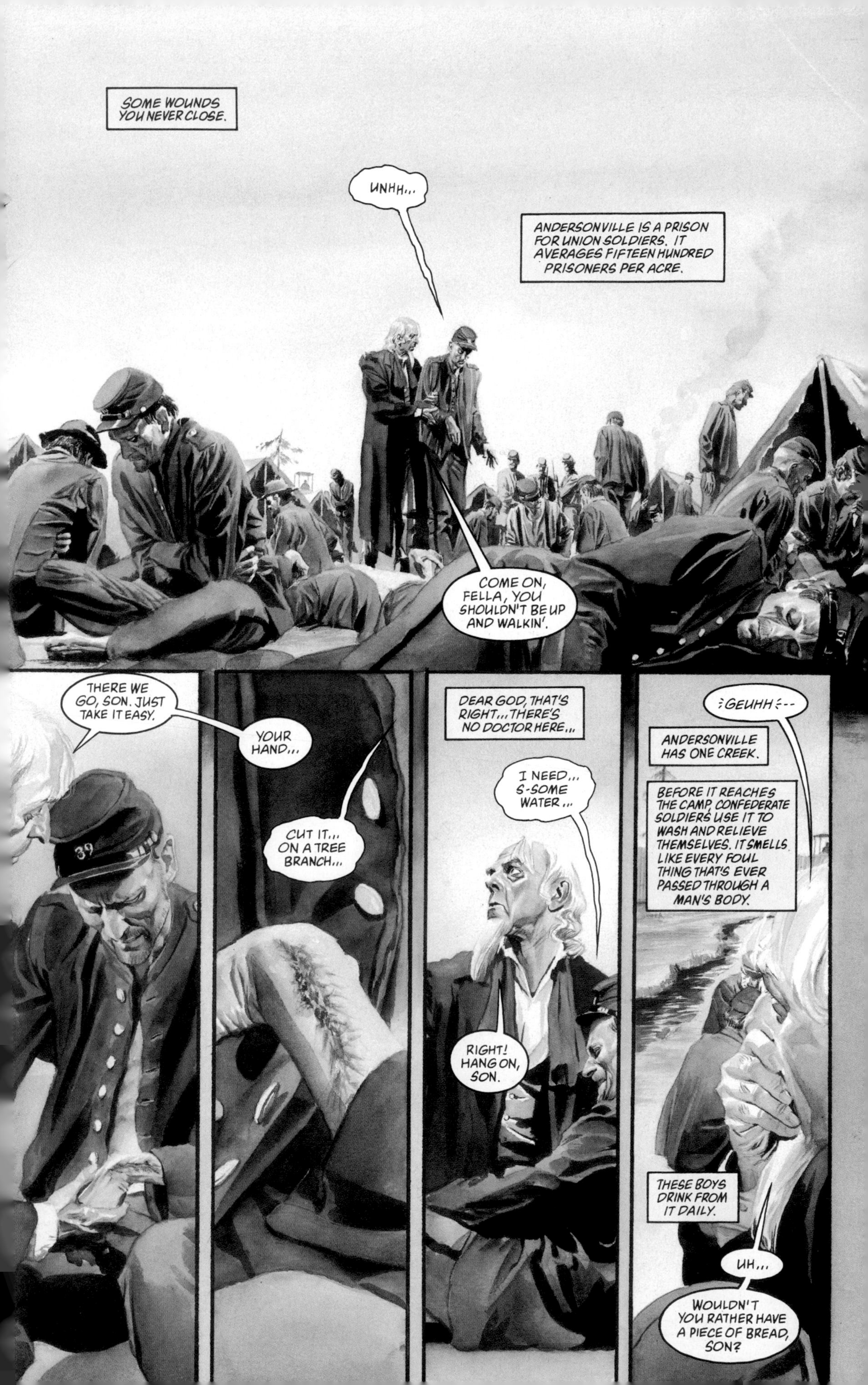
SOME WOUNDS YOU NEVER CLOSE.
UNHH...
ANDERSONVILLE IS A PRISON FOR UNION SOLDIERS. IT AVERAGES FIFTEEN HUNDRED PRISONERS PER ACRE.
COME ON, FELLA, YOU SHOULDN'T BE UP AND WALKIN'.
THERE WE GO, SON. JUST TAKE IT EASY.
YOUR HAND...
CUT IT... ON A TREE BRANCH...
DEAR GOD, THAT'S RIGHT... THERE'S NO DOCTOR HERE...
I NEED... S-SOME WATER...
RIGHT! HANG ON, SON.
GEUHH---
ANDERSONVILLE HAS ONE CREEK.
BEFORE IT REACHES THE CAMP, CONFEDERATE SOLDIERS USE IT TO WASH AND RELIEVE THEMSELVES. IT SMELLS LIKE EVERY FOUL THING THAT'S EVER PASSED THROUGH A MAN'S BODY.
THESE BOYS DRINK FROM IT DAILY.
UH...
WOULDN'T YOU RATHER HAVE A PIECE OF BREAD, SON?

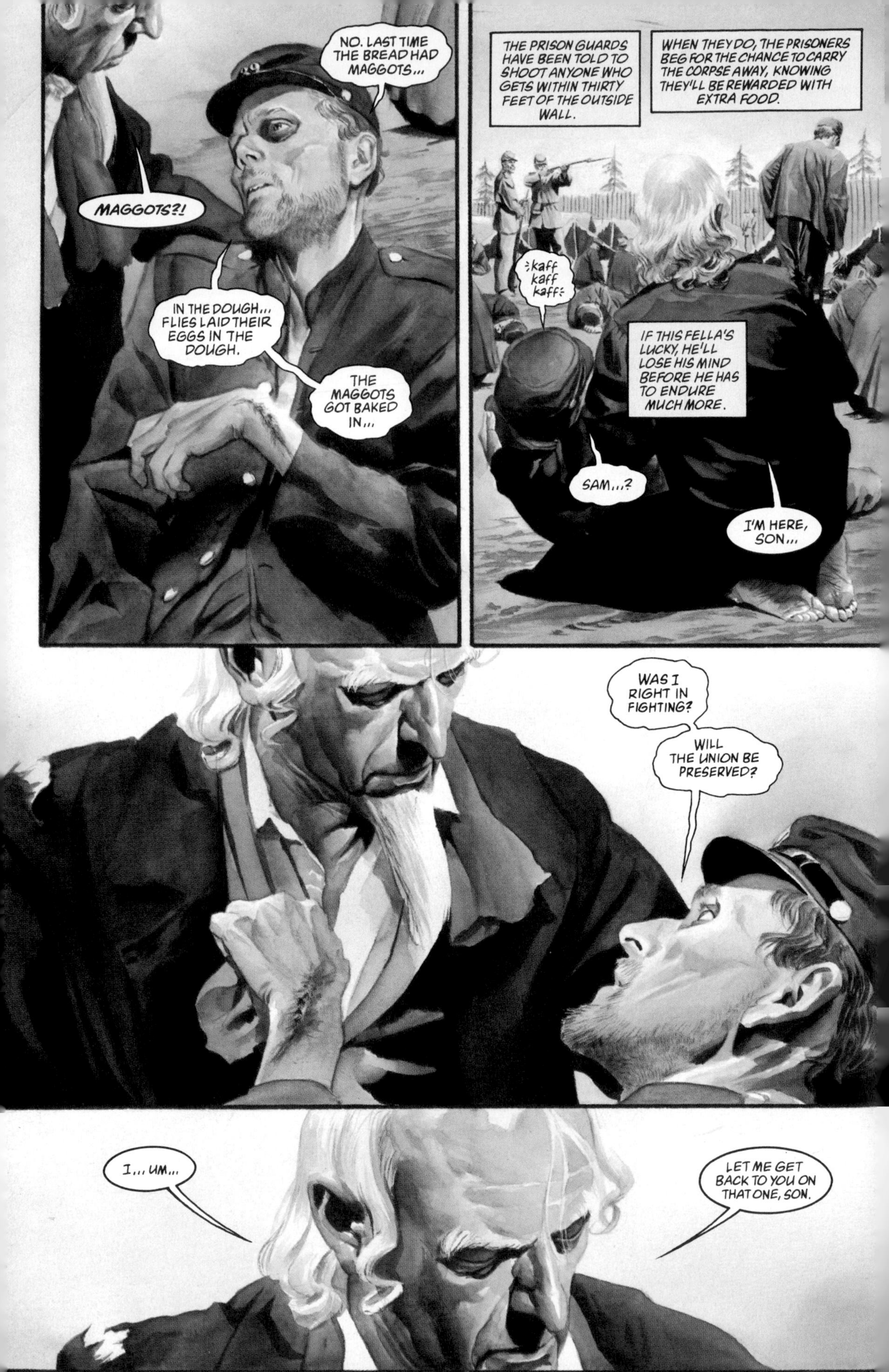
NO. LAST TIME THE BREAD HAD MAGGOTS...
MAGGOTS?!
IN THE DOUGH... FLIES LAID THEIR EGGS IN THE DOUGH.
THE MAGGOTS GOT BAKED IN...
THE PRISON GUARDS HAVE BEEN TOLD TO SHOOT ANYONE WHO GETS WITHIN THIRTY FEET OF THE OUTSIDE WALL.
WHEN THEY DO, THE PRISONERS BEG FOR THE CHANCE TO CARRY THE CORPSE AWAY, KNOWING THEY'LL BE REWARDED WITH EXTRA FOOD.
kaff kaff kaff
IF THIS FELLA'S LUCKY, HE'LL LOSE HIS MIND BEFORE HE HAS TO ENDURE MUCH MORE.
SAM...?
I'M HERE, SON...
WAS I RIGHT IN FIGHTING?
WILL THE UNION BE PRESERVED?
I... UM...
LET ME GET BACK TO YOU ON THAT ONE, SON.

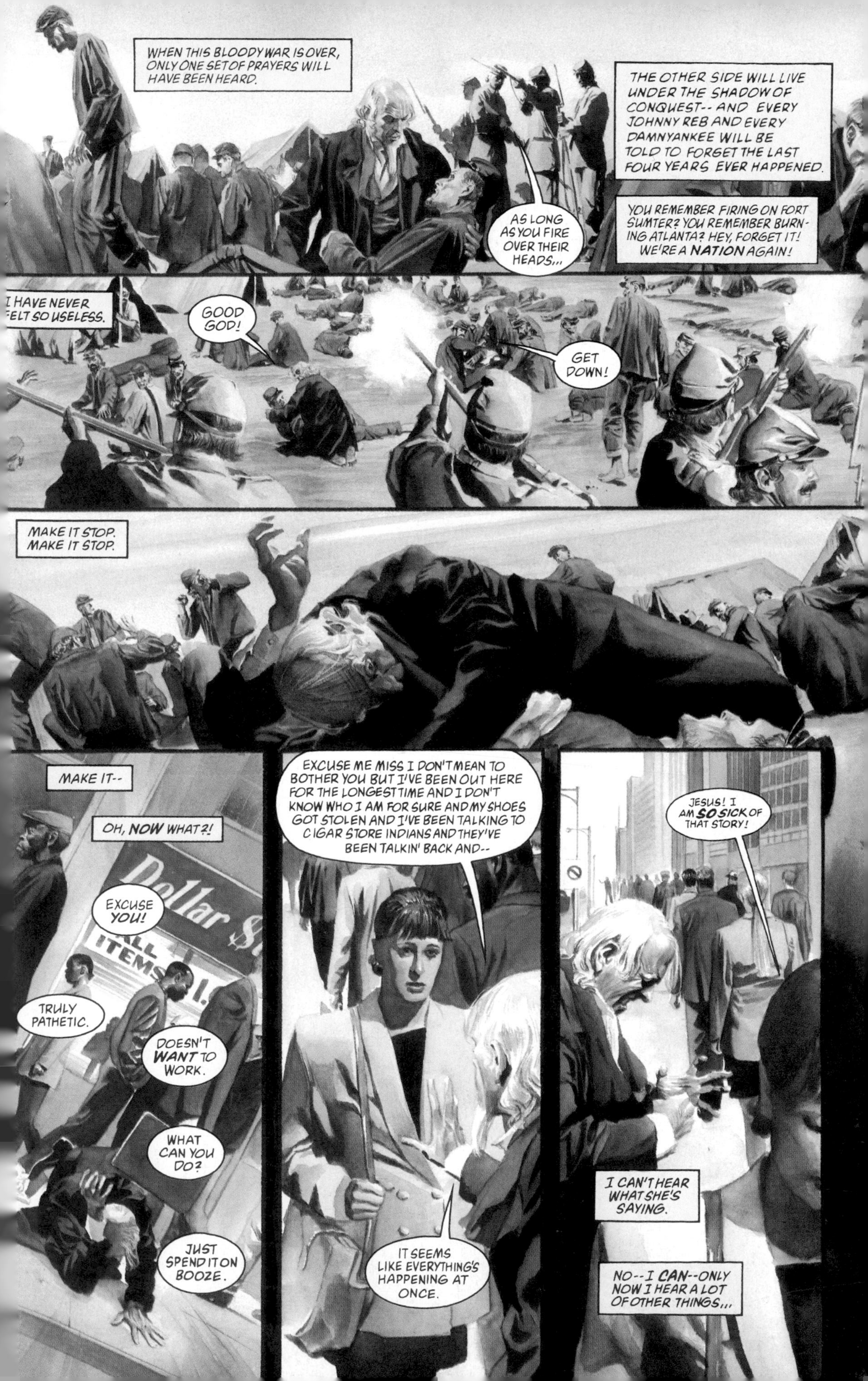
WHEN THIS BLOODY WAR IS OVER, ONLY ONE SET OF PRAYERS WILL HAVE BEEN HEARD.
THE OTHER SIDE WILL LIVE UNDER THE SHADOW OF CONQUEST-- AND EVERY JOHNNY REB AND EVERY DAMNYANKEE WILL BE TOLD TO FORGET THE LAST FOUR YEARS EVER HAPPENED.
AS LONG AS YOU FIRE OVER THEIR HEADS,,,
YOU REMEMBER FIRING ON FORT SUMTER? YOU REMEMBER BURNING ATLANTA? HEY, FORGET IT! WE'RE A NATION AGAIN!
I HAVE NEVER FELT SO USELESS.
GOOD GOD!
GET DOWN!
MAKE IT STOP. MAKE IT STOP.
MAKE IT--
OH, NOW WHAT?!
Dollar St
ALL ITEMS $1.
EXCUSE YOU!
TRULY PATHETIC.
DOESN'T WANT TO WORK.
WHAT CAN YOU DO?
JUST SPEND IT ON BOOZE.
EXCUSE ME MISS I DON'T MEAN TO BOTHER YOU BUT I'VE BEEN OUT HERE FOR THE LONGEST TIME AND I DON'T KNOW WHO I AM FOR SURE AND MY SHOES GOT STOLEN AND I'VE BEEN TALKING TO CIGAR STORE INDIANS AND THEY'VE BEEN TALKIN' BACK AND--
IT SEEMS LIKE EVERYTHING'S HAPPENING AT ONCE.
JESUS! I AM SO SICK OF THAT STORY!
I CAN'T HEAR WHAT SHE'S SAYING.
NO--I CAN--ONLY NOW I HEAR A LOT OF OTHER THINGS,,,

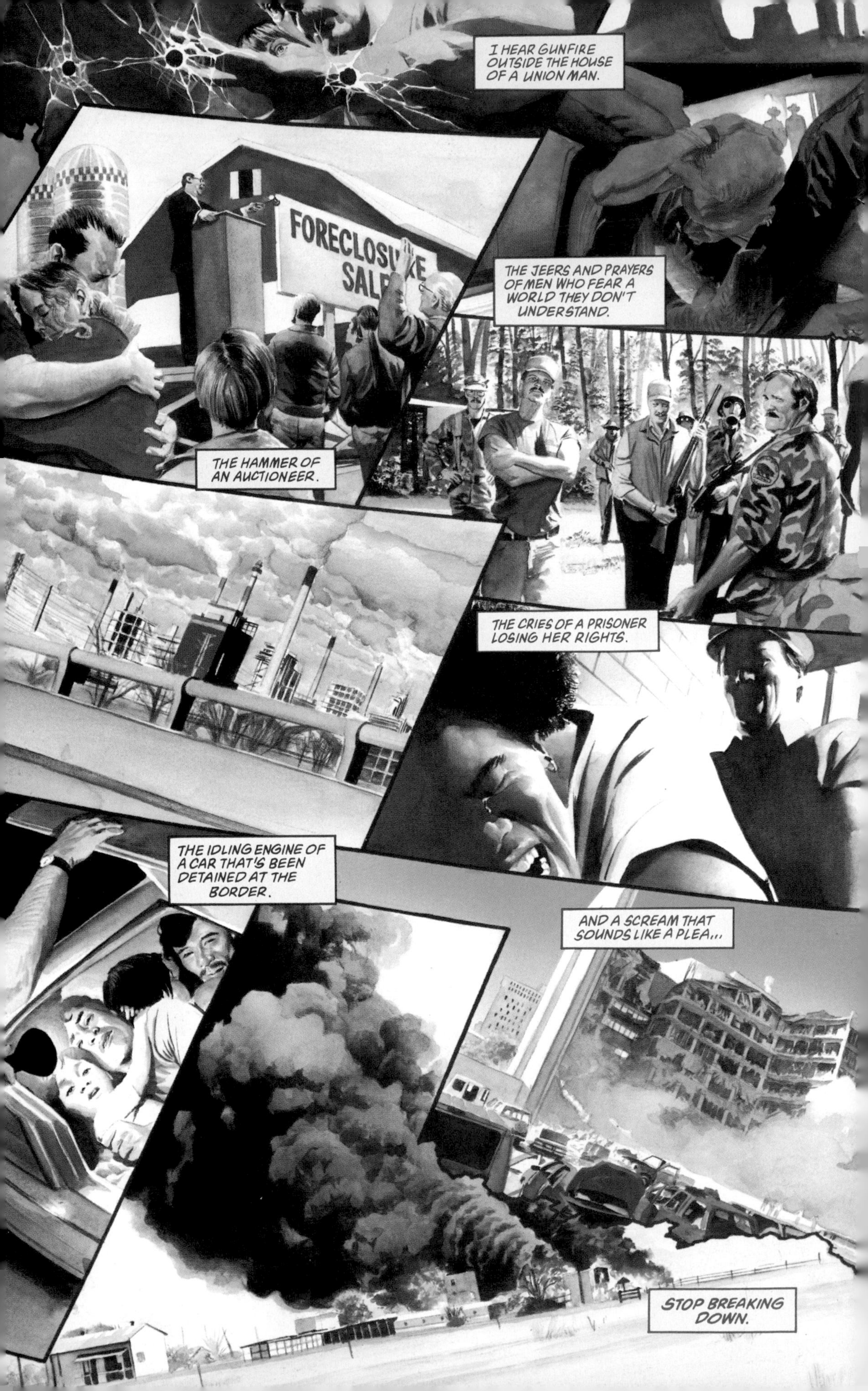
I HEAR GUNFIRE OUTSIDE THE HOUSE OF A UNION MAN.
FORECLOSURE SALE
THE JEERS AND PRAYERS OF MEN WHO FEAR A WORLD THEY DON'T UNDERSTAND.
THE HAMMER OF AN AUCTIONEER.
THE CRIES OF A PRISONER LOSING HER RIGHTS.
THE IDLING ENGINE OF A CAR THAT'S BEEN DETAINED AT THE BORDER.
AND A SCREAM THAT SOUNDS LIKE A PLEA...
STOP BREAKING DOWN.

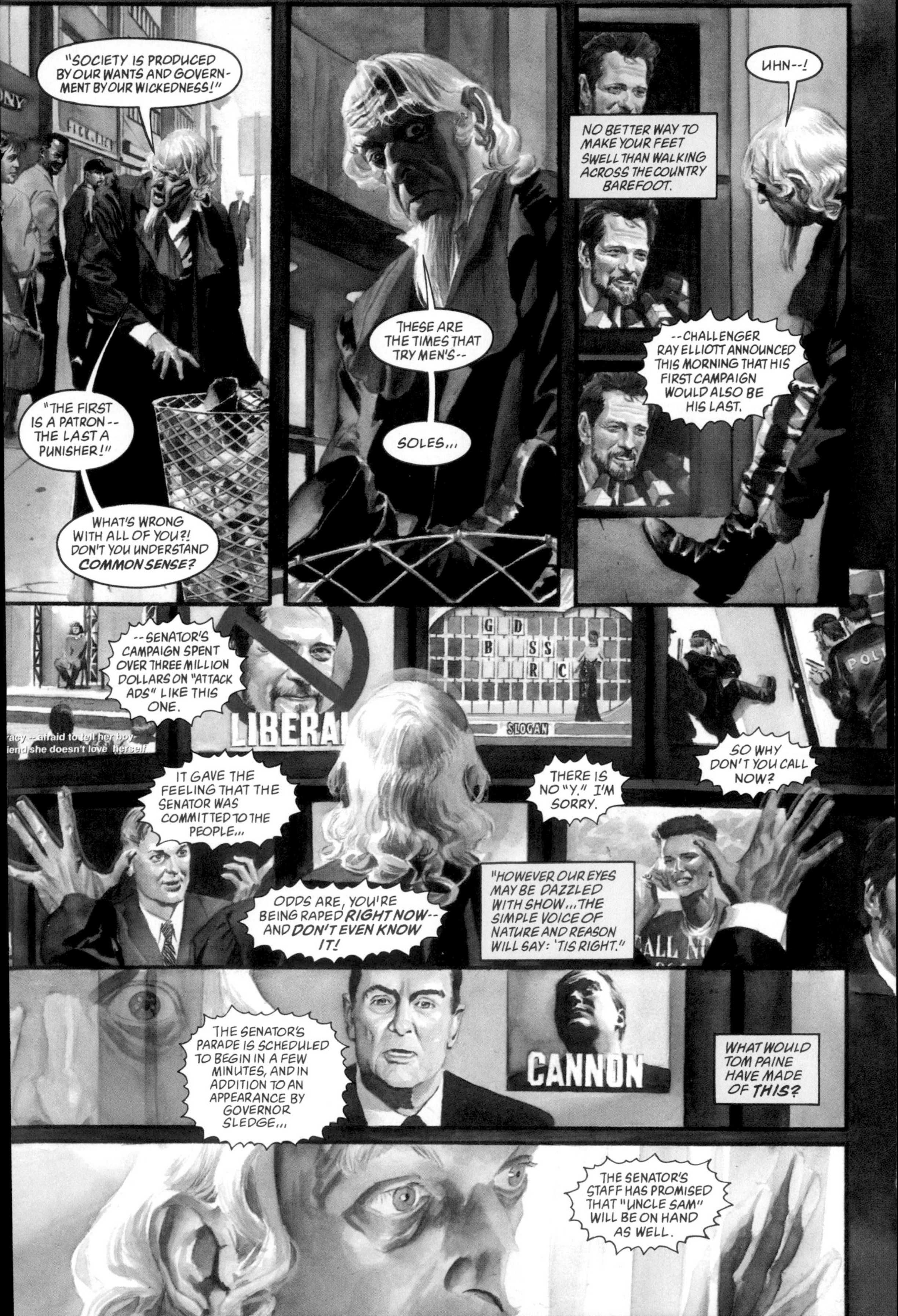
"SOCIETY IS PRODUCED BY OUR WANTS AND GOVERNMENT BY OUR WICKEDNESS!"
"THE FIRST IS A PATRON -- THE LAST A PUNISHER!"
WHAT'S WRONG WITH ALL OF YOU?! DON'T YOU UNDERSTAND **COMMON SENSE?**
THESE ARE THE TIMES THAT TRY MEN'S--
SOLES...
NO BETTER WAY TO MAKE YOUR FEET SWELL THAN WALKING ACROSS THE COUNTRY BAREFOOT.
UHN--!
--CHALLENGER RAY ELLIOTT ANNOUNCED THIS MORNING THAT HIS FIRST CAMPAIGN WOULD ALSO BE HIS LAST.
--SENATOR'S CAMPAIGN SPENT OVER THREE MILLION DOLLARS ON "ATTACK ADS" LIKE THIS ONE.
SLOGAN
SO WHY DON'T YOU CALL NOW?
IT GAVE THE FEELING THAT THE SENATOR WAS COMMITTED TO THE PEOPLE...
THERE IS NO "Y." I'M SORRY.
ODDS ARE, YOU'RE BEING RAPED **RIGHT NOW**-- AND **DON'T EVEN KNOW IT!**
"HOWEVER OUR EYES MAY BE DAZZLED WITH SHOW... THE SIMPLE VOICE OF NATURE AND REASON WILL SAY: 'TIS RIGHT."
THE SENATOR'S PARADE IS SCHEDULED TO BEGIN IN A FEW MINUTES, AND IN ADDITION TO AN APPEARANCE BY GOVERNOR SLEDGE...
CANNON
WHAT WOULD TOM PAINE HAVE MADE OF **THIS?**
THE SENATOR'S STAFF HAS PROMISED THAT "UNCLE SAM" WILL BE ON HAND AS WELL.

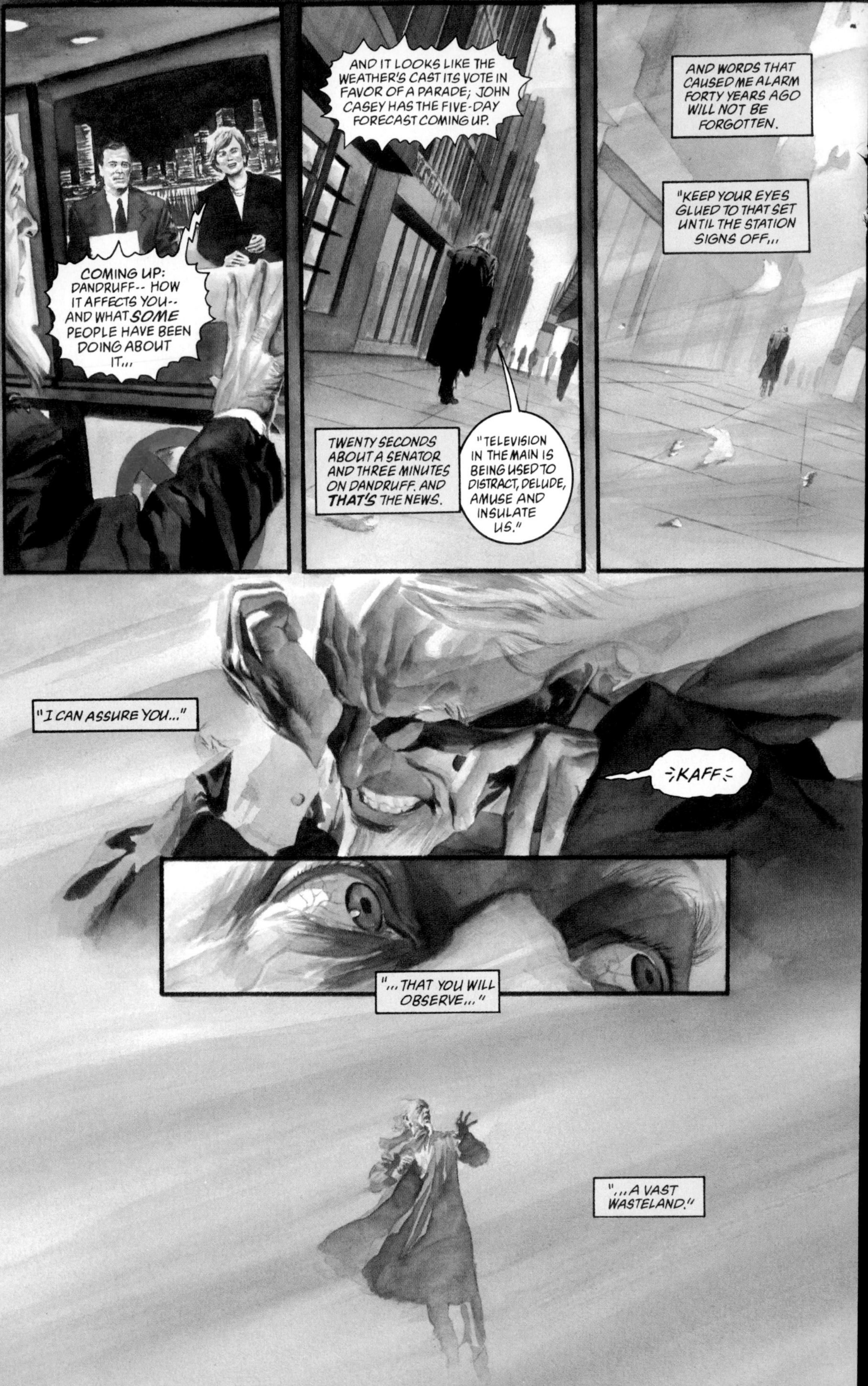
COMING UP: DANDRUFF-- HOW IT AFFECTS YOU-- AND WHAT SOME PEOPLE HAVE BEEN DOING ABOUT IT...
AND IT LOOKS LIKE THE WEATHER'S CAST ITS VOTE IN FAVOR OF A PARADE; JOHN CASEY HAS THE FIVE-DAY FORECAST COMING UP.
TWENTY SECONDS ABOUT A SENATOR AND THREE MINUTES ON DANDRUFF. AND THAT'S THE NEWS.
"TELEVISION IN THE MAIN IS BEING USED TO DISTRACT, DELUDE, AMUSE AND INSULATE US."
AND WORDS THAT CAUSED ME ALARM FORTY YEARS AGO WILL NOT BE FORGOTTEN.
"KEEP YOUR EYES GLUED TO THAT SET UNTIL THE STATION SIGNS OFF,,,
"I CAN ASSURE YOU..."
KAFF
"...THAT YOU WILL OBSERVE..."
"...A VAST WASTELAND."

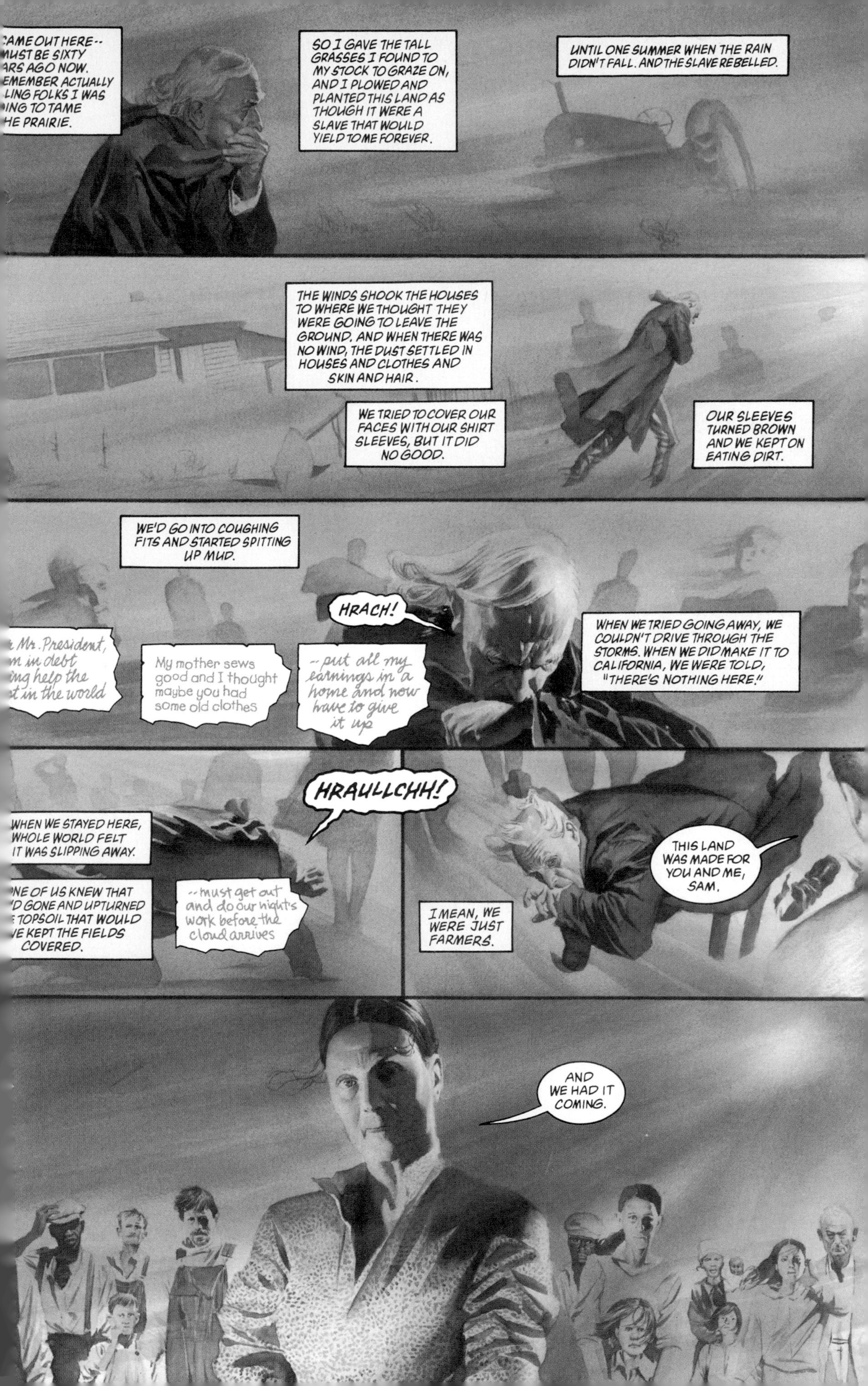
CAME OUT HERE-- MUST BE SIXTY ARS AGO NOW. EMEMBER ACTUALLY LING FOLKS I WAS ING TO TAME HE PRAIRIE.
SO I GAVE THE TALL GRASSES I FOUND TO MY STOCK TO GRAZE ON, AND I PLOWED AND PLANTED THIS LAND AS THOUGH IT WERE A SLAVE THAT WOULD YIELD TO ME FOREVER.
UNTIL ONE SUMMER WHEN THE RAIN DIDN'T FALL. AND THE SLAVE REBELLED.
THE WINDS SHOOK THE HOUSES TO WHERE WE THOUGHT THEY WERE GOING TO LEAVE THE GROUND, AND WHEN THERE WAS NO WIND, THE DUST SETTLED IN HOUSES AND CLOTHES AND SKIN AND HAIR.
WE TRIED TO COVER OUR FACES WITH OUR SHIRT SLEEVES, BUT IT DID NO GOOD.
OUR SLEEVES TURNED BROWN AND WE KEPT ON EATING DIRT.
WE'D GO INTO COUGHING FITS AND STARTED SPITTING UP MUD.
HRACH!
Mr. President, m in debt ing help the t in the world
My mother sews good and I thought maybe you had some old clothes
--put all my earnings in a home and now have to give it up
WHEN WE TRIED GOING AWAY, WE COULDN'T DRIVE THROUGH THE STORMS. WHEN WE DID MAKE IT TO CALIFORNIA, WE WERE TOLD, "THERE'S NOTHING HERE."
HRAULLCHH!
WHEN WE STAYED HERE, WHOLE WORLD FELT IT WAS SLIPPING AWAY.
NE OF US KNEW THAT D GONE AND UPTURNED TOPSOIL THAT WOULD E KEPT THE FIELDS COVERED.
--must get out and do our night's work before the cloud arrives
THIS LAND WAS MADE FOR YOU AND ME, SAM.
I MEAN, WE WERE JUST FARMERS.
AND WE HAD IT COMING.

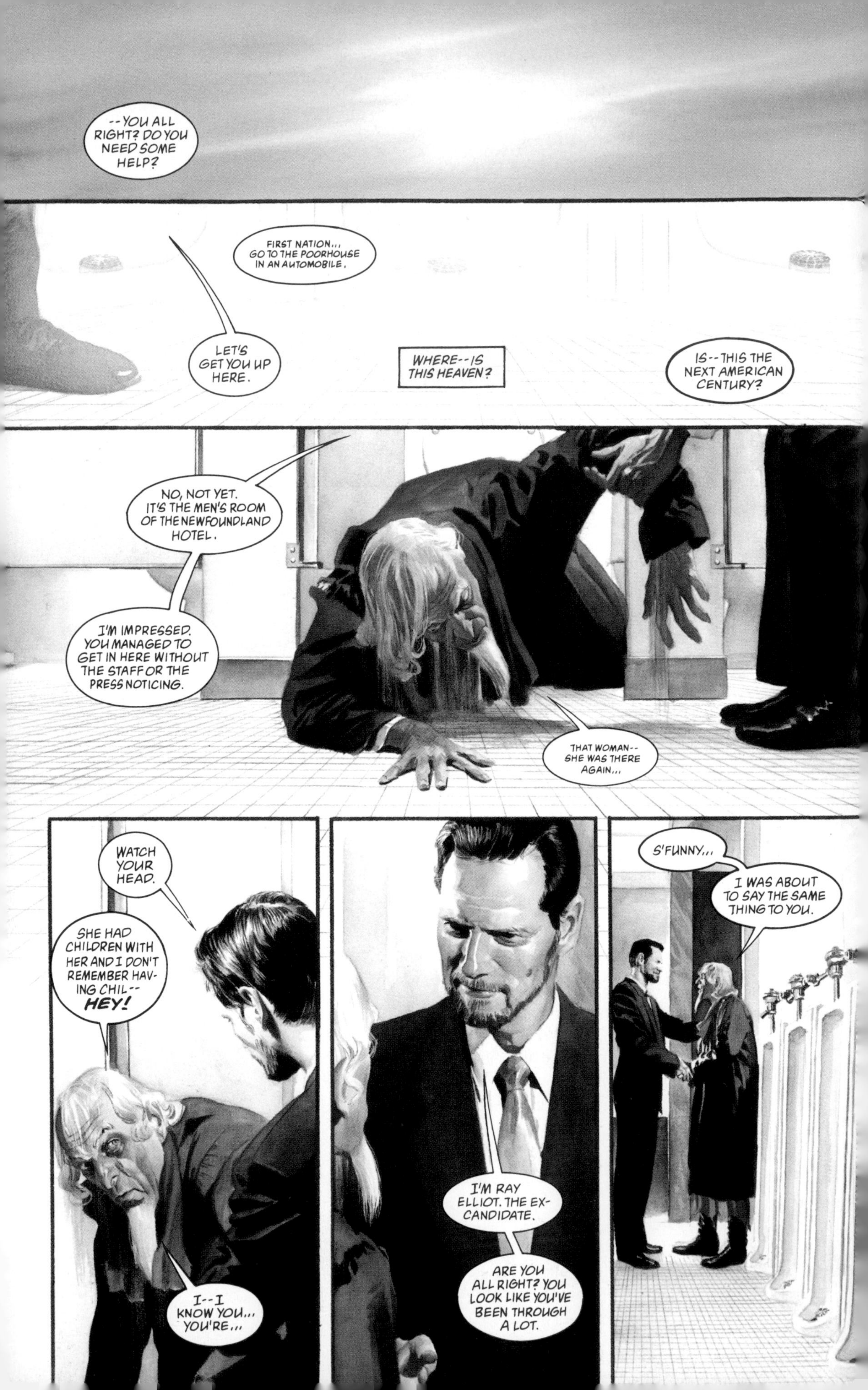
--YOU ALL RIGHT? DO YOU NEED SOME HELP?
FIRST NATION... GO TO THE POORHOUSE IN AN AUTOMOBILE.
LET'S GET YOU UP HERE.
WHERE--IS THIS HEAVEN?
IS--THIS THE NEXT AMERICAN CENTURY?
NO, NOT YET. IT'S THE MEN'S ROOM OF THE NEWFOUNDLAND HOTEL.
I'M IMPRESSED. YOU MANAGED TO GET IN HERE WITHOUT THE STAFF OR THE PRESS NOTICING.
THAT WOMAN--SHE WAS THERE AGAIN...
WATCH YOUR HEAD.
SHE HAD CHILDREN WITH HER AND I DON'T REMEMBER HAVING CHIL--HEY!
I--I KNOW YOU... YOU'RE...
I'M RAY ELLIOT. THE EX-CANDIDATE.
ARE YOU ALL RIGHT? YOU LOOK LIKE YOU'VE BEEN THROUGH A LOT.
S'FUNNY...
I WAS ABOUT TO SAY THE SAME THING TO YOU.

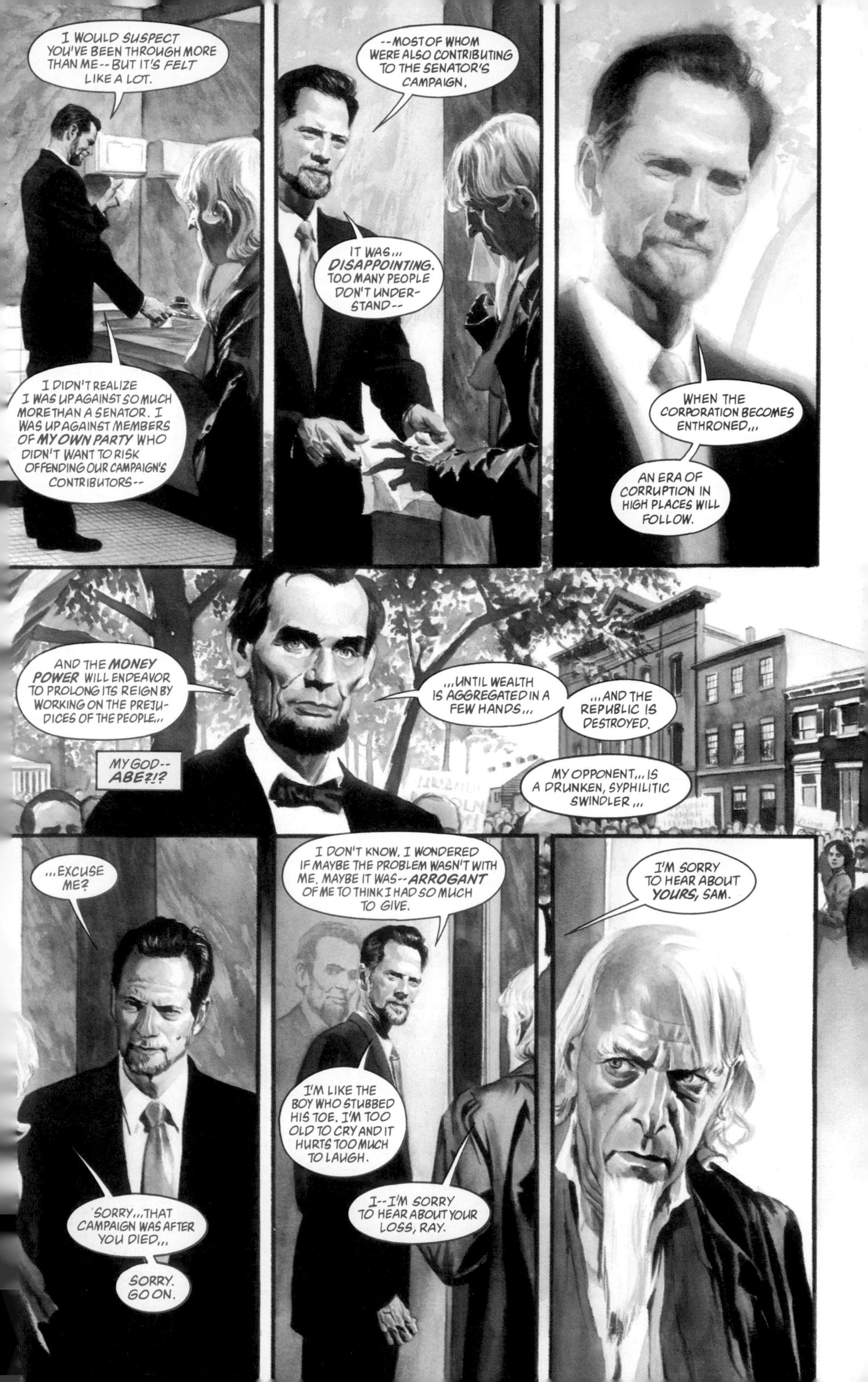
I WOULD SUSPECT YOU'VE BEEN THROUGH MORE THAN ME-- BUT IT'S FELT LIKE A LOT.
I DIDN'T REALIZE I WAS UP AGAINST SO MUCH MORE THAN A SENATOR. I WAS UP AGAINST MEMBERS OF MY OWN PARTY WHO DIDN'T WANT TO RISK OFFENDING OUR CAMPAIGN'S CONTRIBUTORS--
--MOST OF WHOM WERE ALSO CONTRIBUTING TO THE SENATOR'S CAMPAIGN.
IT WAS... DISAPPOINTING. TOO MANY PEOPLE DON'T UNDER-STAND--
WHEN THE CORPORATION BECOMES ENTHRONED...
AN ERA OF CORRUPTION IN HIGH PLACES WILL FOLLOW.
AND THE MONEY POWER WILL ENDEAVOR TO PROLONG ITS REIGN BY WORKING ON THE PREJU-DICES OF THE PEOPLE...
...UNTIL WEALTH IS AGGREGATED IN A FEW HANDS...
...AND THE REPUBLIC IS DESTROYED.
MY GOD-- ABE?!?
MY OPPONENT... IS A DRUNKEN, SYPHILITIC SWINDLER...
...EXCUSE ME?
SORRY... THAT CAMPAIGN WAS AFTER YOU DIED...
SORRY. GO ON.
I DON'T KNOW. I WONDERED IF MAYBE THE PROBLEM WASN'T WITH ME. MAYBE IT WAS-- ARROGANT OF ME TO THINK I HAD SO MUCH TO GIVE.
I'M LIKE THE BOY WHO STUBBED HIS TOE. I'M TOO OLD TO CRY AND IT HURTS TOO MUCH TO LAUGH.
I--I'M SORRY TO HEAR ABOUT YOUR LOSS, RAY.
I'M SORRY TO HEAR ABOUT YOURS, SAM.

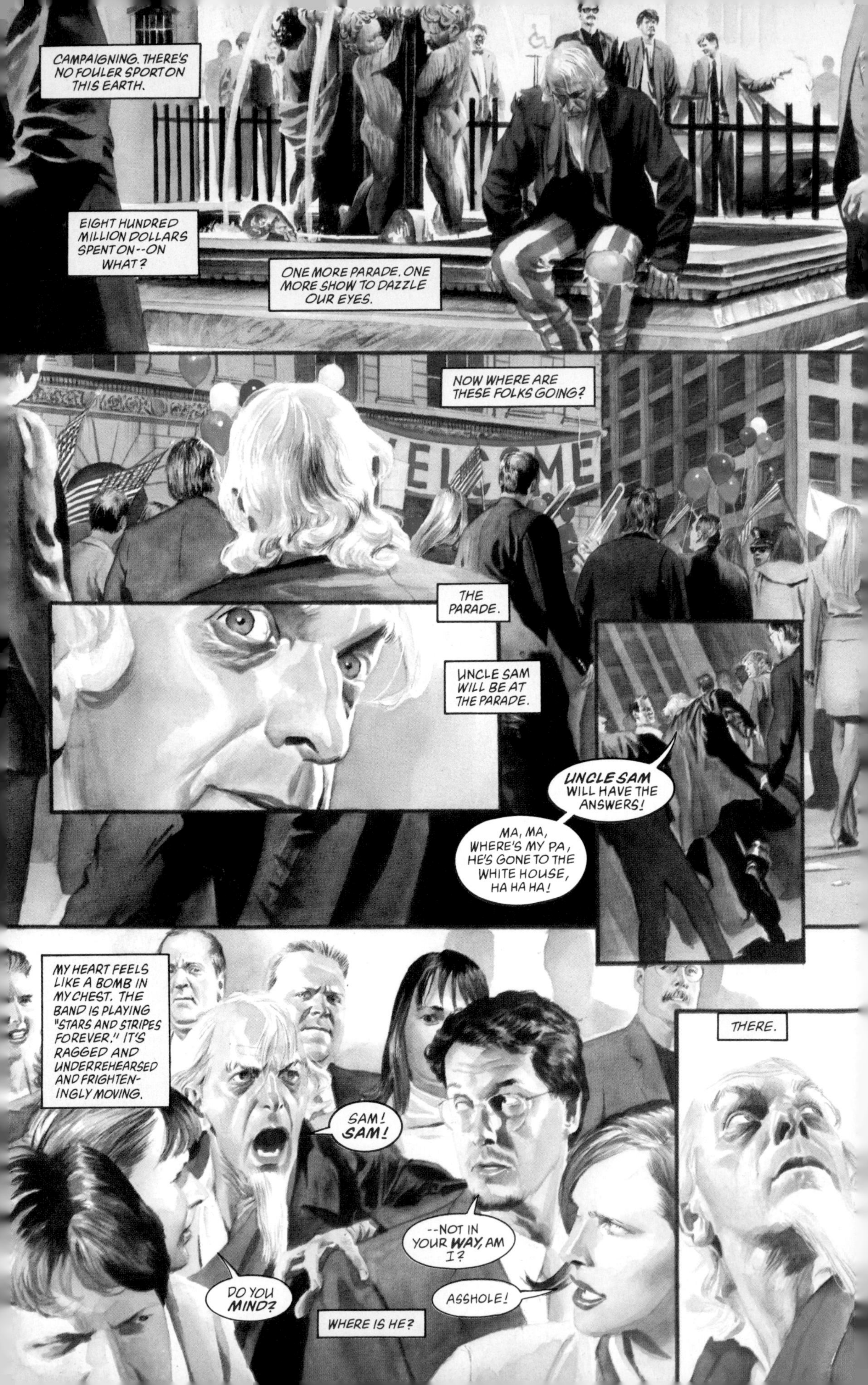

CAMPAIGNING. THERE'S NO FOULER SPORT ON THIS EARTH.
EIGHT HUNDRED MILLION DOLLARS SPENT ON--ON WHAT?
ONE MORE PARADE. ONE MORE SHOW TO DAZZLE OUR EYES.
NOW WHERE ARE THESE FOLKS GOING?
WELCOME
THE PARADE.
UNCLE SAM WILL BE AT THE PARADE.
UNCLE SAM WILL HAVE THE ANSWERS!
MA, MA, WHERE'S MY PA, HE'S GONE TO THE WHITE HOUSE, HA HA HA!
MY HEART FEELS LIKE A BOMB IN MY CHEST. THE BAND IS PLAYING "STARS AND STRIPES FOREVER." IT'S RAGGED AND UNDERREHEARSED AND FRIGHTENINGLY MOVING.
SAM! SAM!
--NOT IN YOUR WAY, AM I?
DO YOU MIND?
ASSHOLE!
WHERE IS HE?
THERE.

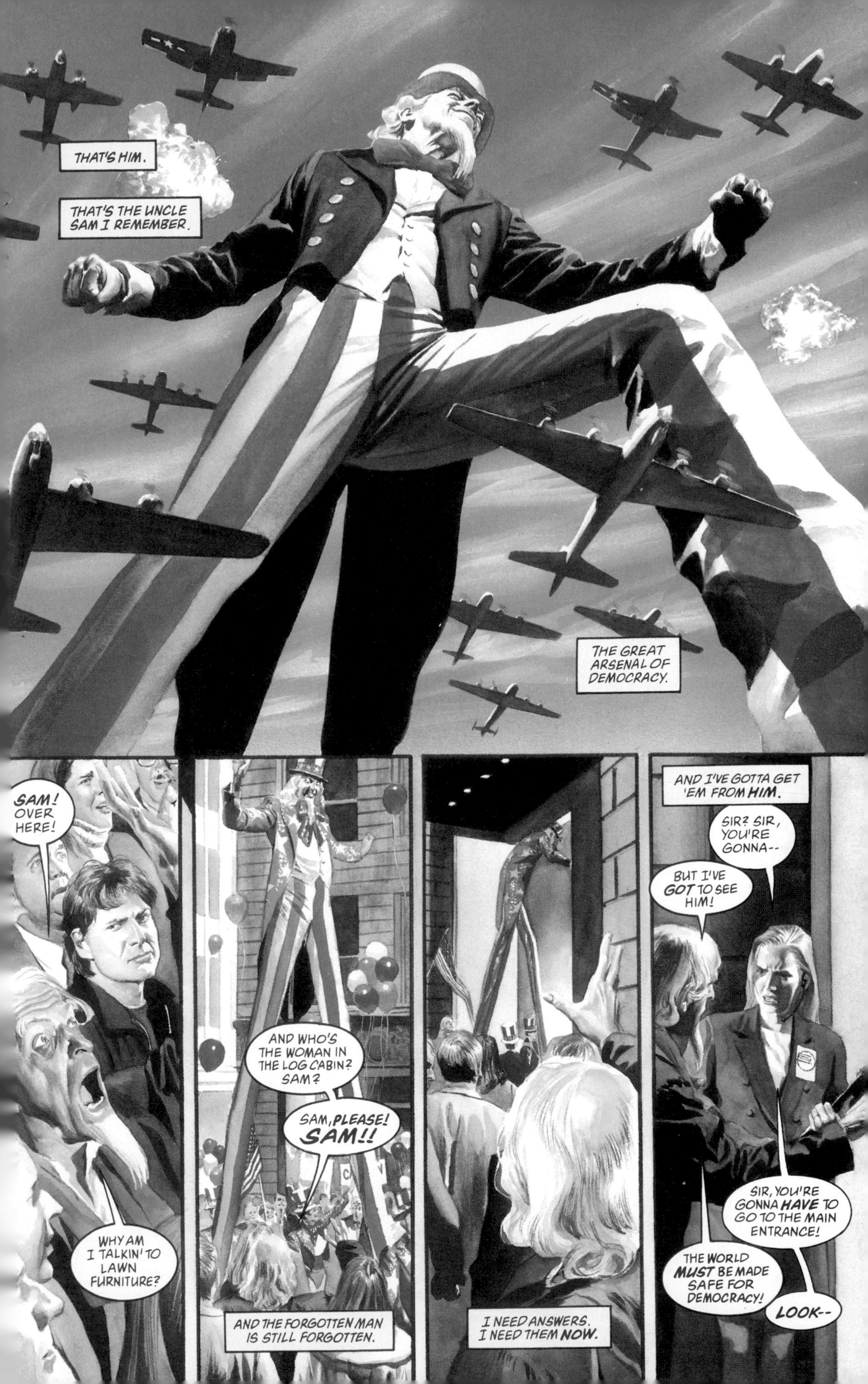
THAT'S HIM.
THAT'S THE UNCLE SAM I REMEMBER.
THE GREAT ARSENAL OF DEMOCRACY.
SAM! OVER HERE!
WHY AM I TALKIN' TO LAWN FURNITURE?
AND WHO'S THE WOMAN IN THE LOG CABIN? SAM?
SAM, PLEASE! SAM!!
AND THE FORGOTTEN MAN IS STILL FORGOTTEN.
I NEED ANSWERS. I NEED THEM NOW.
AND I'VE GOTTA GET 'EM FROM HIM.
SIR? SIR, YOU'RE GONNA--
BUT I'VE GOT TO SEE HIM!
SIR, YOU'RE GONNA HAVE TO GO TO THE MAIN ENTRANCE!
THE WORLD MUST BE MADE SAFE FOR DEMOCRACY!
LOOK--

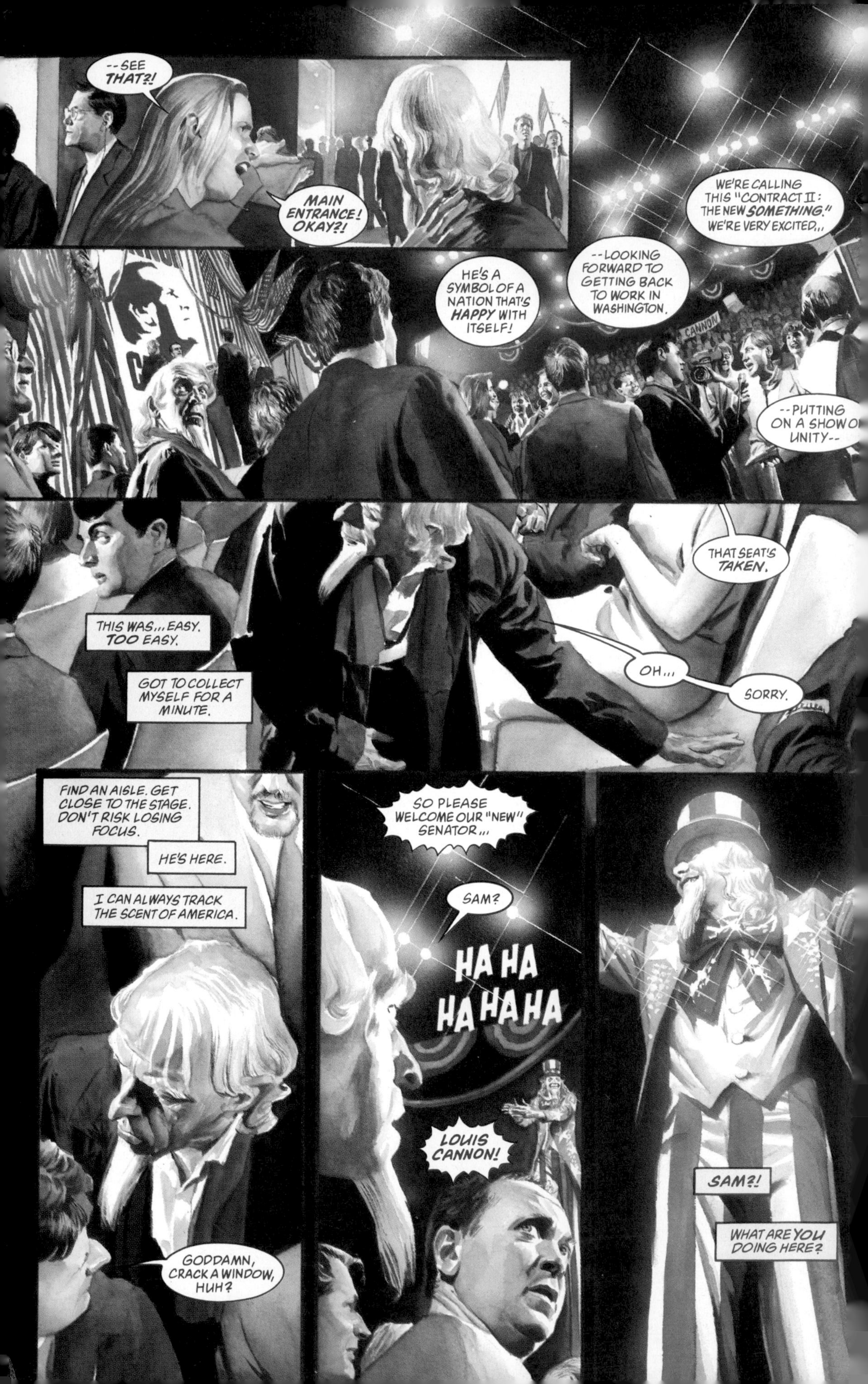
--SEE THAT?!
MAIN ENTRANCE! OKAY?!
WE'RE CALLING THIS "CONTRACT II: THE NEW SOMETHING." WE'RE VERY EXCITED,,,
HE'S A SYMBOL OF A NATION THAT'S HAPPY WITH ITSELF!
--LOOKING FORWARD TO GETTING BACK TO WORK IN WASHINGTON.
CANNON
--PUTTING ON A SHOW OF UNITY--
THAT SEAT'S TAKEN.
THIS WAS,,, EASY. TOO EASY.
GOT TO COLLECT MYSELF FOR A MINUTE.
OH,,,
SORRY.
FIND AN AISLE. GET CLOSE TO THE STAGE. DON'T RISK LOSING FOCUS.
HE'S HERE.
I CAN ALWAYS TRACK THE SCENT OF AMERICA.
GODDAMN, CRACK A WINDOW, HUH?
SO PLEASE WELCOME OUR "NEW" SENATOR,,,
SAM?
HA HA HA HA HA
LOUIS CANNON!
SAM?!
WHAT ARE YOU DOING HERE?

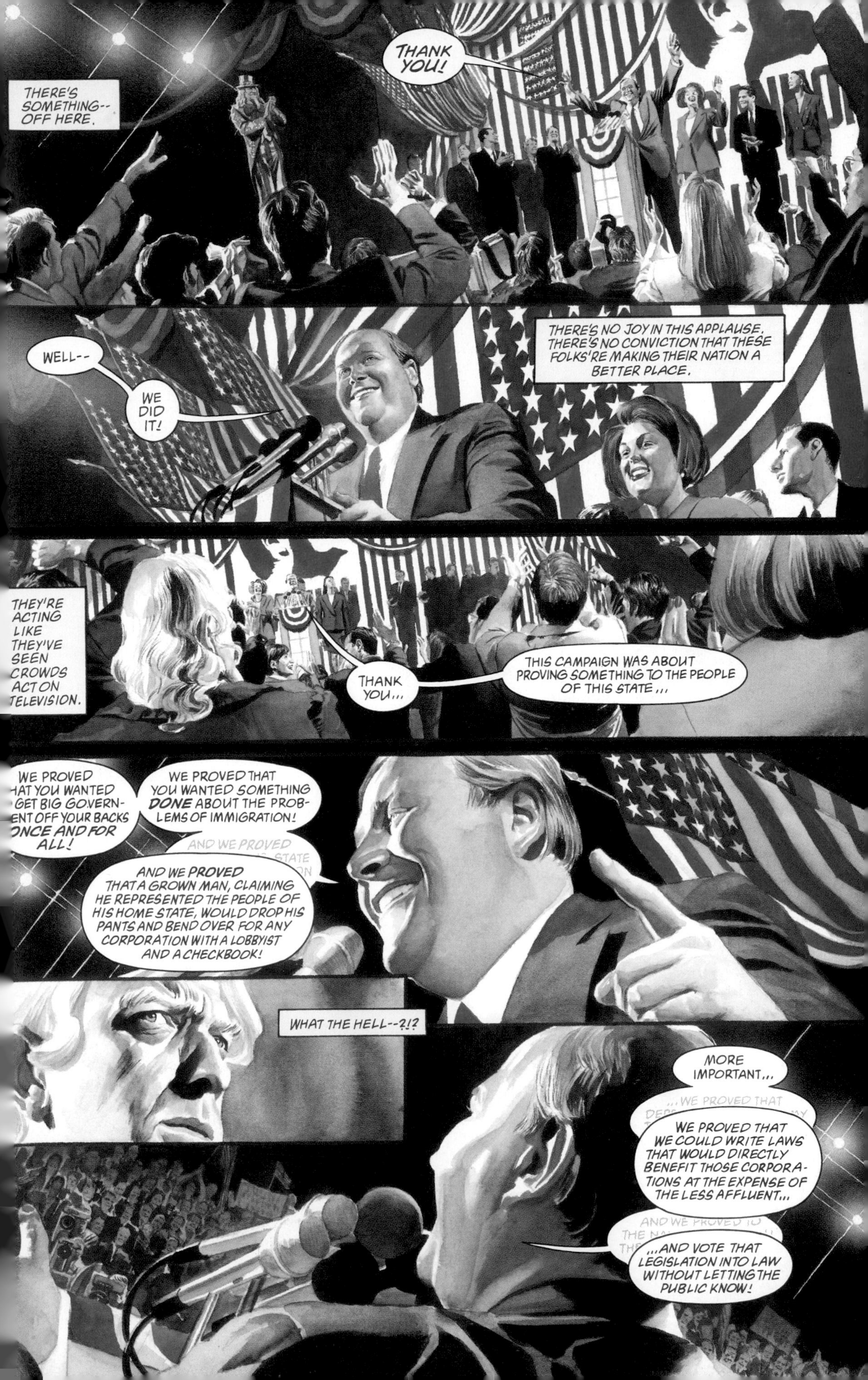

THERE'S SOMETHING-- OFF HERE.
THANK YOU!
WELL--
WE DID IT!
THERE'S NO JOY IN THIS APPLAUSE. THERE'S NO CONVICTION THAT THESE FOLKS'RE MAKING THEIR NATION A BETTER PLACE.
THEY'RE ACTING LIKE THEY'VE SEEN CROWDS ACT ON TELEVISION.
THANK YOU...
THIS CAMPAIGN WAS ABOUT PROVING SOMETHING TO THE PEOPLE OF THIS STATE...
WE PROVED HAT YOU WANTED GET BIG GOVERN- ENT OFF YOUR BACKS ONCE AND FOR ALL!
WE PROVED THAT YOU WANTED SOMETHING DONE ABOUT THE PROB- LEMS OF IMMIGRATION!
AND WE PROVED
AND WE PROVED THAT A GROWN MAN, CLAIMING HE REPRESENTED THE PEOPLE OF HIS HOME STATE, WOULD DROP HIS PANTS AND BEND OVER FOR ANY CORPORATION WITH A LOBBYIST AND A CHECKBOOK!
WHAT THE HELL--?!?
MORE IMPORTANT...
...WE PROVED THAT
WE PROVED THAT WE COULD WRITE LAWS THAT WOULD DIRECTLY BENEFIT THOSE CORPORA- TIONS AT THE EXPENSE OF THE LESS AFFLUENT...
AND WE PROVED TO
...AND VOTE THAT LEGISLATION INTO LAW WITHOUT LETTING THE PUBLIC KNOW!

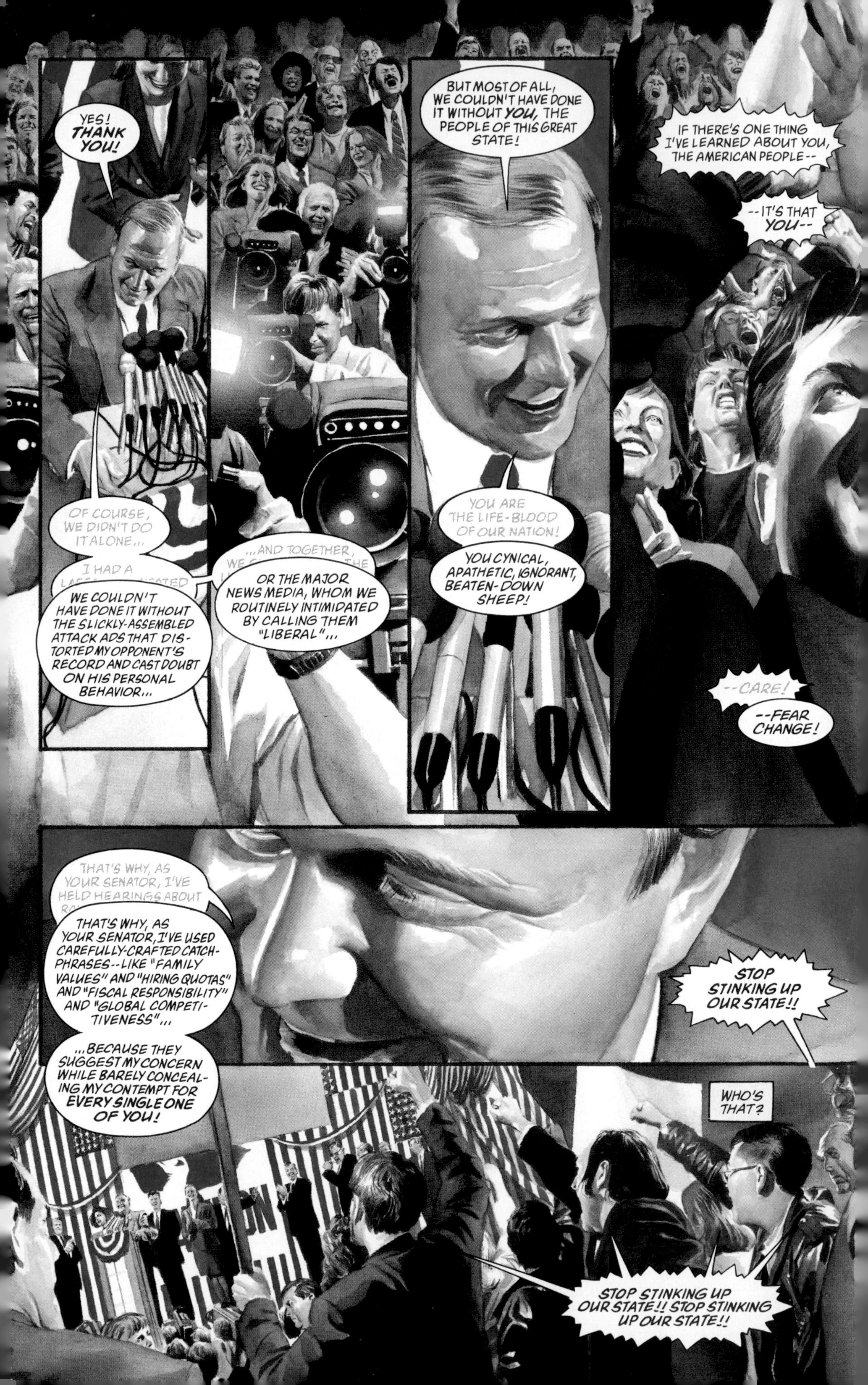
YES! THANK YOU!
OF COURSE, WE DIDN'T DO IT ALONE...
I HAD A
WE COULDN'T HAVE DONE IT WITHOUT THE SLICKLY-ASSEMBLED ATTACK ADS THAT DISTORTED MY OPPONENT'S RECORD AND CAST DOUBT ON HIS PERSONAL BEHAVIOR...
...AND TOGETHER,
OR THE MAJOR NEWS MEDIA, WHOM WE ROUTINELY INTIMIDATED BY CALLING THEM "LIBERAL"...
BUT MOST OF ALL, WE COULDN'T HAVE DONE IT WITHOUT YOU, THE PEOPLE OF THIS GREAT STATE!
YOU ARE THE LIFE-BLOOD OF OUR NATION!
YOU CYNICAL, APATHETIC, IGNORANT, BEATEN-DOWN SHEEP!
IF THERE'S ONE THING I'VE LEARNED ABOUT YOU, THE AMERICAN PEOPLE--
--IT'S THAT YOU--
--CARE!
--FEAR CHANGE!
THAT'S WHY, AS YOUR SENATOR, I'VE HELD HEARINGS ABOUT
THAT'S WHY, AS YOUR SENATOR, I'VE USED CAREFULLY-CRAFTED CATCH-PHRASES--LIKE "FAMILY VALUES" AND "HIRING QUOTAS" AND "FISCAL RESPONSIBILITY" AND "GLOBAL COMPETITIVENESS"...
...BECAUSE THEY SUGGEST MY CONCERN WHILE BARELY CONCEALING MY CONTEMPT FOR EVERY SINGLE ONE OF YOU!
STOP STINKING UP OUR STATE!!
WHO'S THAT?
STOP STINKING UP OUR STATE!! STOP STINKING UP OUR STATE!!

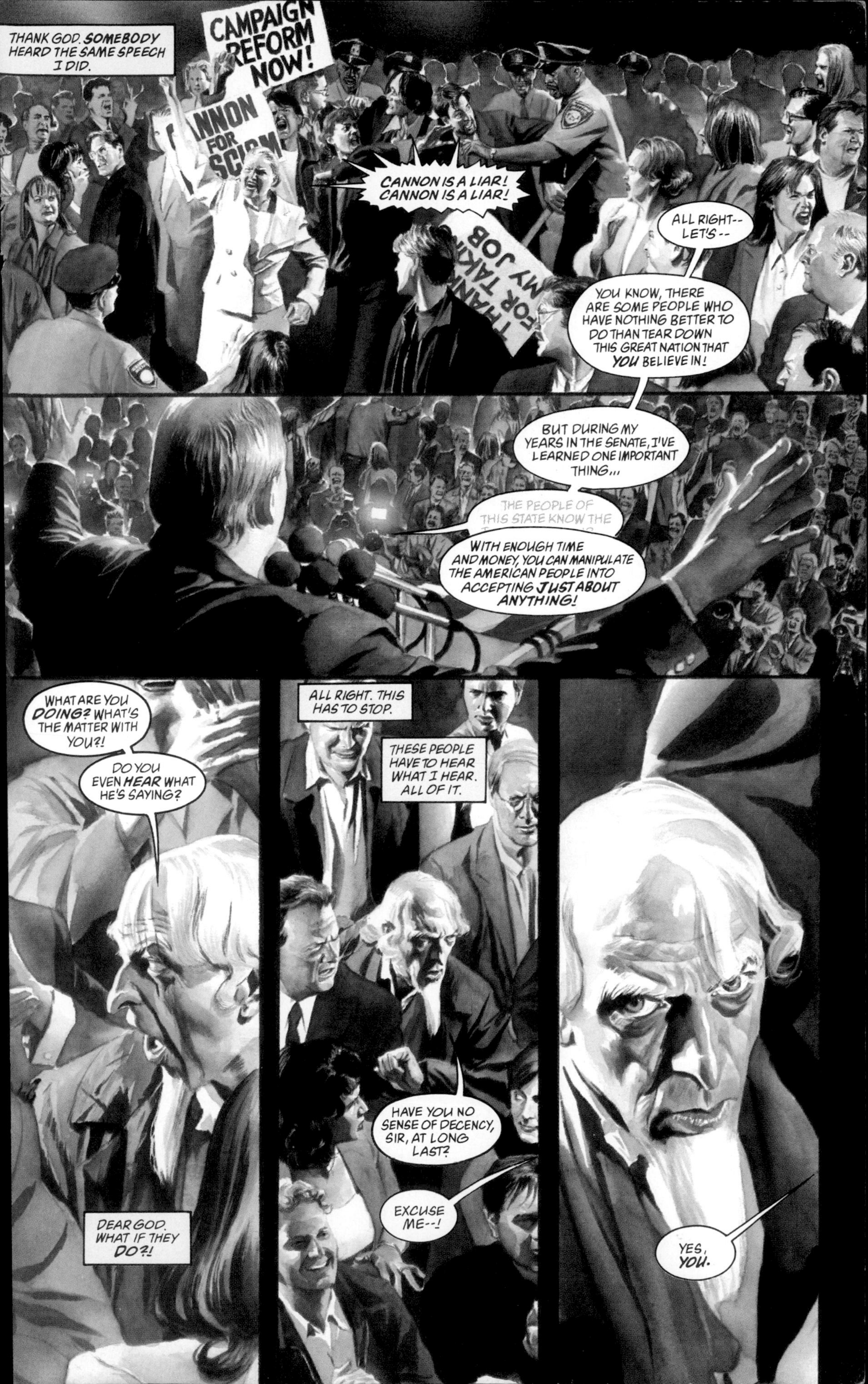

THANK GOD. SOMEBODY HEARD THE SAME SPEECH I DID.
CAMPAIGN REFORM NOW!
CANNON IS A LIAR! CANNON IS A LIAR!
ALL RIGHT-- LET'S --
YOU KNOW, THERE ARE SOME PEOPLE WHO HAVE NOTHING BETTER TO DO THAN TEAR DOWN THIS GREAT NATION THAT YOU BELIEVE IN!
BUT DURING MY YEARS IN THE SENATE, I'VE LEARNED ONE IMPORTANT THING...
THE PEOPLE OF THIS STATE KNOW THE
WITH ENOUGH TIME AND MONEY, YOU CAN MANIPULATE THE AMERICAN PEOPLE INTO ACCEPTING JUST ABOUT ANYTHING!
WHAT ARE YOU DOING? WHAT'S THE MATTER WITH YOU?!
DO YOU EVEN HEAR WHAT HE'S SAYING?
DEAR GOD. WHAT IF THEY DO?!
ALL RIGHT. THIS HAS TO STOP.
THESE PEOPLE HAVE TO HEAR WHAT I HEAR. ALL OF IT.
HAVE YOU NO SENSE OF DECENCY, SIR, AT LONG LAST?
EXCUSE ME--!
YES, YOU.

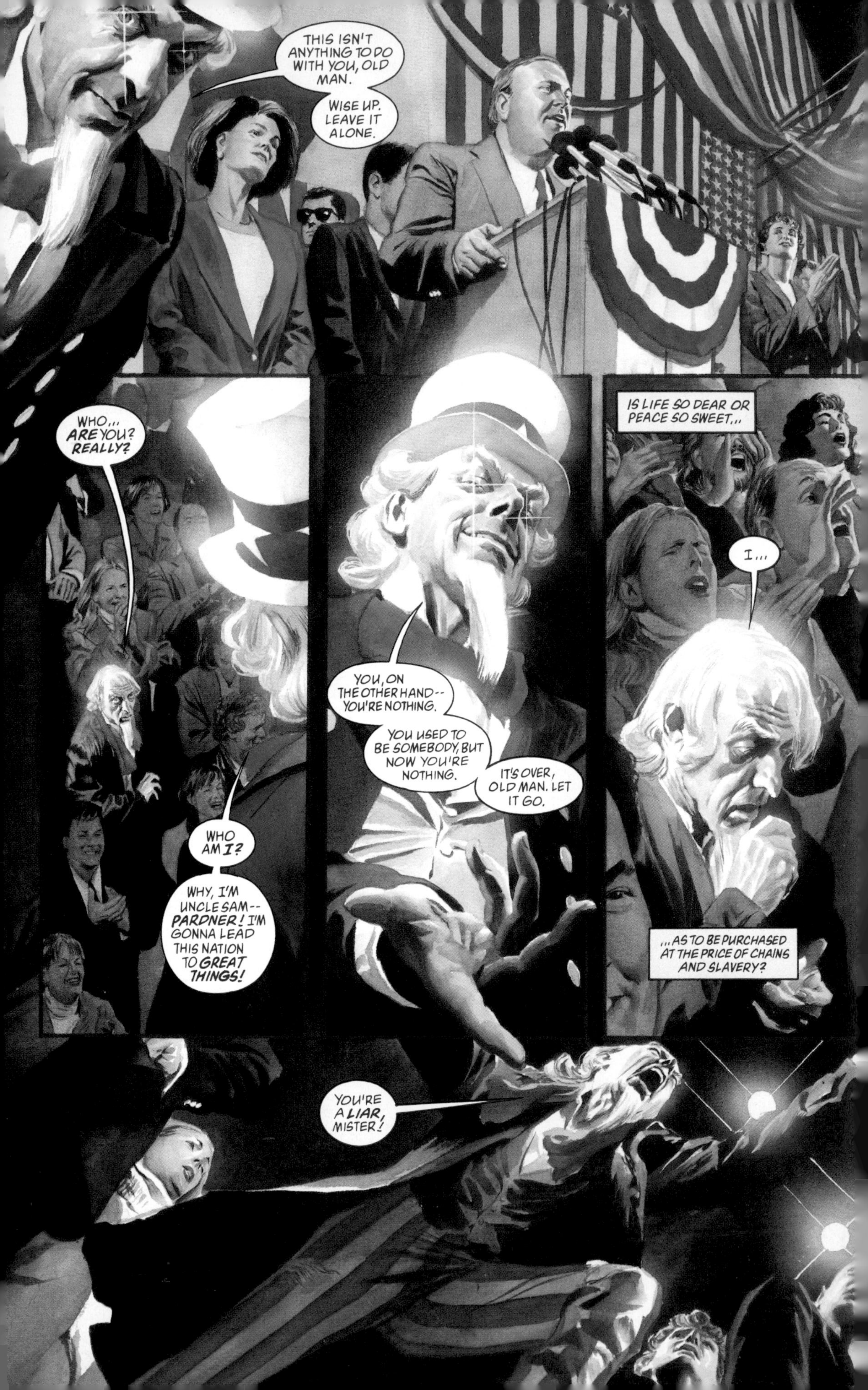
THIS ISN'T ANYTHING TO DO WITH YOU, OLD MAN.
WISE UP. LEAVE IT ALONE.
WHO... ARE YOU? REALLY?
WHO AM I?
WHY, I'M UNCLE SAM-- PARDNER! I'M GONNA LEAD THIS NATION TO GREAT THINGS!
YOU, ON THE OTHER HAND-- YOU'RE NOTHING.
YOU USED TO BE SOMEBODY, BUT NOW YOU'RE NOTHING.
IT'S OVER, OLD MAN. LET IT GO.
IS LIFE SO DEAR OR PEACE SO SWEET...
I...
...AS TO BE PURCHASED AT THE PRICE OF CHAINS AND SLAVERY?
YOU'RE A LIAR, MISTER!

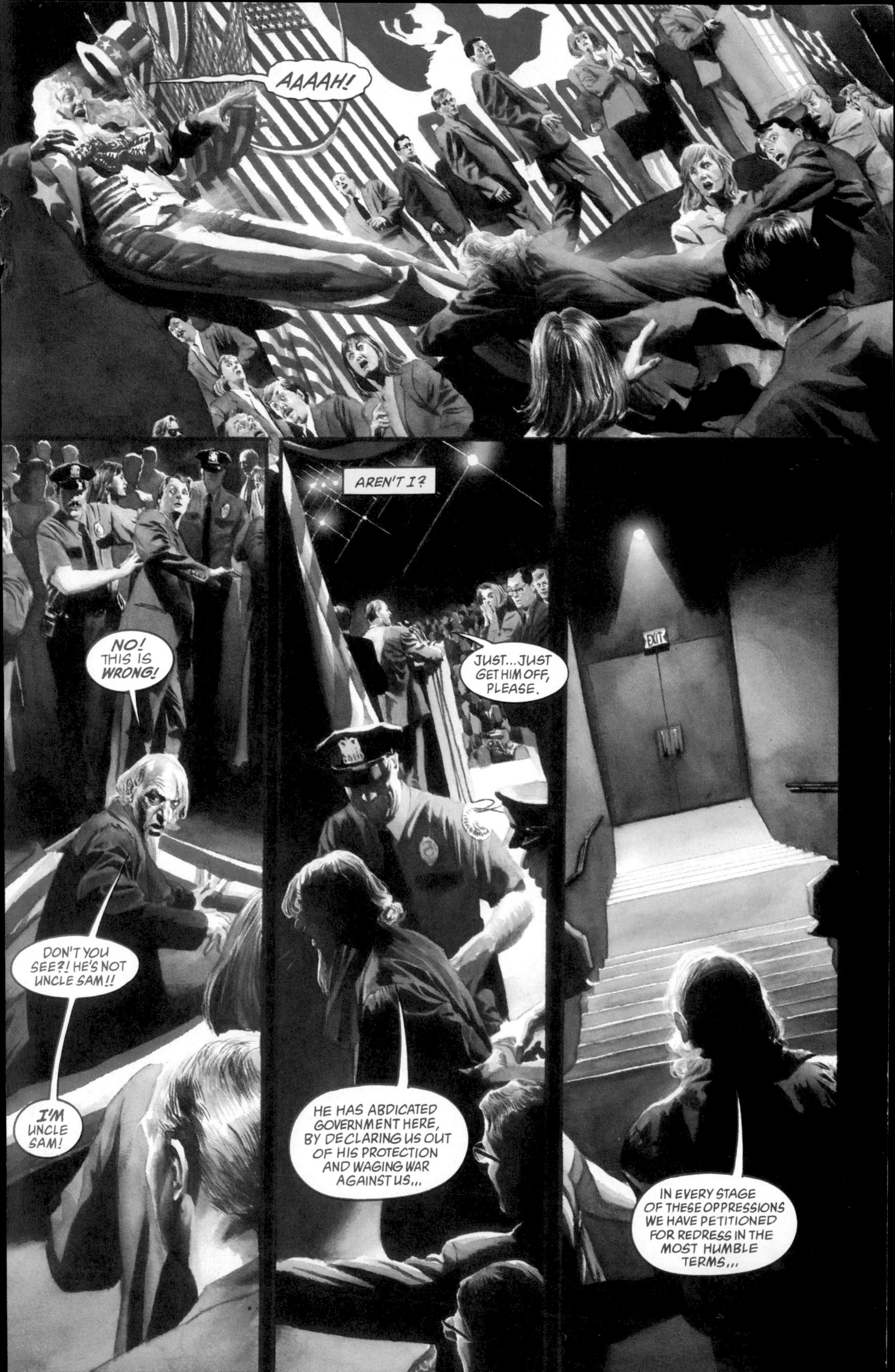
AAAAH!
NO! THIS IS WRONG!
DON'T YOU SEE?! HE'S NOT UNCLE SAM!!
I'M UNCLE SAM!
AREN'T I?
JUST...JUST GET HIM OFF, PLEASE.
HE HAS ABDICATED GOVERNMENT HERE, BY DECLARING US OUT OF HIS PROTECTION AND WAGING WAR AGAINST US...
EXIT
IN EVERY STAGE OF THESE OPPRESSIONS WE HAVE PETITIONED FOR REDRESS IN THE MOST HUMBLE TERMS...

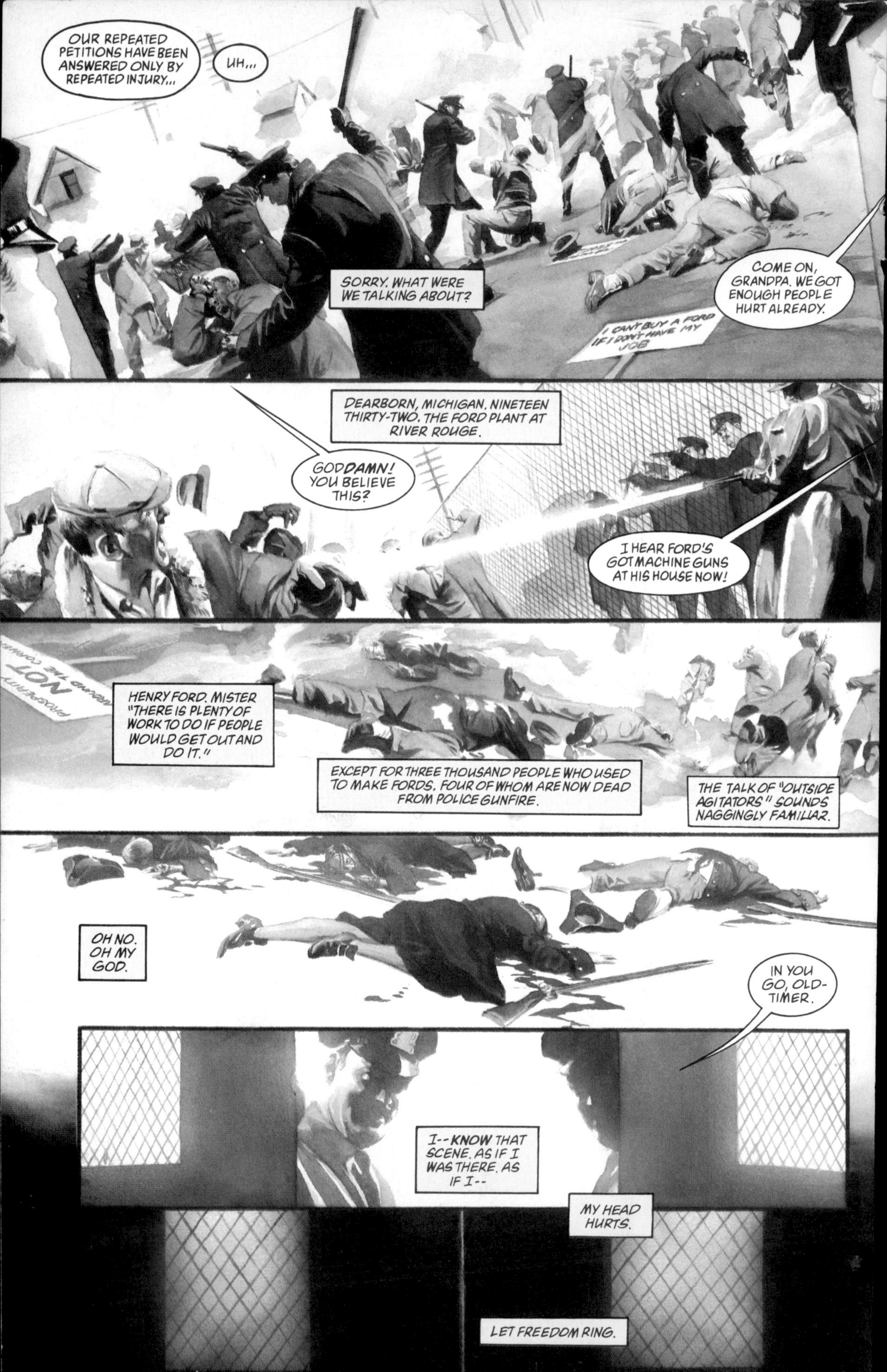
OUR REPEATED PETITIONS HAVE BEEN ANSWERED ONLY BY REPEATED INJURY...
UH...
SORRY. WHAT WERE WE TALKING ABOUT?
COME ON, GRANDPA. WE GOT ENOUGH PEOPLE HURT ALREADY.
I CANT BUY A FORD IF I DONT HAVE MY JOB
DEARBORN, MICHIGAN. NINETEEN THIRTY-TWO. THE FORD PLANT AT RIVER ROUGE.
GOD**DAMN**! YOU BELIEVE THIS?
I HEAR FORD'S GOT MACHINE GUNS AT HIS HOUSE NOW!
HENRY FORD. MISTER "THERE IS PLENTY OF WORK TO DO IF PEOPLE WOULD GET OUT AND DO IT."
EXCEPT FOR THREE THOUSAND PEOPLE WHO USED TO MAKE FORDS. FOUR OF WHOM ARE NOW DEAD FROM POLICE GUNFIRE.
THE TALK OF "OUTSIDE AGITATORS" SOUNDS NAGGINGLY FAMILIAR.
OH NO. OH MY GOD.
IN YOU GO, OLD-TIMER.
I--**KNOW** THAT SCENE. AS IF I WAS THERE. AS IF I--
MY HEAD HURTS.
LET FREEDOM RING.

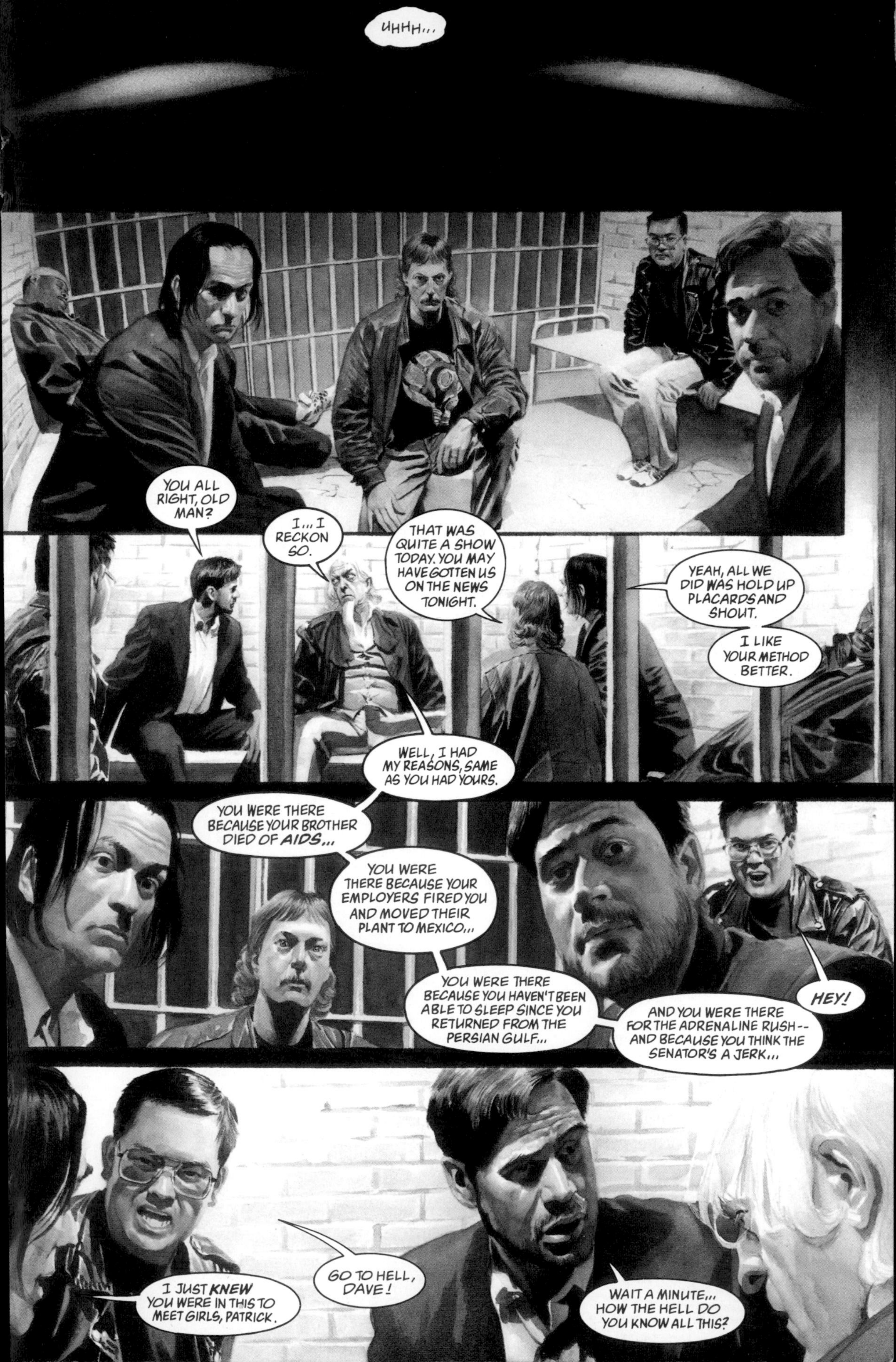
UHHH...
YOU ALL RIGHT, OLD MAN?
I... I RECKON SO.
THAT WAS QUITE A SHOW TODAY. YOU MAY HAVE GOTTEN US ON THE NEWS TONIGHT.
YEAH, ALL WE DID WAS HOLD UP PLACARDS AND SHOUT.
I LIKE YOUR METHOD BETTER.
WELL, I HAD MY REASONS, SAME AS YOU HAD YOURS.
YOU WERE THERE BECAUSE YOUR BROTHER DIED OF AIDS...
YOU WERE THERE BECAUSE YOUR EMPLOYERS FIRED YOU AND MOVED THEIR PLANT TO MEXICO...
YOU WERE THERE BECAUSE YOU HAVEN'T BEEN ABLE TO SLEEP SINCE YOU RETURNED FROM THE PERSIAN GULF...
AND YOU WERE THERE FOR THE ADRENALINE RUSH -- AND BECAUSE YOU THINK THE SENATOR'S A JERK...
HEY!
I JUST KNEW YOU WERE IN THIS TO MEET GIRLS, PATRICK.
GO TO HELL, DAVE!
WAIT A MINUTE... HOW THE HELL DO YOU KNOW ALL THIS?

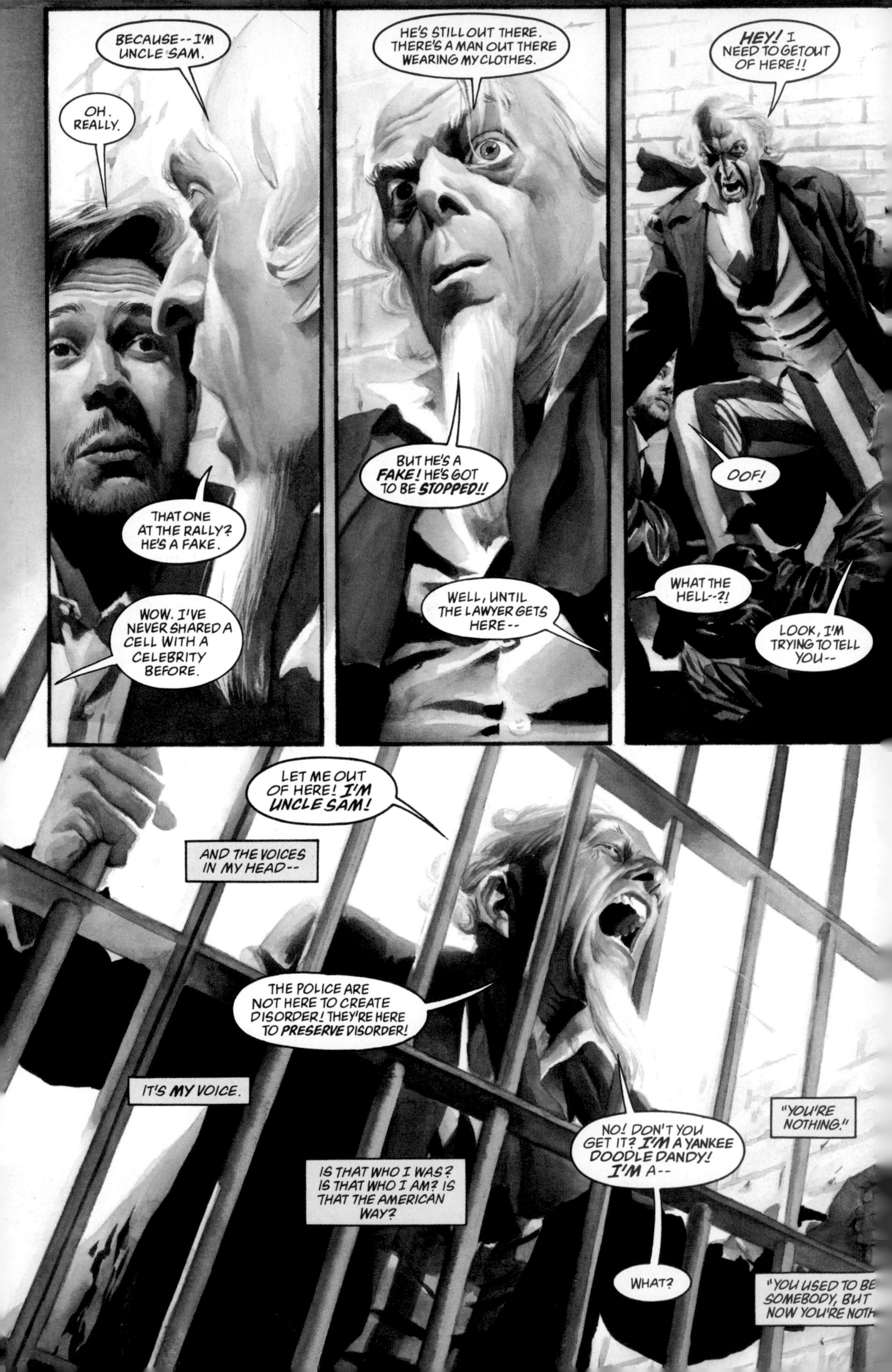
BECAUSE--I'M UNCLE SAM.
OH. REALLY.
THAT ONE AT THE RALLY? HE'S A FAKE.
WOW. I'VE NEVER SHARED A CELL WITH A CELEBRITY BEFORE.
HE'S STILL OUT THERE. THERE'S A MAN OUT THERE WEARING MY CLOTHES.
BUT HE'S A FAKE! HE'S GOT TO BE STOPPED!!
WELL, UNTIL THE LAWYER GETS HERE--
HEY! I NEED TO GET OUT OF HERE!!
OOF!
WHAT THE HELL--?!
LOOK, I'M TRYING TO TELL YOU--
LET ME OUT OF HERE! I'M UNCLE SAM!
AND THE VOICES IN MY HEAD--
THE POLICE ARE NOT HERE TO CREATE DISORDER! THEY'RE HERE TO PRESERVE DISORDER!
IT'S MY VOICE.
IS THAT WHO I WAS? IS THAT WHO I AM? IS THAT THE AMERICAN WAY?
NO! DON'T YOU GET IT? I'M A YANKEE DOODLE DANDY! I'M A--
WHAT?
"YOU'RE NOTHING."
"YOU USED TO BE SOMEBODY, BUT NOW YOU'RE NOTH

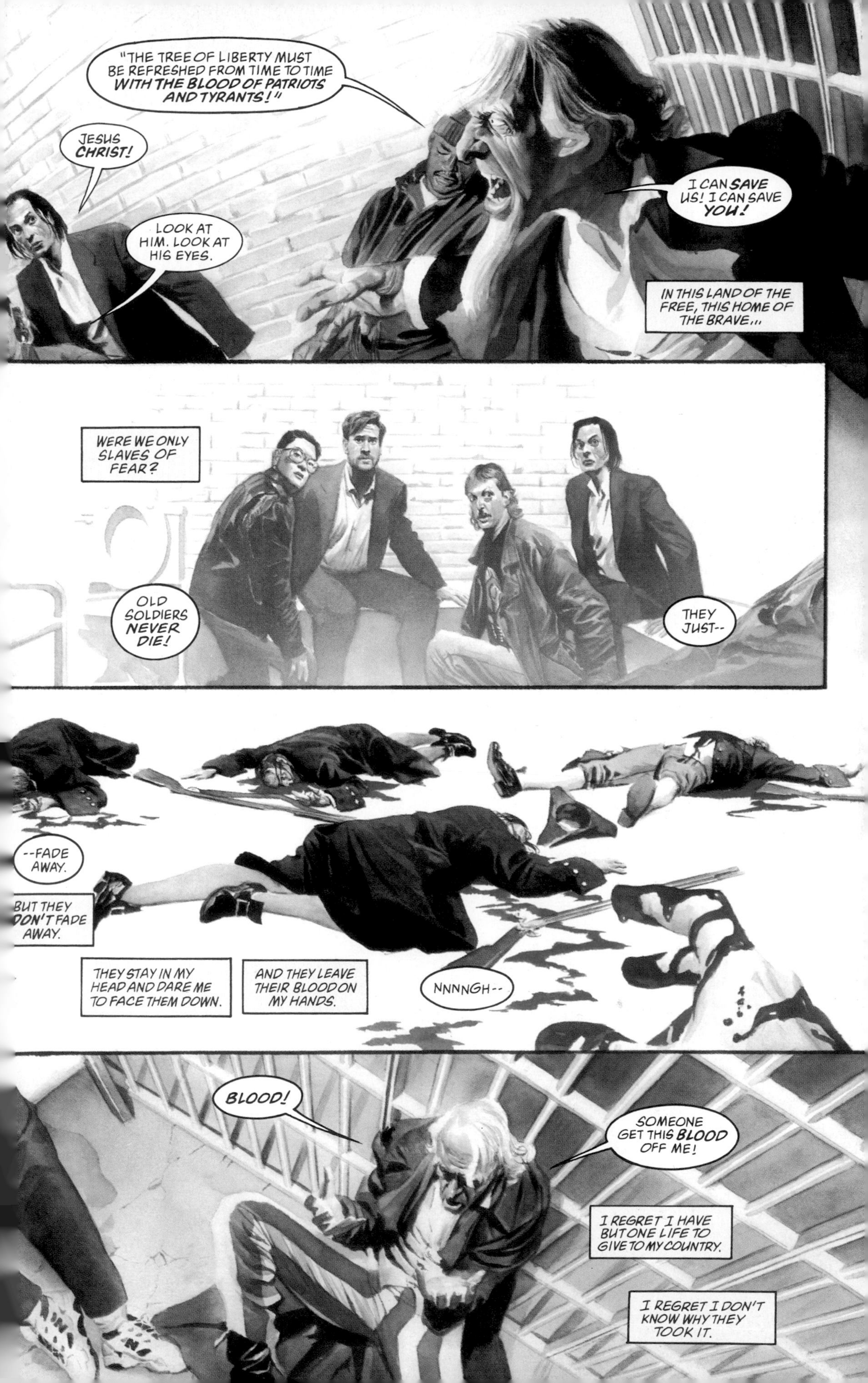
"THE TREE OF LIBERTY MUST BE REFRESHED FROM TIME TO TIME WITH THE BLOOD OF PATRIOTS AND TYRANTS!"
JESUS CHRIST!
LOOK AT HIM. LOOK AT HIS EYES.
I CAN SAVE US! I CAN SAVE YOU!
IN THIS LAND OF THE FREE, THIS HOME OF THE BRAVE...
WERE WE ONLY SLAVES OF FEAR?
OLD SOLDIERS NEVER DIE!
THEY JUST--
--FADE AWAY.
BUT THEY DON'T FADE AWAY.
THEY STAY IN MY HEAD AND DARE ME TO FACE THEM DOWN.
AND THEY LEAVE THEIR BLOOD ON MY HANDS.
NNNNGH--
BLOOD!
SOMEONE GET THIS BLOOD OFF ME!
I REGRET I HAVE BUT ONE LIFE TO GIVE TO MY COUNTRY.
I REGRET I DON'T KNOW WHY THEY TOOK IT.

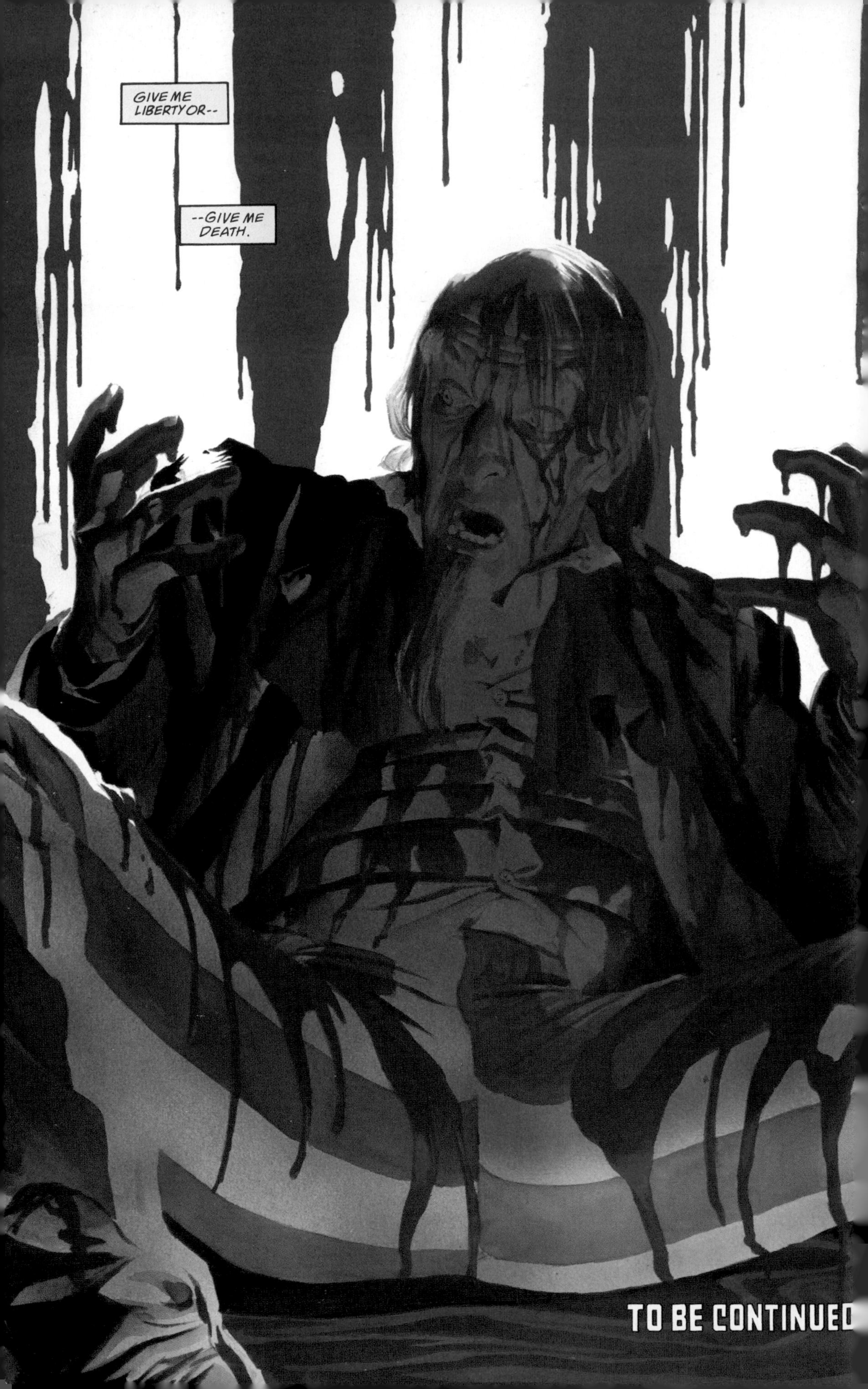
GIVE ME LIBERTY OR--
--GIVE ME DEATH.
TO BE CONTINUED

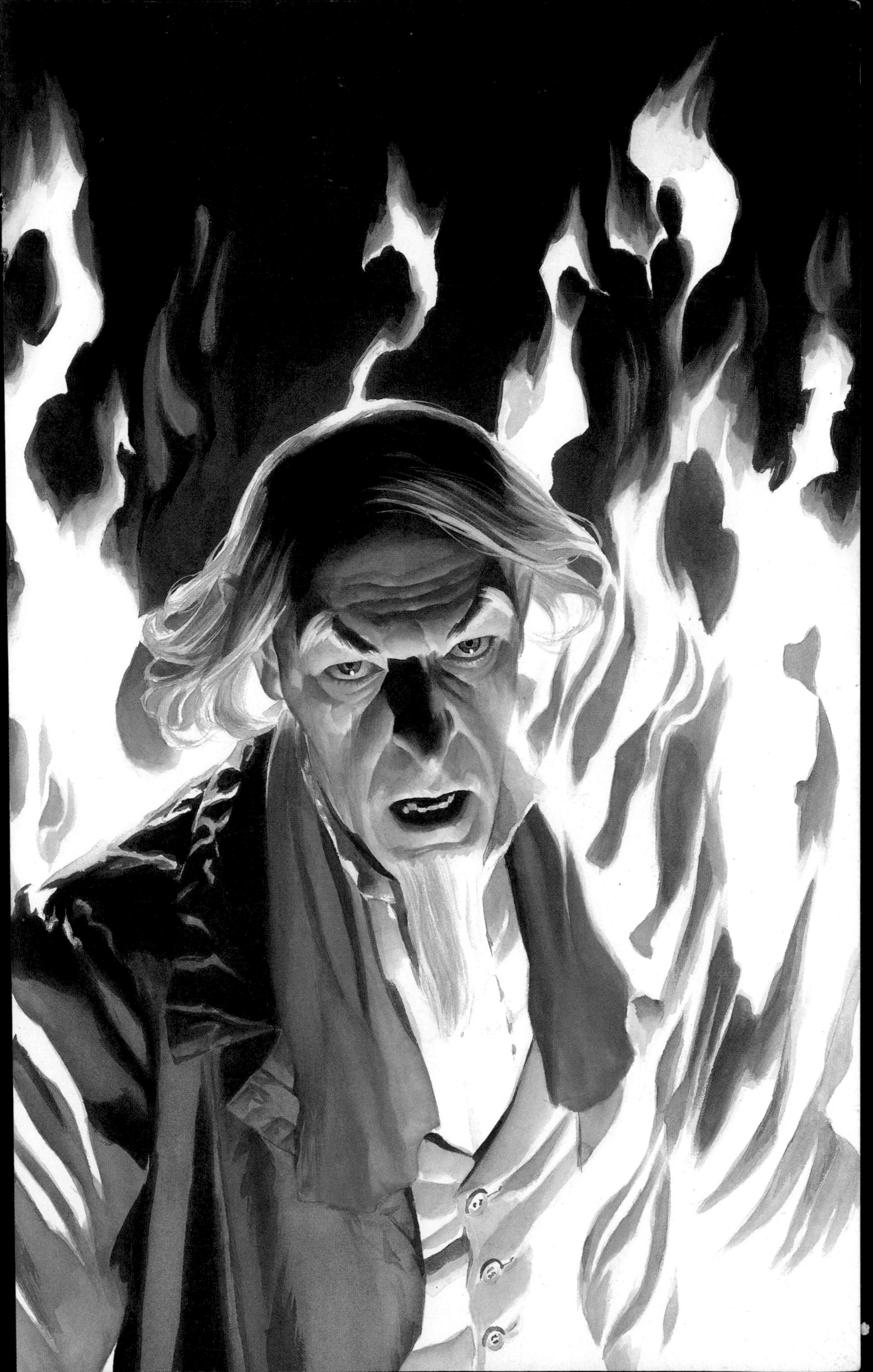

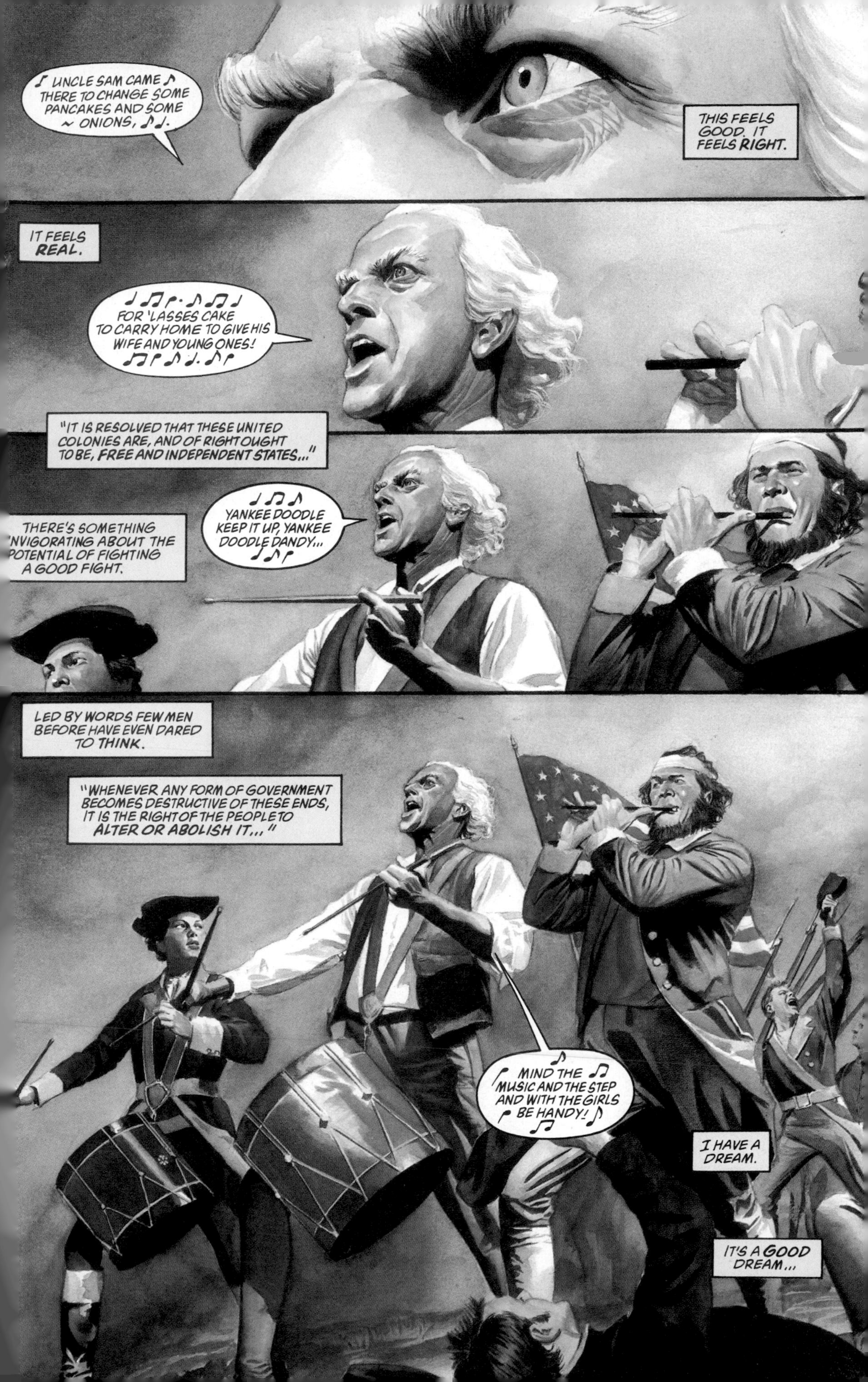
♪ UNCLE SAM CAME ♪ THERE TO CHANGE SOME PANCAKES AND SOME ~ ONIONS, ♪♩.
THIS FEELS GOOD. IT FEELS RIGHT.
IT FEELS REAL.
♩♫♪♪♫♩ FOR 'LASSES CAKE TO CARRY HOME TO GIVE HIS WIFE AND YOUNG ONES! ♫♪♪♩♪♪
"IT IS RESOLVED THAT THESE UNITED COLONIES ARE, AND OF RIGHT OUGHT TO BE, FREE AND INDEPENDENT STATES..."
♩♫♪ YANKEE DOODLE KEEP IT UP, YANKEE DOODLE DANDY... ♩♪♪
THERE'S SOMETHING INVIGORATING ABOUT THE POTENTIAL OF FIGHTING A GOOD FIGHT.
LED BY WORDS FEW MEN BEFORE HAVE EVEN DARED TO THINK.
"WHENEVER ANY FORM OF GOVERNMENT BECOMES DESTRUCTIVE OF THESE ENDS, IT IS THE RIGHT OF THE PEOPLE TO ALTER OR ABOLISH IT..."
♪ MIND THE ♫ MUSIC AND THE STEP AND WITH THE GIRLS BE HANDY! ♪ ♫
I HAVE A DREAM.
IT'S A GOOD DREAM...

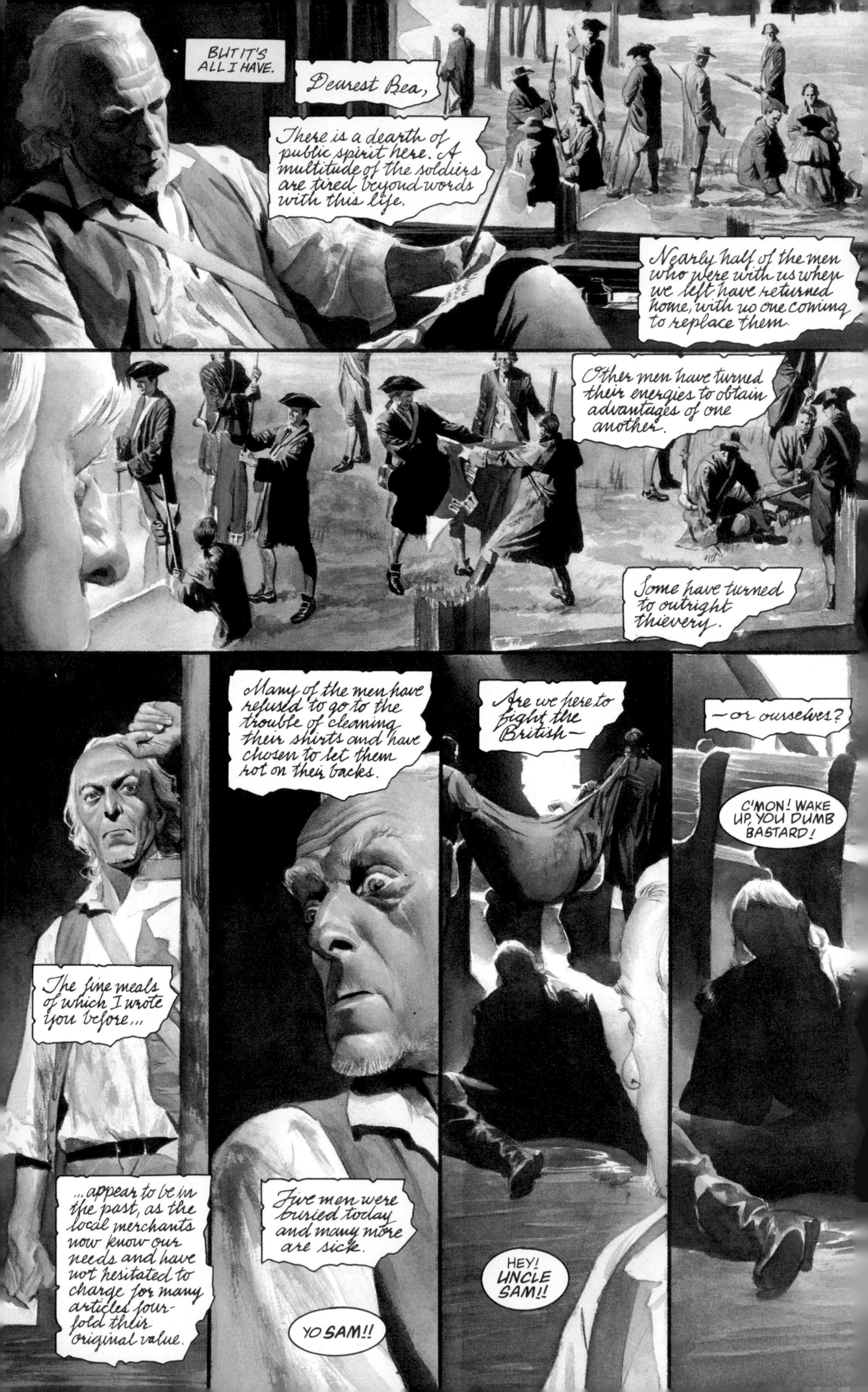
BUT IT'S ALL I HAVE.
Dearest Bea,
There is a dearth of public spirit here. A multitude of the soldiers are tired beyond words with this life.
Nearly half of the men who were with us when we left have returned home, with no one coming to replace them.
Other men have turned their energies to obtain advantages of one another.
Some have turned to outright thievery.
The fine meals of which I wrote you before...
...appear to be in the past, as the local merchants now know our needs and have not hesitated to charge for many articles four-fold their original value.
Many of the men have refused to go to the trouble of cleaning their shirts and have chosen to let them rot on their backs.
Five men were buried today and many more are sick.
YO SAM!!
Are we here to fight the British—
HEY! UNCLE SAM!!
—or ourselves?
C'MON! WAKE UP, YOU DUMB BASTARD!

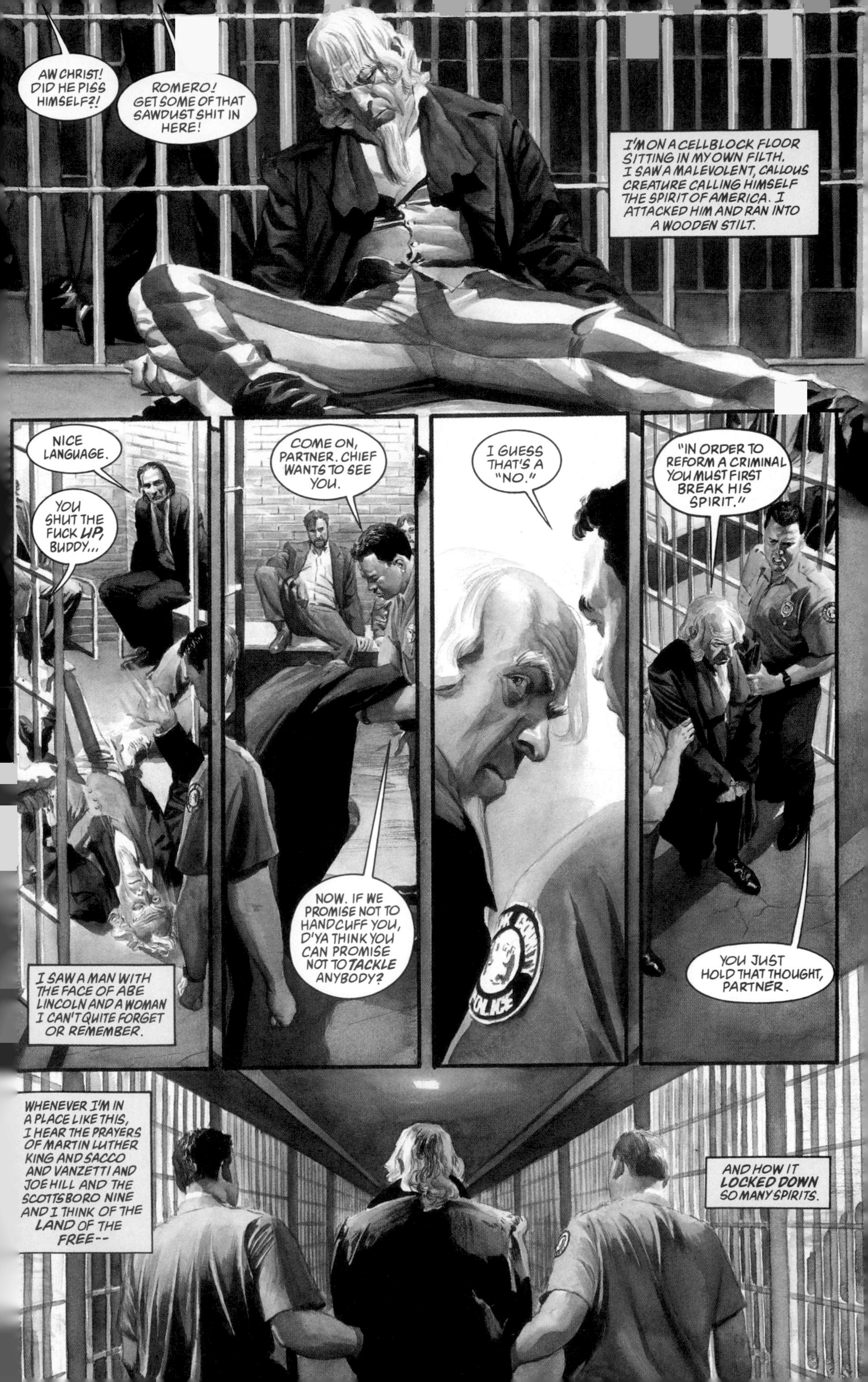
AW CHRIST! DID HE PISS HIMSELF?!
ROMERO! GET SOME OF THAT SAWDUST SHIT IN HERE!
I'M ON A CELLBLOCK FLOOR SITTING IN MY OWN FILTH. I SAW A MALEVOLENT, CALLOUS CREATURE CALLING HIMSELF THE SPIRIT OF AMERICA. I ATTACKED HIM AND RAN INTO A WOODEN STILT.
NICE LANGUAGE.
YOU SHUT THE FUCK UP, BUDDY...
I SAW A MAN WITH THE FACE OF ABE LINCOLN AND A WOMAN I CAN'T QUITE FORGET OR REMEMBER.
COME ON, PARTNER. CHIEF WANTS TO SEE YOU.
NOW. IF WE PROMISE NOT TO HANDCUFF YOU, D'YA THINK YOU CAN PROMISE NOT TO TACKLE ANYBODY?
I GUESS THAT'S A "NO."
"IN ORDER TO REFORM A CRIMINAL YOU MUST FIRST BREAK HIS SPIRIT."
YOU JUST HOLD THAT THOUGHT, PARTNER.
WHENEVER I'M IN A PLACE LIKE THIS, I HEAR THE PRAYERS OF MARTIN LUTHER KING AND SACCO AND VANZETTI AND JOE HILL AND THE SCOTTSBORO NINE AND I THINK OF THE LAND OF THE FREE--
AND HOW IT LOCKED DOWN SO MANY SPIRITS.

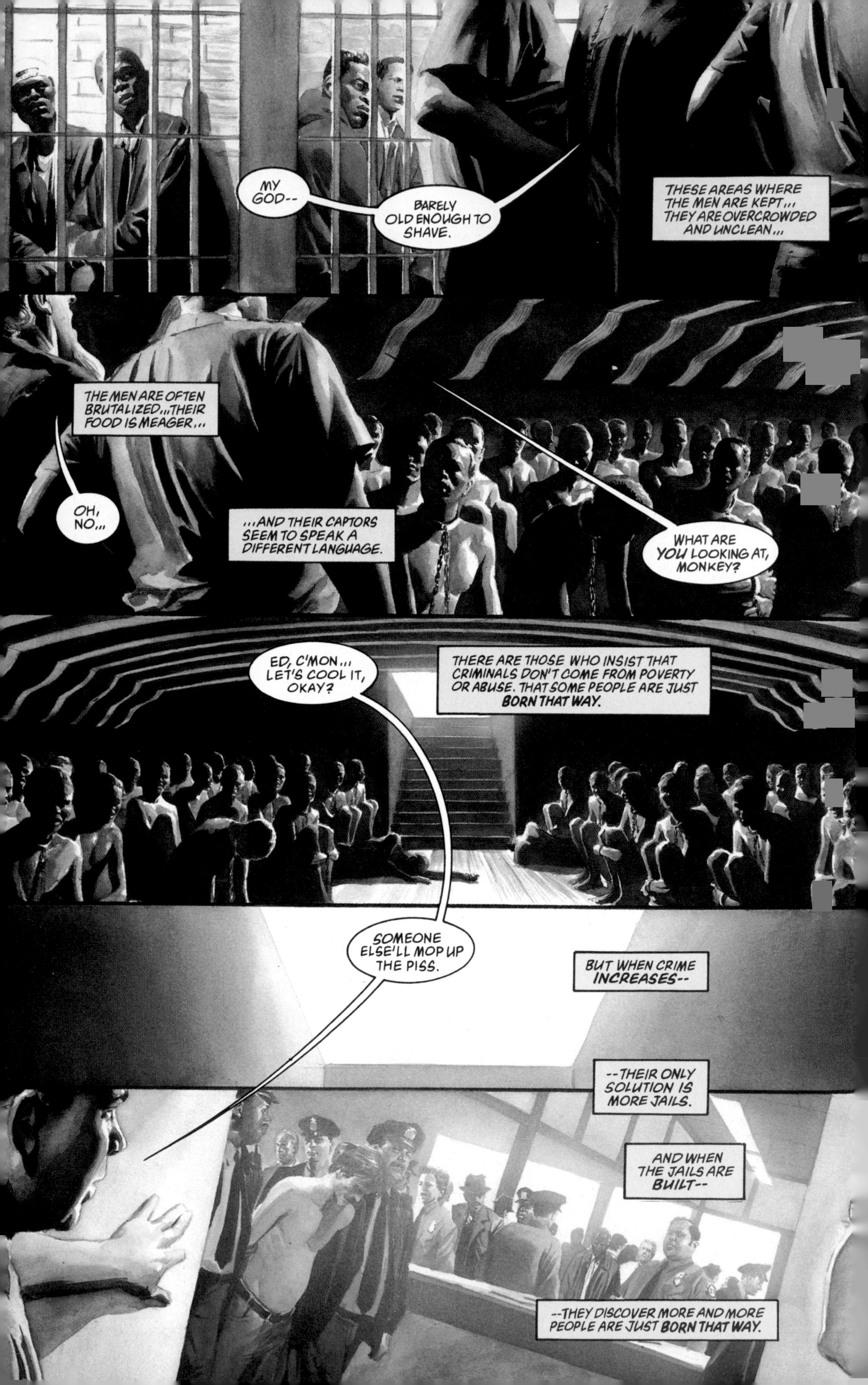
MY GOD--
BARELY OLD ENOUGH TO SHAVE.
THESE AREAS WHERE THE MEN ARE KEPT... THEY ARE OVERCROWDED AND UNCLEAN...
THE MEN ARE OFTEN BRUTALIZED...THEIR FOOD IS MEAGER...
OH, NO...
...AND THEIR CAPTORS SEEM TO SPEAK A DIFFERENT LANGUAGE.
WHAT ARE YOU LOOKING AT, MONKEY?
ED, C'MON... LET'S COOL IT, OKAY?
THERE ARE THOSE WHO INSIST THAT CRIMINALS DON'T COME FROM POVERTY OR ABUSE. THAT SOME PEOPLE ARE JUST BORN THAT WAY.
SOMEONE ELSE'LL MOP UP THE PISS.
BUT WHEN CRIME INCREASES--
--THEIR ONLY SOLUTION IS MORE JAILS.
AND WHEN THE JAILS ARE BUILT--
--THEY DISCOVER MORE AND MORE PEOPLE ARE JUST BORN THAT WAY.

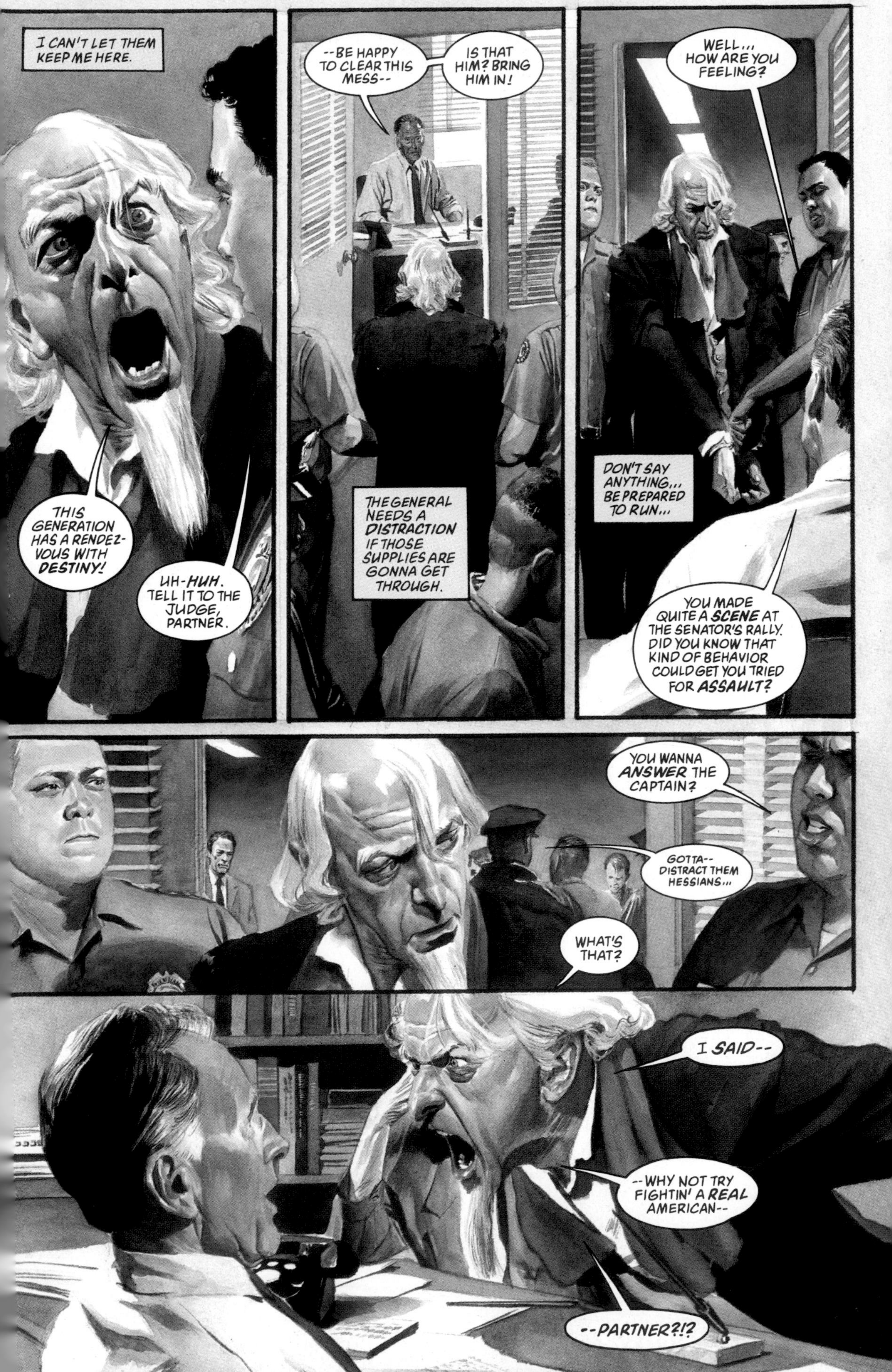
I CAN'T LET THEM KEEP ME HERE.
THIS GENERATION HAS A RENDEZ-VOUS WITH DESTINY!
UH-HUH. TELL IT TO THE JUDGE, PARTNER.
--BE HAPPY TO CLEAR THIS MESS--
IS THAT HIM? BRING HIM IN!
THE GENERAL NEEDS A DISTRACTION IF THOSE SUPPLIES ARE GONNA GET THROUGH.
WELL... HOW ARE YOU FEELING?
DON'T SAY ANYTHING... BE PREPARED TO RUN...
YOU MADE QUITE A SCENE AT THE SENATOR'S RALLY. DID YOU KNOW THAT KIND OF BEHAVIOR COULD GET YOU TRIED FOR ASSAULT?
YOU WANNA ANSWER THE CAPTAIN?
GOTTA-- DISTRACT THEM HESSIANS...
WHAT'S THAT?
I SAID--
--WHY NOT TRY FIGHTIN' A REAL AMERICAN--
--PARTNER?!?

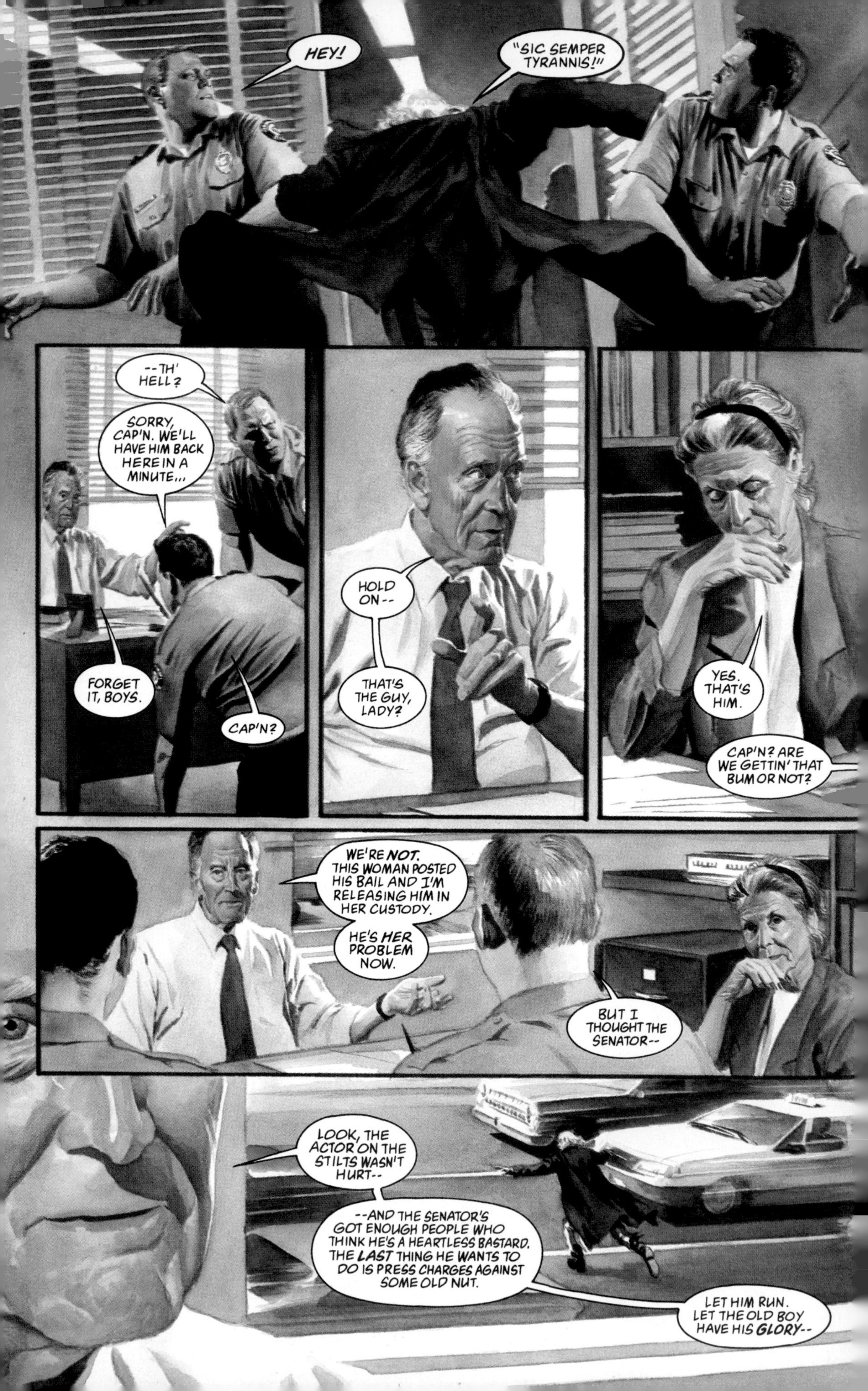
HEY!
"SIC SEMPER TYRANNIS!"
--TH' HELL?
SORRY, CAP'N. WE'LL HAVE HIM BACK HERE IN A MINUTE...
FORGET IT, BOYS.
CAP'N?
HOLD ON--
THAT'S THE GUY, LADY?
YES. THAT'S HIM.
CAP'N? ARE WE GETTIN' THAT BUM OR NOT?
WE'RE NOT. THIS WOMAN POSTED HIS BAIL AND I'M RELEASING HIM IN HER CUSTODY.
HE'S HER PROBLEM NOW.
BUT I THOUGHT THE SENATOR--
LOOK, THE ACTOR ON THE STILTS WASN'T HURT--
--AND THE SENATOR'S GOT ENOUGH PEOPLE WHO THINK HE'S A HEARTLESS BASTARD. THE LAST THING HE WANTS TO DO IS PRESS CHARGES AGAINST SOME OLD NUT.
LET HIM RUN. LET THE OLD BOY HAVE HIS GLORY--

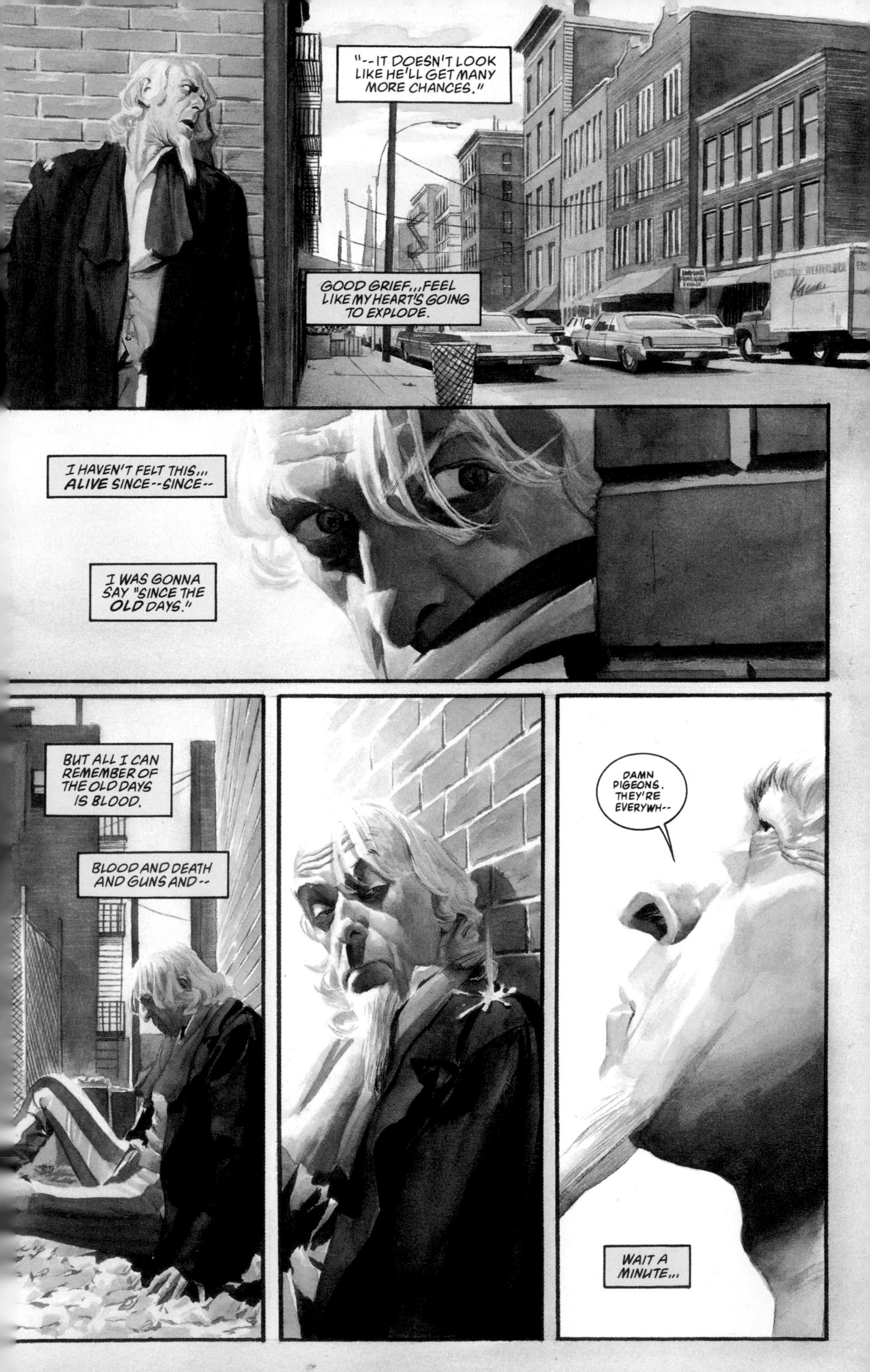
"--IT DOESN'T LOOK LIKE HE'LL GET MANY MORE CHANCES."
GOOD GRIEF... FEEL LIKE MY HEART'S GOING TO EXPLODE.
I HAVEN'T FELT THIS... ALIVE SINCE--SINCE--
I WAS GONNA SAY "SINCE THE OLD DAYS."
BUT ALL I CAN REMEMBER OF THE OLD DAYS IS BLOOD.
BLOOD AND DEATH AND GUNS AND--
DAMN PIGEONS. THEY'RE EVERYWH--
WAIT A MINUTE...

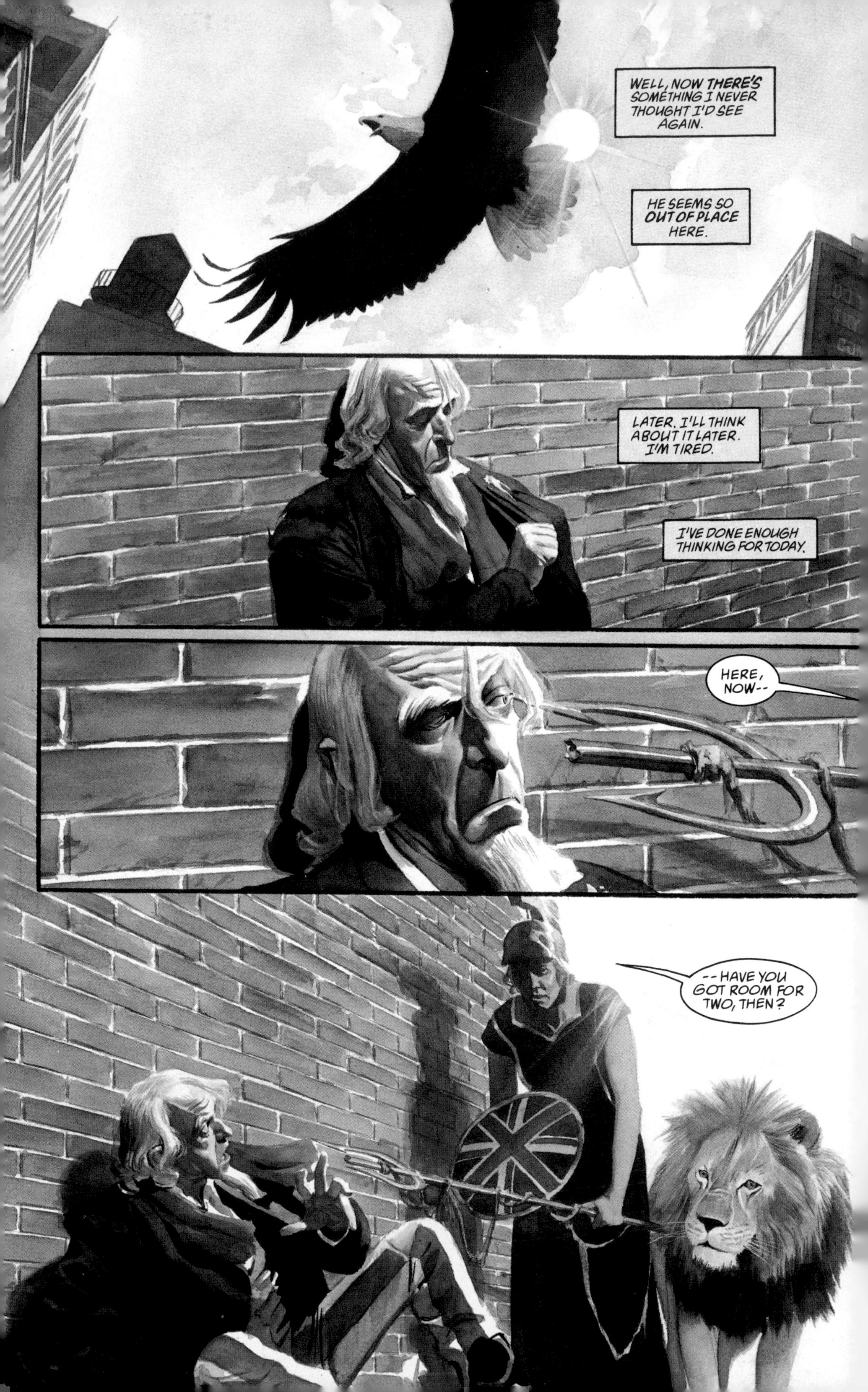
WELL, NOW THERE'S SOMETHING I NEVER THOUGHT I'D SEE AGAIN.
HE SEEMS SO OUT OF PLACE HERE.
LATER. I'LL THINK ABOUT IT LATER. I'M TIRED.
I'VE DONE ENOUGH THINKING FOR TODAY.
HERE, NOW--
--HAVE YOU GOT ROOM FOR TWO, THEN?

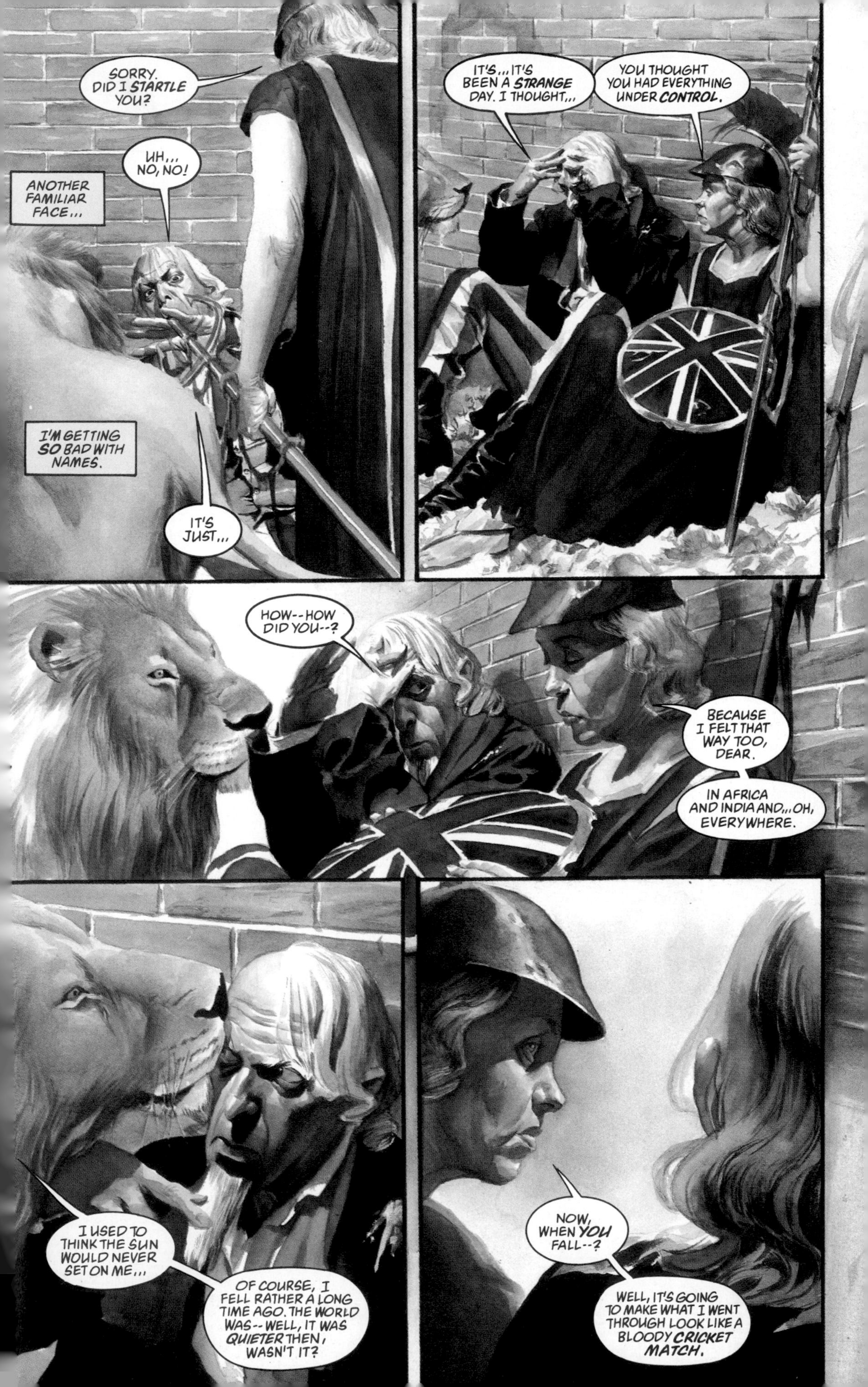
SORRY. DID I STARTLE YOU?
ANOTHER FAMILIAR FACE...
UH... NO, NO!
I'M GETTING SO BAD WITH NAMES.
IT'S JUST...
IT'S... IT'S BEEN A STRANGE DAY. I THOUGHT...
YOU THOUGHT YOU HAD EVERYTHING UNDER CONTROL.
HOW--HOW DID YOU--?
BECAUSE I FELT THAT WAY TOO, DEAR.
IN AFRICA AND INDIA AND... OH, EVERYWHERE.
I USED TO THINK THE SUN WOULD NEVER SET ON ME...
OF COURSE, I FELL RATHER A LONG TIME AGO. THE WORLD WAS--WELL, IT WAS QUIETER THEN, WASN'T IT?
NOW, WHEN YOU FALL--?
WELL, IT'S GOING TO MAKE WHAT I WENT THROUGH LOOK LIKE A BLOODY CRICKET MATCH.

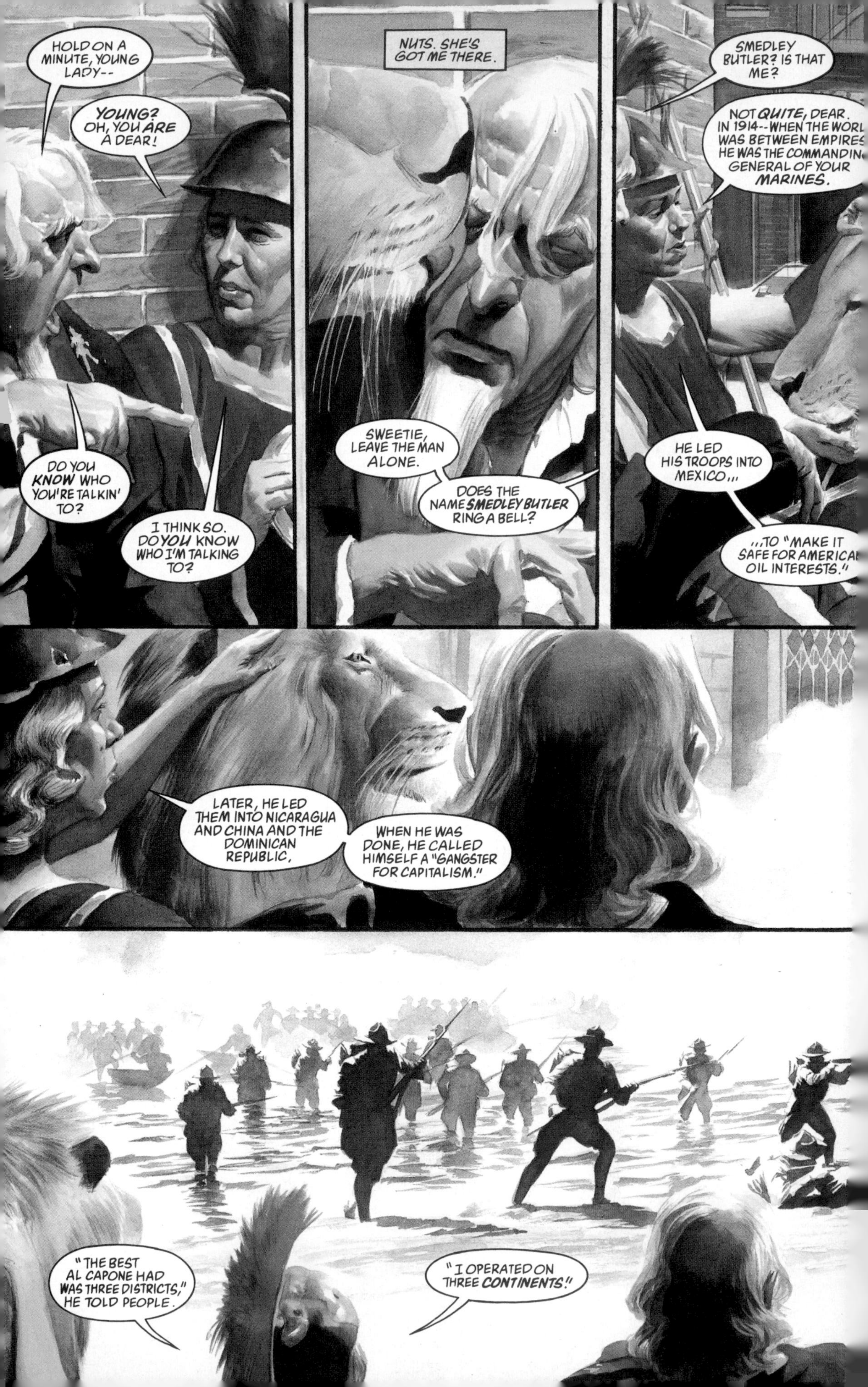
HOLD ON A MINUTE, YOUNG LADY--
YOUNG? OH, YOU ARE A DEAR!
DO YOU KNOW WHO YOU'RE TALKIN' TO?
I THINK SO. DO YOU KNOW WHO I'M TALKING TO?
NUTS. SHE'S GOT ME THERE.
SWEETIE, LEAVE THE MAN ALONE.
DOES THE NAME SMEDLEY BUTLER RING A BELL?
SMEDLEY BUTLER? IS THAT ME?
NOT QUITE, DEAR. IN 1914--WHEN THE WORL WAS BETWEEN EMPIRES HE WAS THE COMMANDIN GENERAL OF YOUR MARINES.
HE LED HIS TROOPS INTO MEXICO...
...TO "MAKE IT SAFE FOR AMERICA OIL INTERESTS."
LATER, HE LED THEM INTO NICARAGUA AND CHINA AND THE DOMINICAN REPUBLIC.
WHEN HE WAS DONE, HE CALLED HIMSELF A "GANGSTER FOR CAPITALISM."
"THE BEST AL CAPONE HAD WAS THREE DISTRICTS," HE TOLD PEOPLE.
"I OPERATED ON THREE CONTINENTS!"

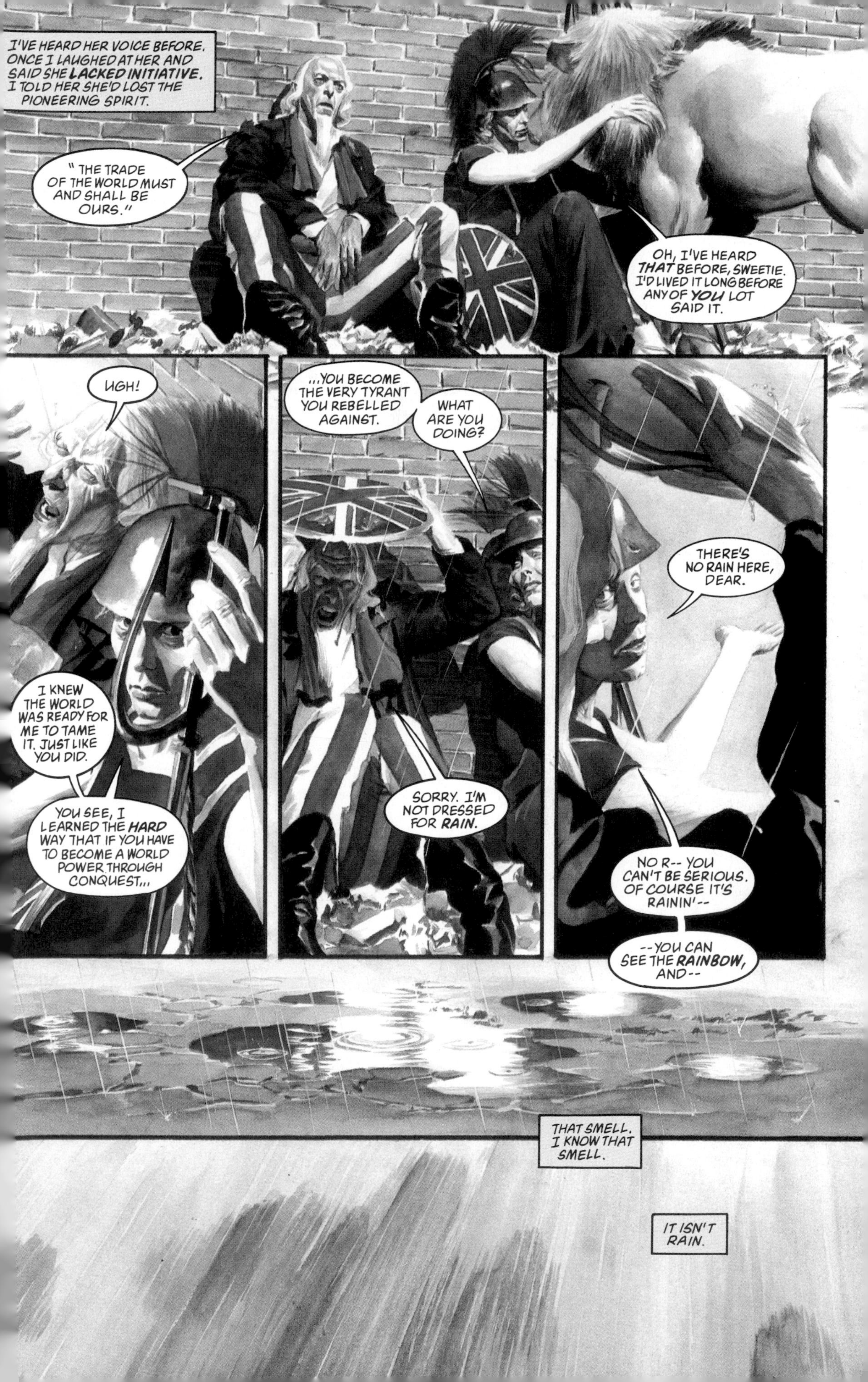
I'VE HEARD HER VOICE BEFORE. ONCE I LAUGHED AT HER AND SAID SHE LACKED INITIATIVE. I TOLD HER SHE'D LOST THE PIONEERING SPIRIT.
"THE TRADE OF THE WORLD MUST AND SHALL BE OURS."
OH, I'VE HEARD THAT BEFORE, SWEETIE. I'D LIVED IT LONG BEFORE ANY OF YOU LOT SAID IT.
UGH!
I KNEW THE WORLD WAS READY FOR ME TO TAME IT. JUST LIKE YOU DID.
YOU SEE, I LEARNED THE HARD WAY THAT IF YOU HAVE TO BECOME A WORLD POWER THROUGH CONQUEST...
...YOU BECOME THE VERY TYRANT YOU REBELLED AGAINST.
WHAT ARE YOU DOING?
SORRY. I'M NOT DRESSED FOR RAIN.
THERE'S NO RAIN HERE, DEAR.
NO R-- YOU CAN'T BE SERIOUS. OF COURSE IT'S RAININ'--
--YOU CAN SEE THE RAINBOW, AND--
THAT SMELL. I KNOW THAT SMELL.
IT ISN'T RAIN.

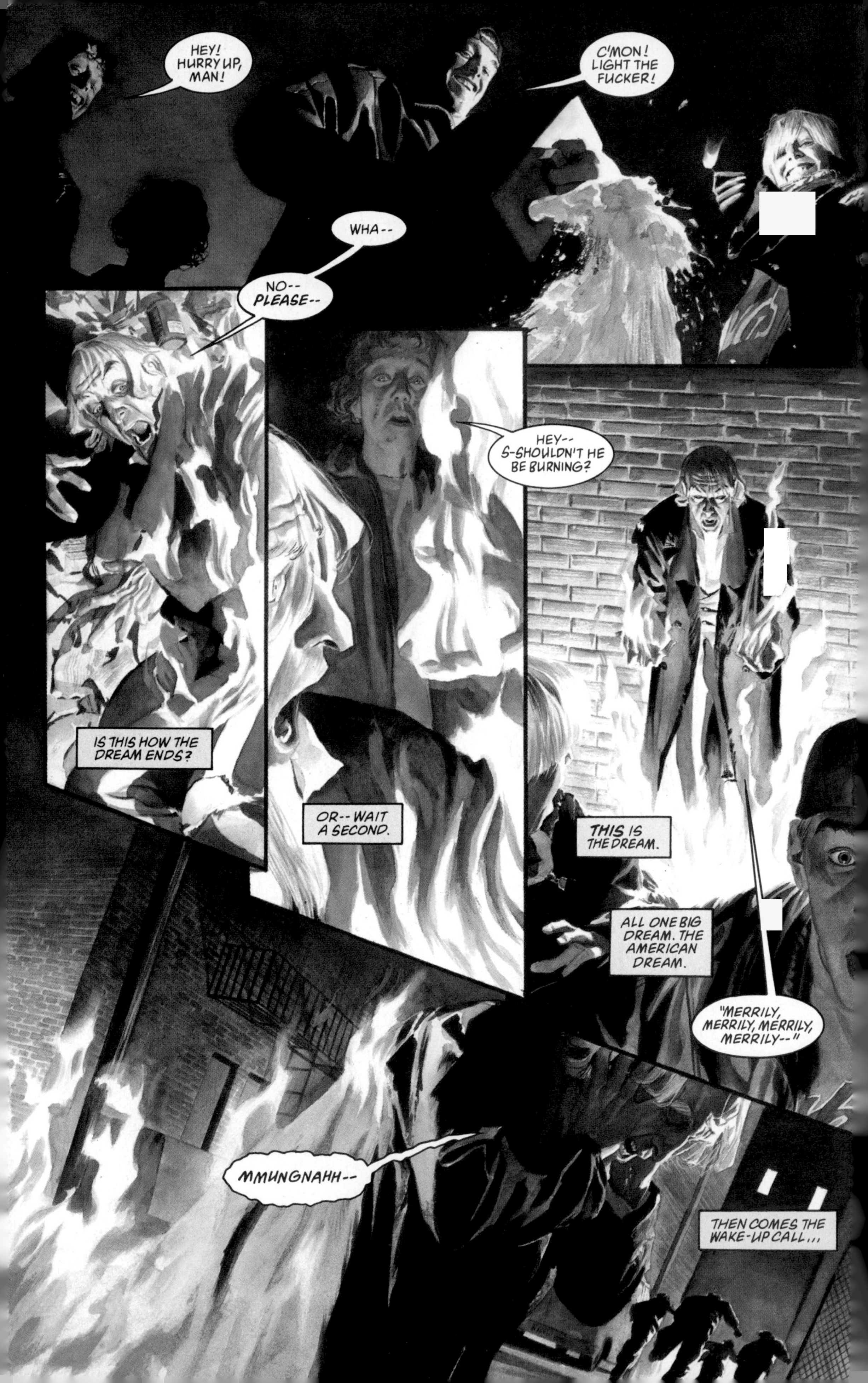
HEY! HURRY UP, MAN!
C'MON! LIGHT THE FUCKER!
WHA--
NO-- PLEASE--
IS THIS HOW THE DREAM ENDS?
HEY-- S-SHOULDN'T HE BE BURNING?
OR-- WAIT A SECOND.
THIS IS THE DREAM.
ALL ONE BIG DREAM. THE AMERICAN DREAM.
"MERRILY, MERRILY, MERRILY, MERRILY--"
MMUNGNAHH--
THEN COMES THE WAKE-UP CALL...

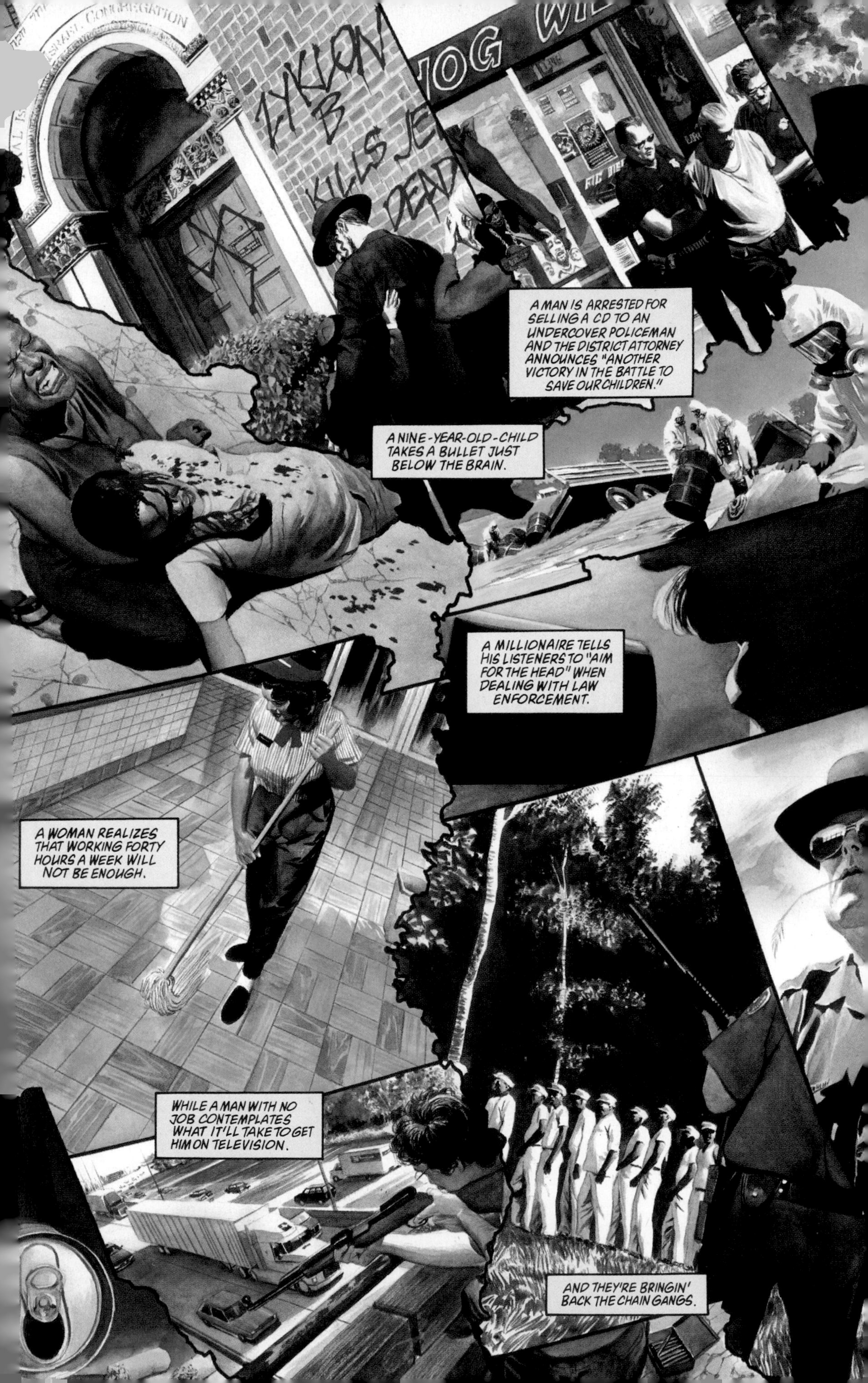
A MAN IS ARRESTED FOR SELLING A CD TO AN UNDERCOVER POLICEMAN AND THE DISTRICT ATTORNEY ANNOUNCES "ANOTHER VICTORY IN THE BATTLE TO SAVE OUR CHILDREN."
A NINE-YEAR-OLD-CHILD TAKES A BULLET JUST BELOW THE BRAIN.
A MILLIONAIRE TELLS HIS LISTENERS TO "AIM FOR THE HEAD" WHEN DEALING WITH LAW ENFORCEMENT.
A WOMAN REALIZES THAT WORKING FORTY HOURS A WEEK WILL NOT BE ENOUGH.
WHILE A MAN WITH NO JOB CONTEMPLATES WHAT IT'LL TAKE TO GET HIM ON TELEVISION.
AND THEY'RE BRINGIN' BACK THE CHAIN GANGS.

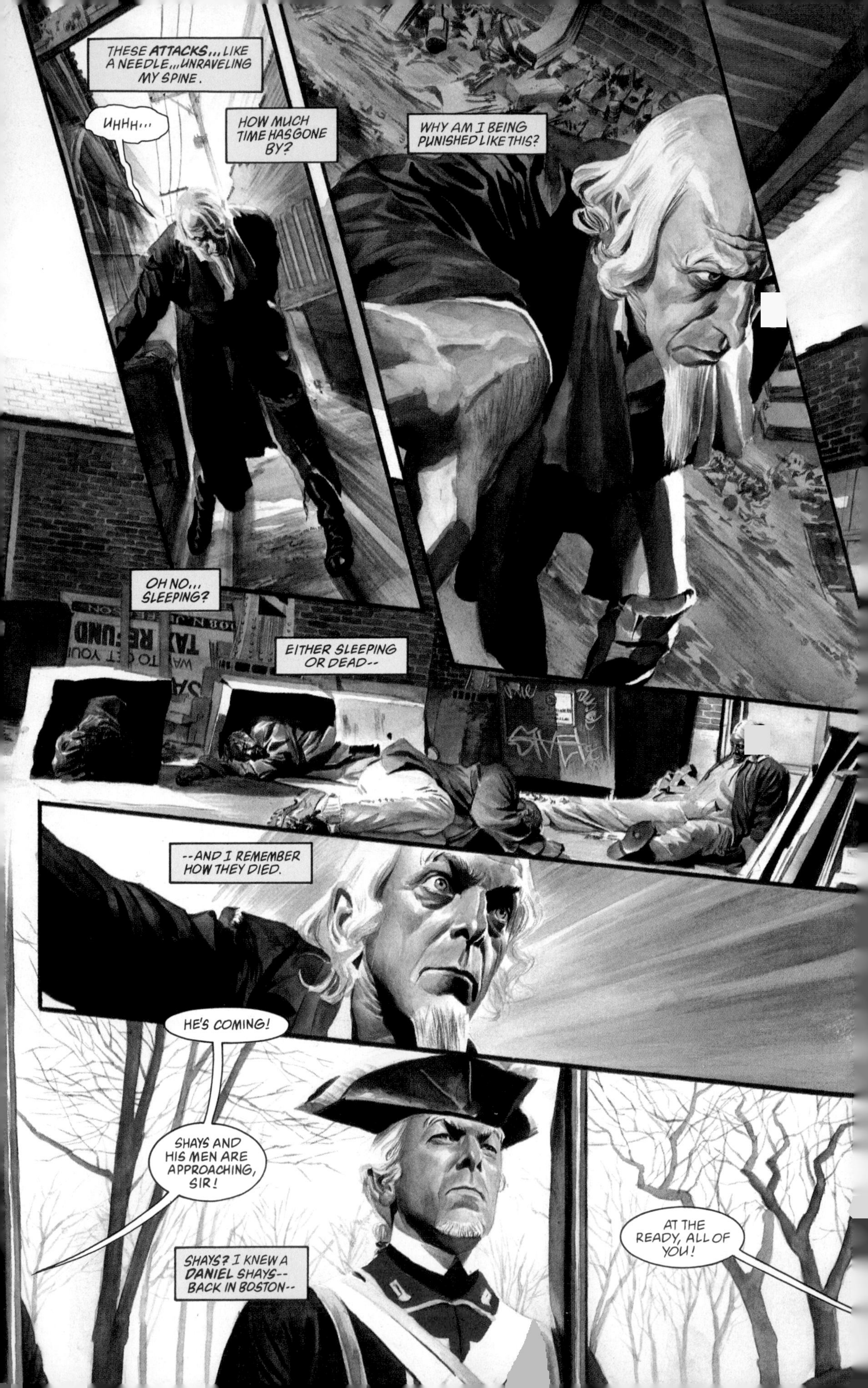
THESE ATTACKS... LIKE A NEEDLE... UNRAVELING MY SPINE.
UHHH...
HOW MUCH TIME HAS GONE BY?
WHY AM I BEING PUNISHED LIKE THIS?
OH NO... SLEEPING?
EITHER SLEEPING OR DEAD--
--AND I REMEMBER HOW THEY DIED.
HE'S COMING!
SHAYS AND HIS MEN ARE APPROACHING, SIR!
SHAYS? I KNEW A DANIEL SHAYS-- BACK IN BOSTON--
AT THE READY, ALL OF YOU!

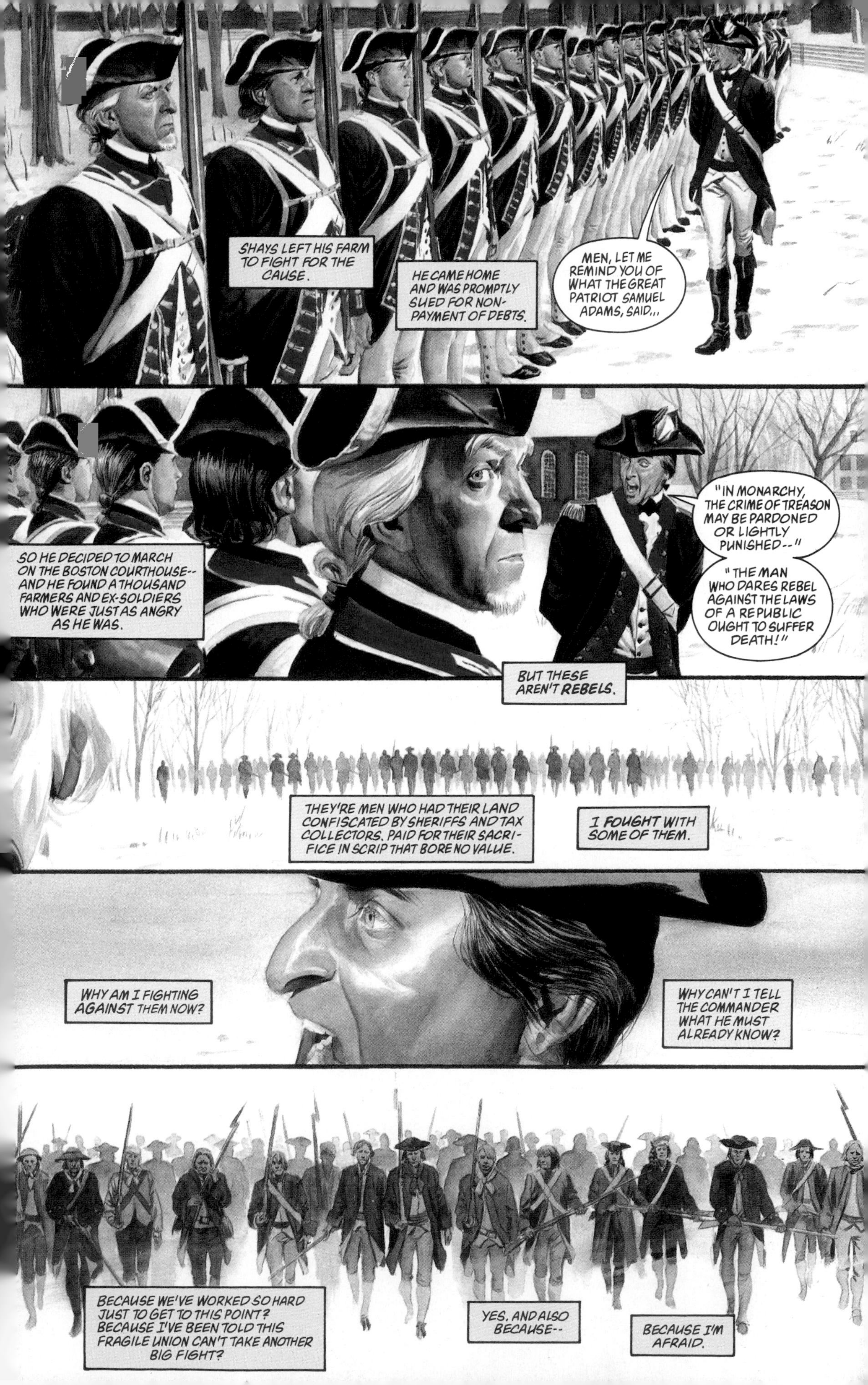
SHAYS LEFT HIS FARM TO FIGHT FOR THE CAUSE.
HE CAME HOME AND WAS PROMPTLY SUED FOR NON-PAYMENT OF DEBTS.
MEN, LET ME REMIND YOU OF WHAT THE GREAT PATRIOT SAMUEL ADAMS, SAID...
SO HE DECIDED TO MARCH ON THE BOSTON COURTHOUSE-- AND HE FOUND A THOUSAND FARMERS AND EX-SOLDIERS WHO WERE JUST AS ANGRY AS HE WAS.
"IN MONARCHY, THE CRIME OF TREASON MAY BE PARDONED OR LIGHTLY PUNISHED--"
"THE MAN WHO DARES REBEL AGAINST THE LAWS OF A REPUBLIC OUGHT TO SUFFER DEATH!"
BUT THESE AREN'T REBELS.
THEY'RE MEN WHO HAD THEIR LAND CONFISCATED BY SHERIFFS AND TAX COLLECTORS. PAID FOR THEIR SACRIFICE IN SCRIP THAT BORE NO VALUE.
I FOUGHT WITH SOME OF THEM.
WHY AM I FIGHTING AGAINST THEM NOW?
WHY CAN'T I TELL THE COMMANDER WHAT HE MUST ALREADY KNOW?
BECAUSE WE'VE WORKED SO HARD JUST TO GET TO THIS POINT? BECAUSE I'VE BEEN TOLD THIS FRAGILE UNION CAN'T TAKE ANOTHER BIG FIGHT?
YES, AND ALSO BECAUSE--
BECAUSE I'M AFRAID.

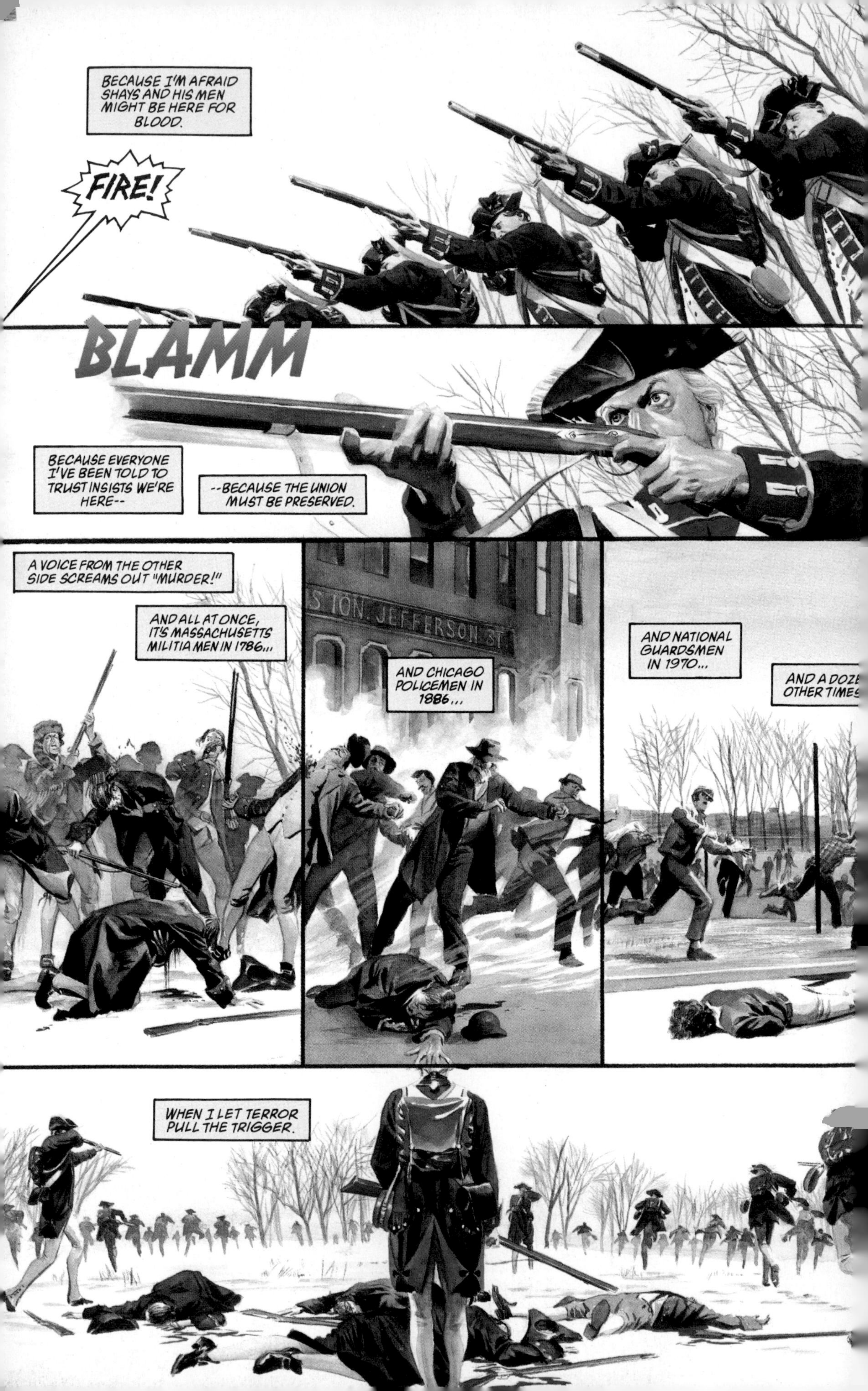

BECAUSE I'M AFRAID SHAYS AND HIS MEN MIGHT BE HERE FOR BLOOD.
FIRE!
BLAMM
BECAUSE EVERYONE I'VE BEEN TOLD TO TRUST INSISTS WE'RE HERE--
--BECAUSE THE UNION MUST BE PRESERVED.
A VOICE FROM THE OTHER SIDE SCREAMS OUT "MURDER!"
AND ALL AT ONCE, IT'S MASSACHUSETTS MILITIA MEN IN 1786...
JEFFERSON ST
AND CHICAGO POLICEMEN IN 1886...
AND NATIONAL GUARDSMEN IN 1970...
AND A DOZE
OTHER TIMES
WHEN I LET TERROR PULL THE TRIGGER.

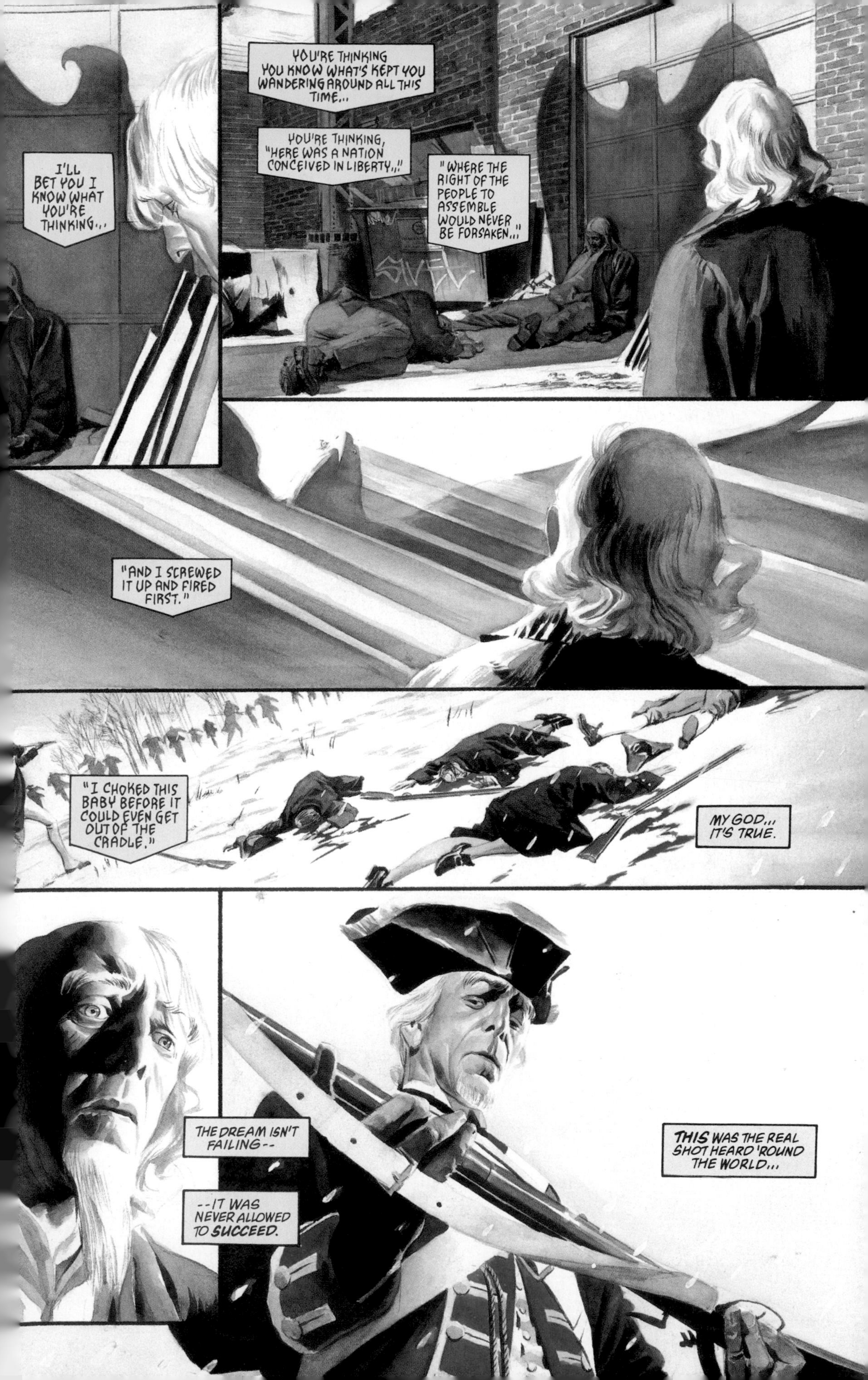
I'LL BET YOU I KNOW WHAT YOU'RE THINKING...
YOU'RE THINKING YOU KNOW WHAT'S KEPT YOU WANDERING AROUND ALL THIS TIME...
YOU'RE THINKING, "HERE WAS A NATION CONCEIVED IN LIBERTY..."
"WHERE THE RIGHT OF THE PEOPLE TO ASSEMBLE WOULD NEVER BE FORSAKEN..."
"AND I SCREWED IT UP AND FIRED FIRST."
"I CHOKED THIS BABY BEFORE IT COULD EVEN GET OUT OF THE CRADLE."
MY GOD... IT'S TRUE.
THE DREAM ISN'T FAILING--
--IT WAS NEVER ALLOWED TO SUCCEED.
THIS WAS THE REAL SHOT HEARD 'ROUND THE WORLD...

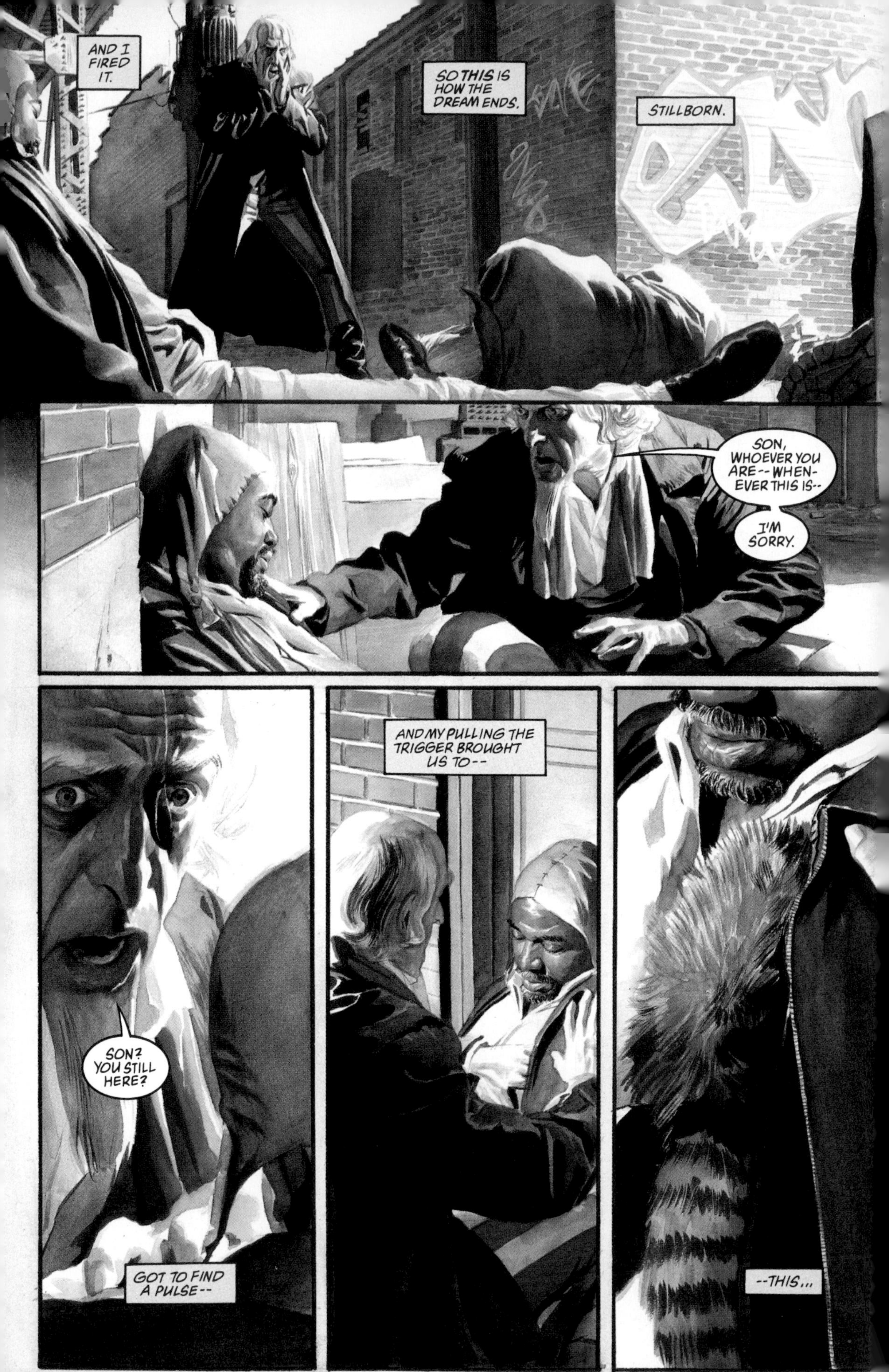
AND I FIRED IT.
SO THIS IS HOW THE DREAM ENDS.
STILLBORN.
SON, WHOEVER YOU ARE--WHEN-EVER THIS IS--
I'M SORRY.
SON? YOU STILL HERE?
GOT TO FIND A PULSE--
AND MY PULLING THE TRIGGER BROUGHT US TO--
--THIS...

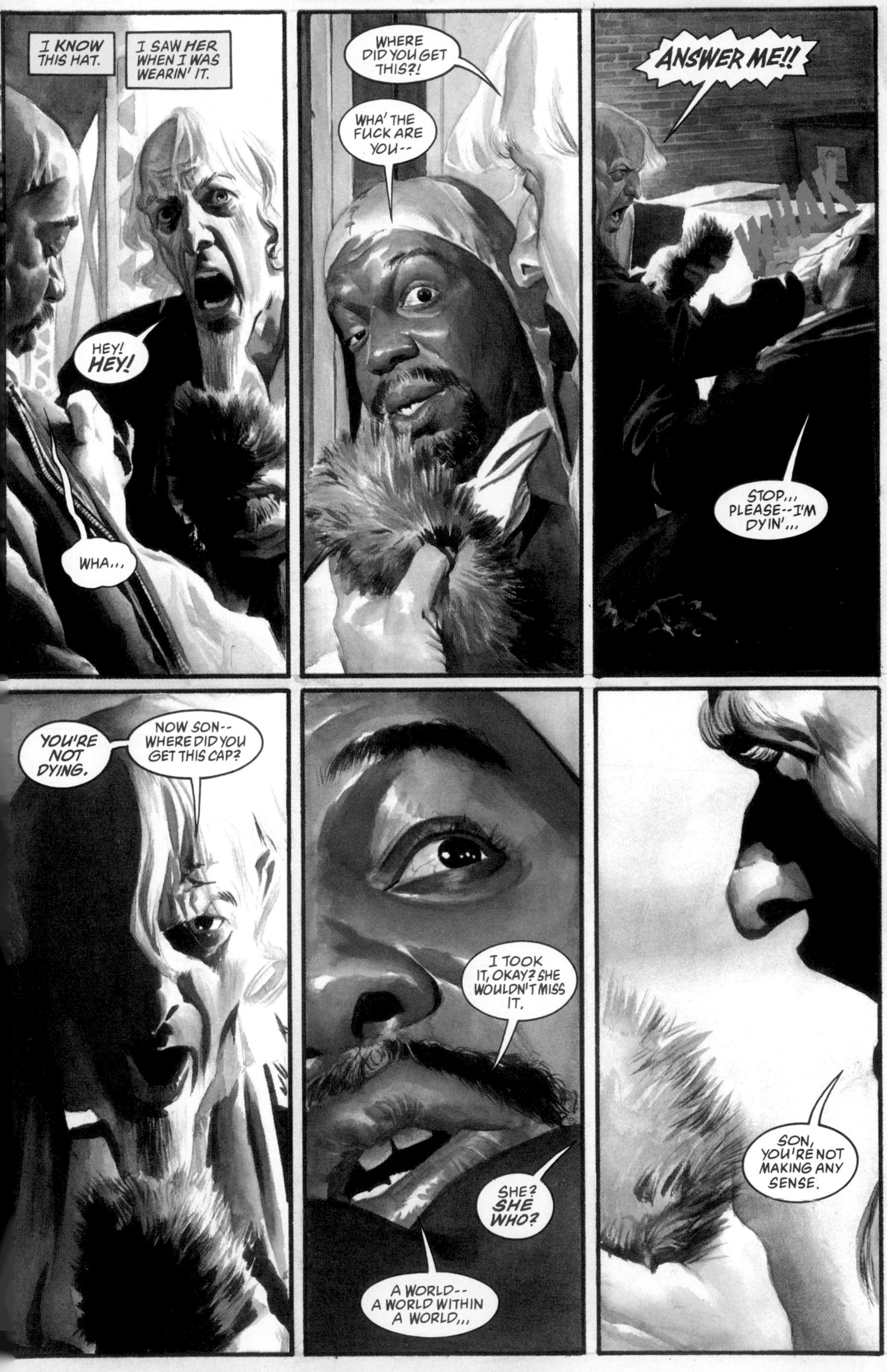
I KNOW THIS HAT.
I SAW HER WHEN I WAS WEARIN' IT.
HEY! HEY!
WHA...
WHERE DID YOU GET THIS?!
WHA' THE FUCK ARE YOU--
ANSWER ME!!
WHAK
STOP... PLEASE--I'M DYIN'...
YOU'RE NOT DYING.
NOW SON-- WHERE DID YOU GET THIS CAP?
I TOOK IT, OKAY? SHE WOULDN'T MISS IT.
SHE? SHE WHO?
A WORLD-- A WORLD WITHIN A WORLD...
SON, YOU'RE NOT MAKING ANY SENSE.

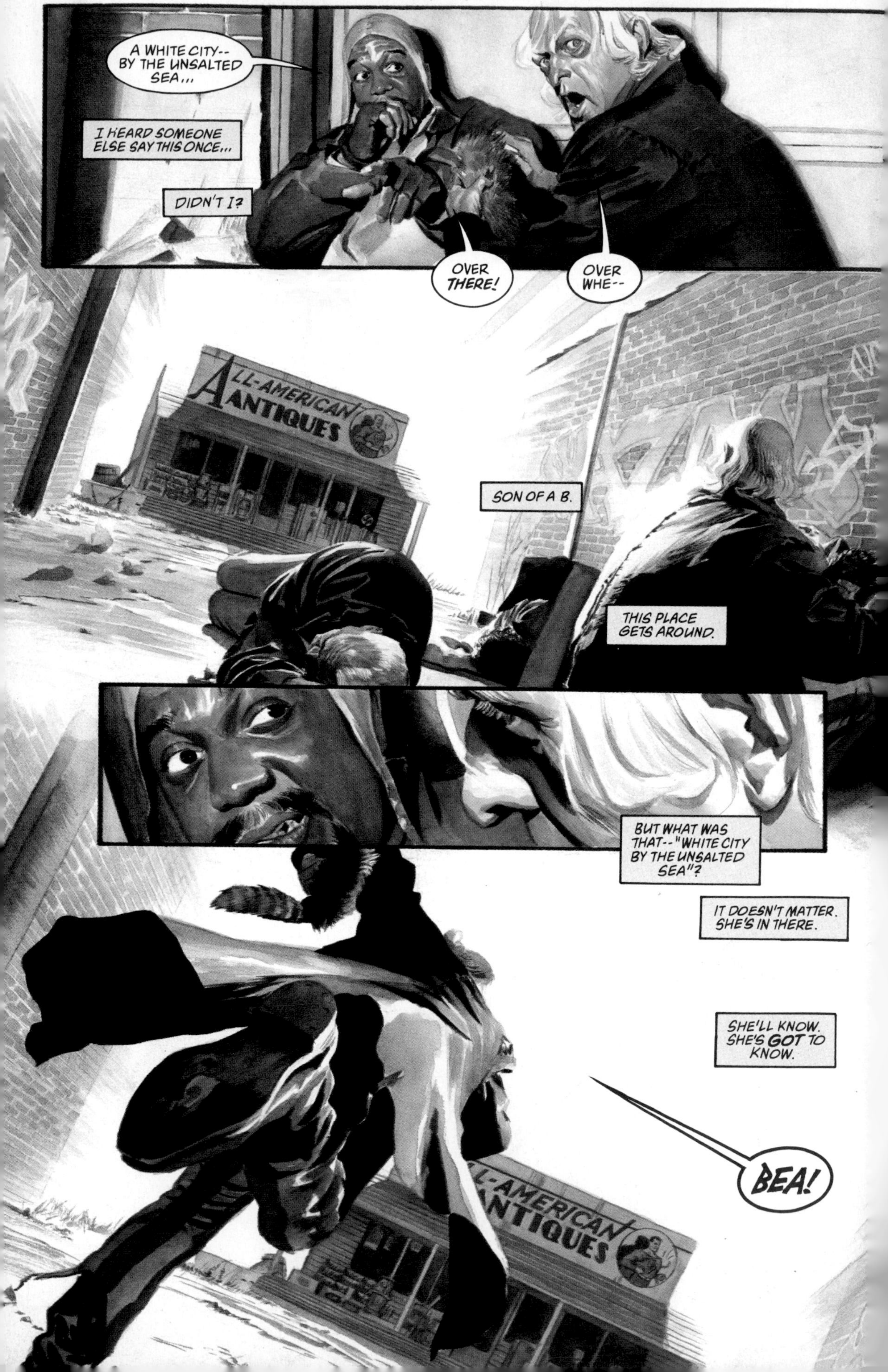
A WHITE CITY-- BY THE UNSALTED SEA...
I HEARD SOMEONE ELSE SAY THIS ONCE...
DIDN'T I?
OVER THERE!
OVER WHE--
ALL-AMERICAN ANTIQUES
SON OF A B.
THIS PLACE GETS AROUND.
BUT WHAT WAS THAT--"WHITE CITY BY THE UNSALTED SEA"?
IT DOESN'T MATTER. SHE'S IN THERE.
SHE'LL KNOW. SHE'S GOT TO KNOW.
BEA!
ALL-AMERICAN ANTIQUES

WHERE--

WHERE IS EVERYONE?

BEA?

IT'S THE SAME STORE. IT'S GOT TO BE.

THE JOCKEY. THE WOODEN INDIAN. LAST TIME, THEY WERE RIGHT--

--AGAINST THE WALL.

♪ THE VERY THOUGHT OF YOU... ♪

♪ ...AND I FORGET TO DO... ♪

BEA?!

THAT VOICE-- IT'S HER.

WHERE ARE YOU?!

♪ ...THE LITTLE ORDINARY THINGS... ♪

BEA, I CAME BACK! I--

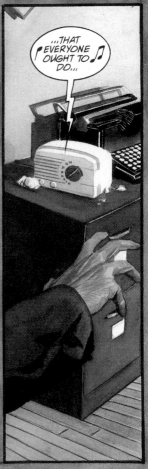

♪ ...THAT EVERYONE OUGHT TO DO... ♪

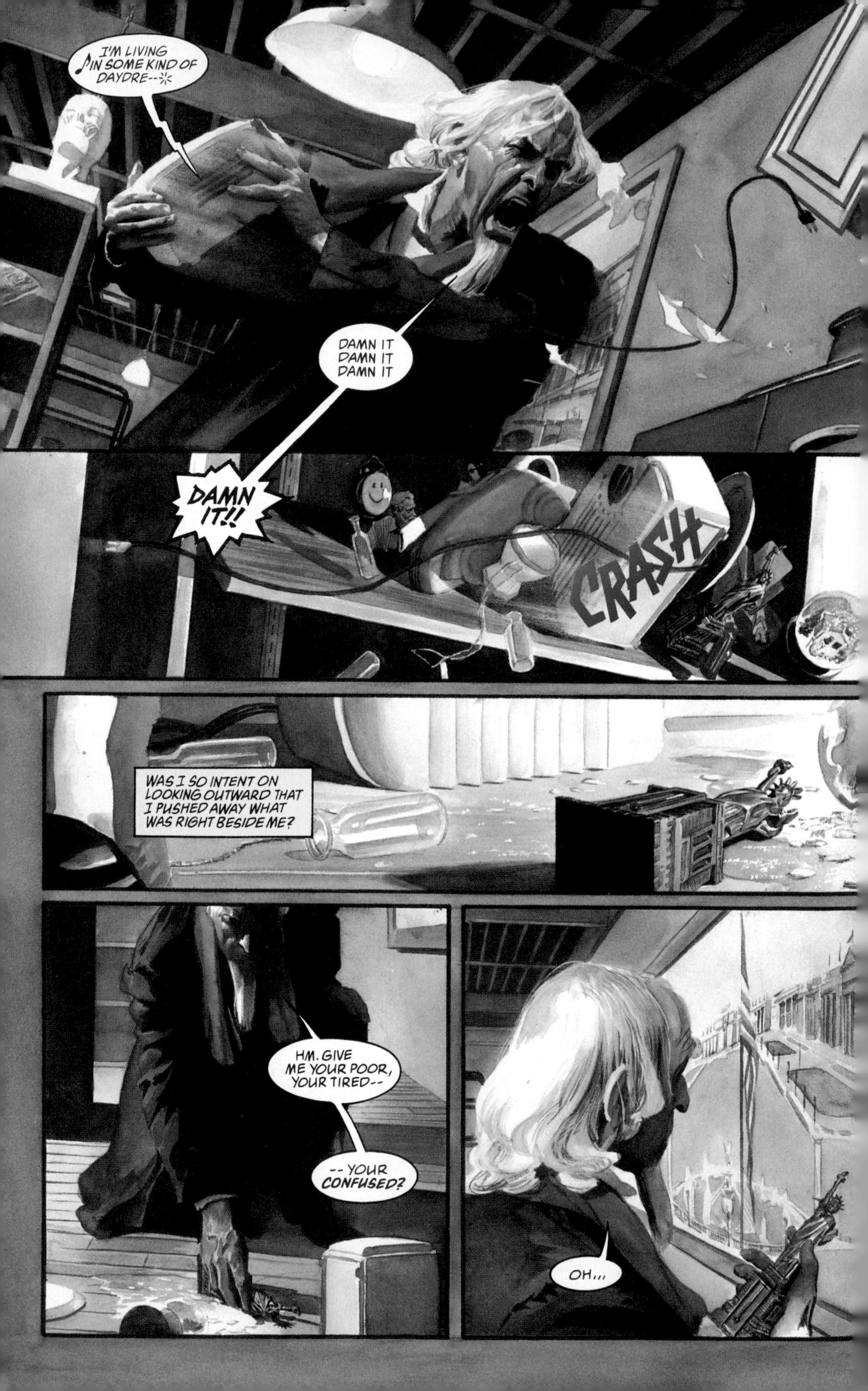
I'M LIVING
IN SOME KIND OF
DAYDRE--
DAMN IT
DAMN IT
DAMN IT
DAMN IT!!
CRASH
WAS I SO INTENT ON LOOKING OUTWARD THAT I PUSHED AWAY WHAT WAS RIGHT BESIDE ME?
HM. GIVE ME YOUR POOR, YOUR TIRED--
--YOUR CONFUSED?
OH...

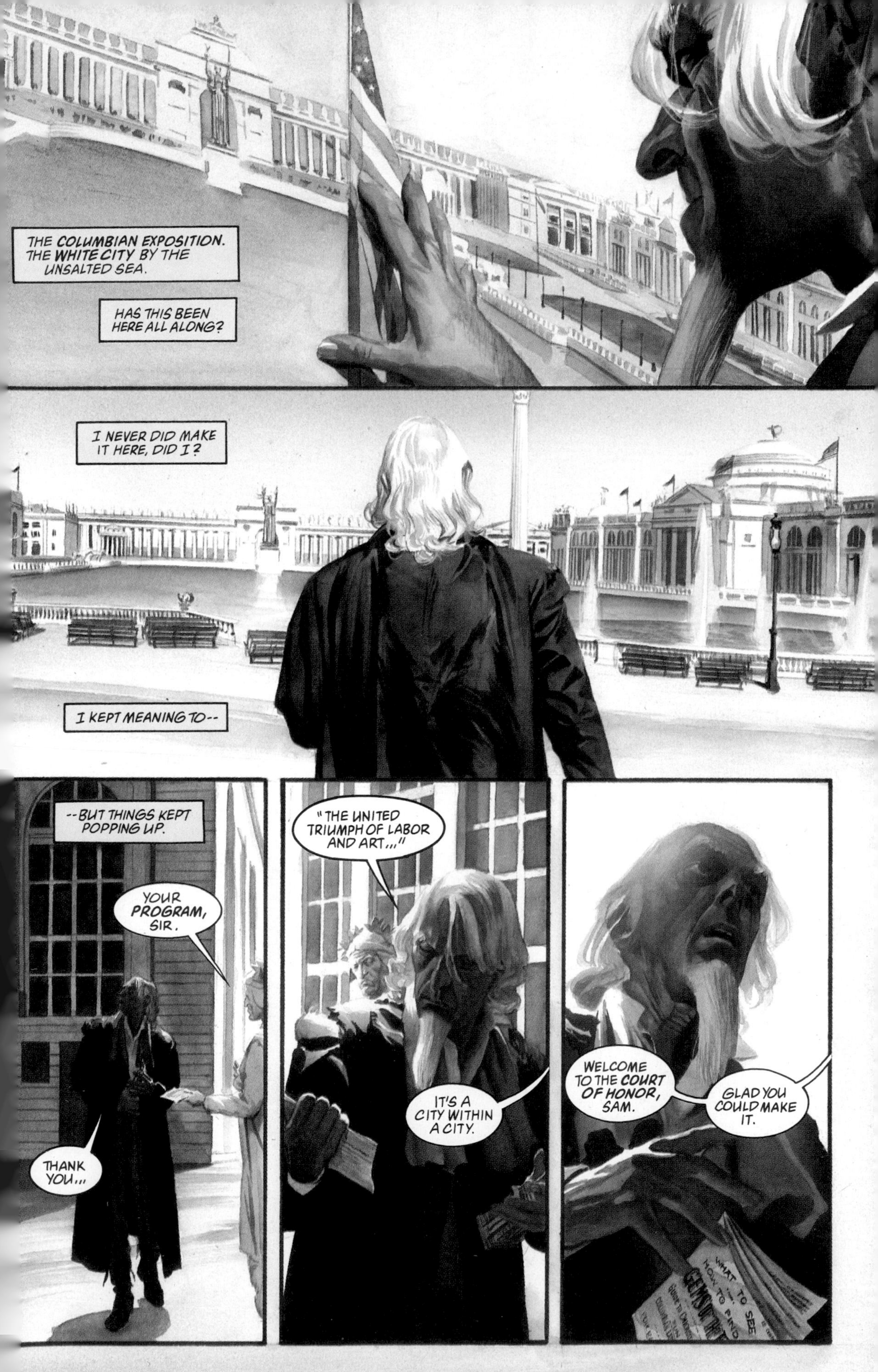
THE COLUMBIAN EXPOSITION. THE WHITE CITY BY THE UNSALTED SEA.
HAS THIS BEEN HERE ALL ALONG?
I NEVER DID MAKE IT HERE, DID I?
I KEPT MEANING TO--
--BUT THINGS KEPT POPPING UP.
YOUR PROGRAM, SIR.
THANK YOU...
"THE UNITED TRIUMPH OF LABOR AND ART..."
IT'S A CITY WITHIN A CITY.
WELCOME TO THE COURT OF HONOR, SAM.
GLAD YOU COULD MAKE IT.

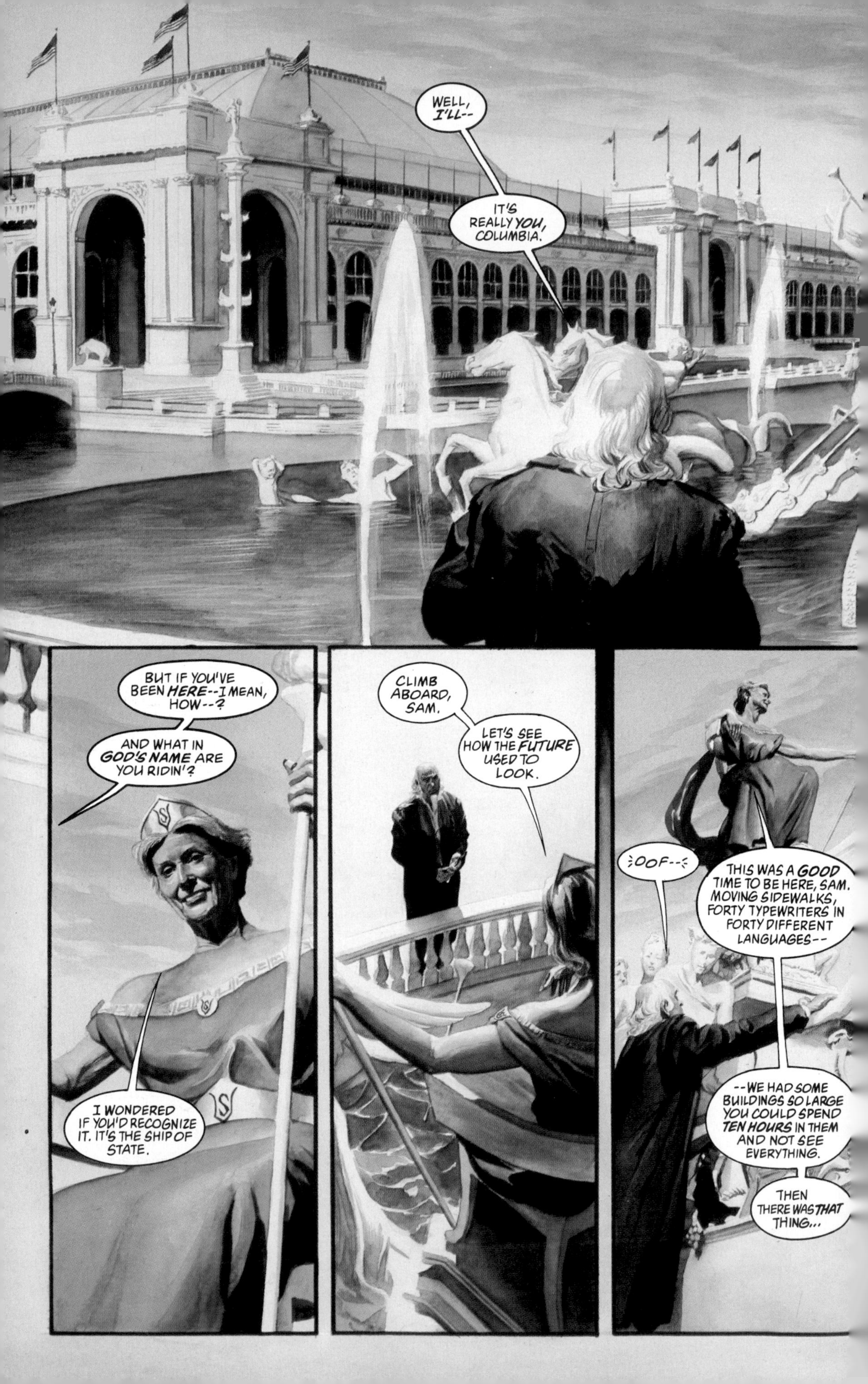
WELL, I'LL--
IT'S REALLY YOU, COLUMBIA.
BUT IF YOU'VE BEEN HERE--I MEAN, HOW--?
AND WHAT IN GOD'S NAME ARE YOU RIDIN'?
I WONDERED IF YOU'D RECOGNIZE IT. IT'S THE SHIP OF STATE.
CLIMB ABOARD, SAM.
LET'S SEE HOW THE FUTURE USED TO LOOK.
OOF--
THIS WAS A GOOD TIME TO BE HERE, SAM. MOVING SIDEWALKS, FORTY TYPEWRITERS IN FORTY DIFFERENT LANGUAGES--
--WE HAD SOME BUILDINGS SO LARGE YOU COULD SPEND TEN HOURS IN THEM AND NOT SEE EVERYTHING.
THEN THERE WAS THAT THING...

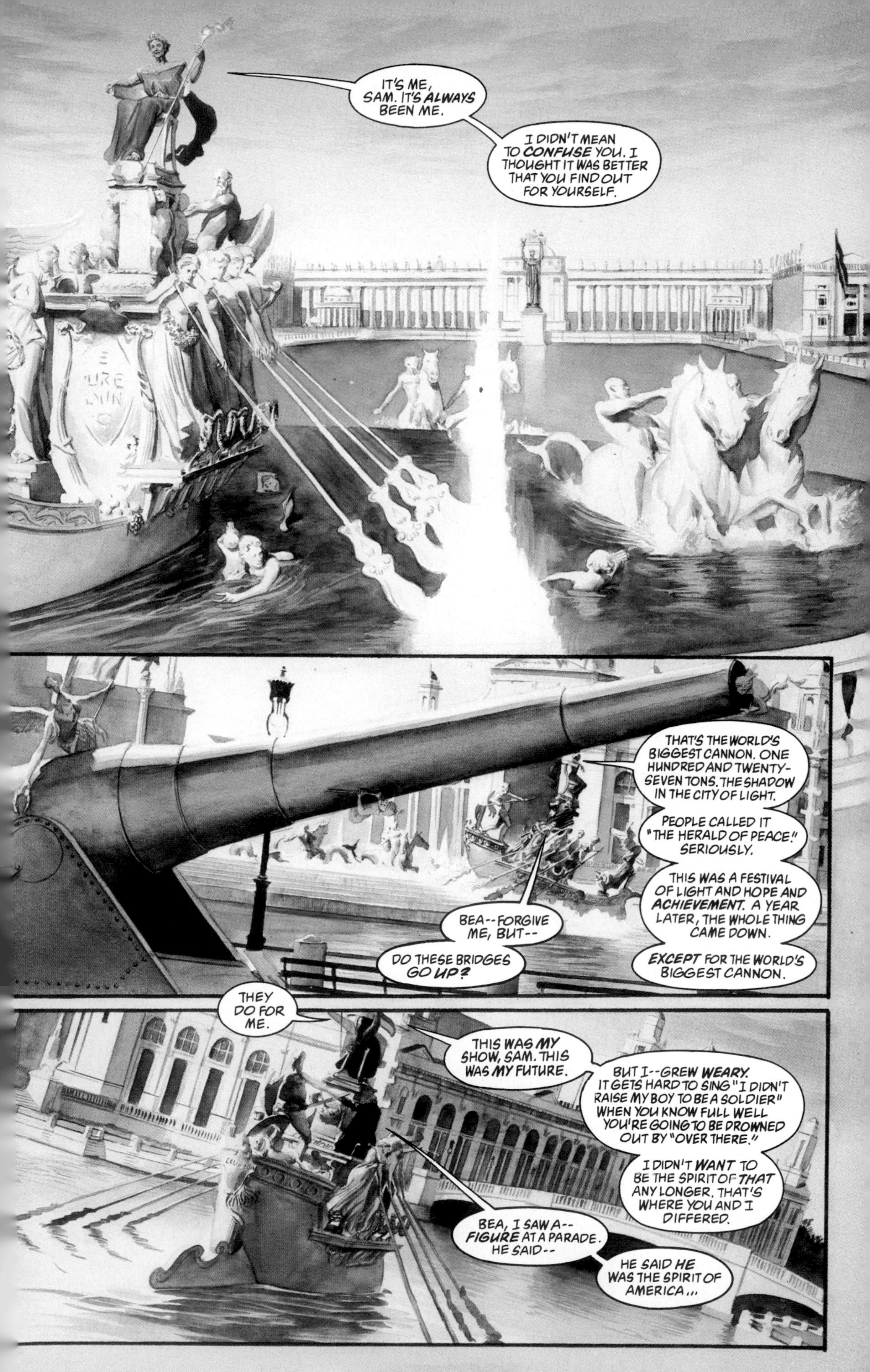
IT'S ME, SAM. IT'S ALWAYS BEEN ME.
I DIDN'T MEAN TO CONFUSE YOU. I THOUGHT IT WAS BETTER THAT YOU FIND OUT FOR YOURSELF.
THAT'S THE WORLD'S BIGGEST CANNON. ONE HUNDRED AND TWENTY-SEVEN TONS. THE SHADOW IN THE CITY OF LIGHT.
PEOPLE CALLED IT "THE HERALD OF PEACE." SERIOUSLY.
THIS WAS A FESTIVAL OF LIGHT AND HOPE AND ACHIEVEMENT. A YEAR LATER, THE WHOLE THING CAME DOWN.
EXCEPT FOR THE WORLD'S BIGGEST CANNON.
BEA--FORGIVE ME, BUT--
DO THESE BRIDGES GO UP?
THEY DO FOR ME.
THIS WAS MY SHOW, SAM. THIS WAS MY FUTURE.
BUT I--GREW WEARY. IT GETS HARD TO SING "I DIDN'T RAISE MY BOY TO BE A SOLDIER" WHEN YOU KNOW FULL WELL YOU'RE GOING TO BE DROWNED OUT BY "OVER THERE."
I DIDN'T WANT TO BE THE SPIRIT OF THAT ANY LONGER. THAT'S WHERE YOU AND I DIFFERED.
BEA, I SAW A--FIGURE AT A PARADE. HE SAID--
HE SAID HE WAS THE SPIRIT OF AMERICA...

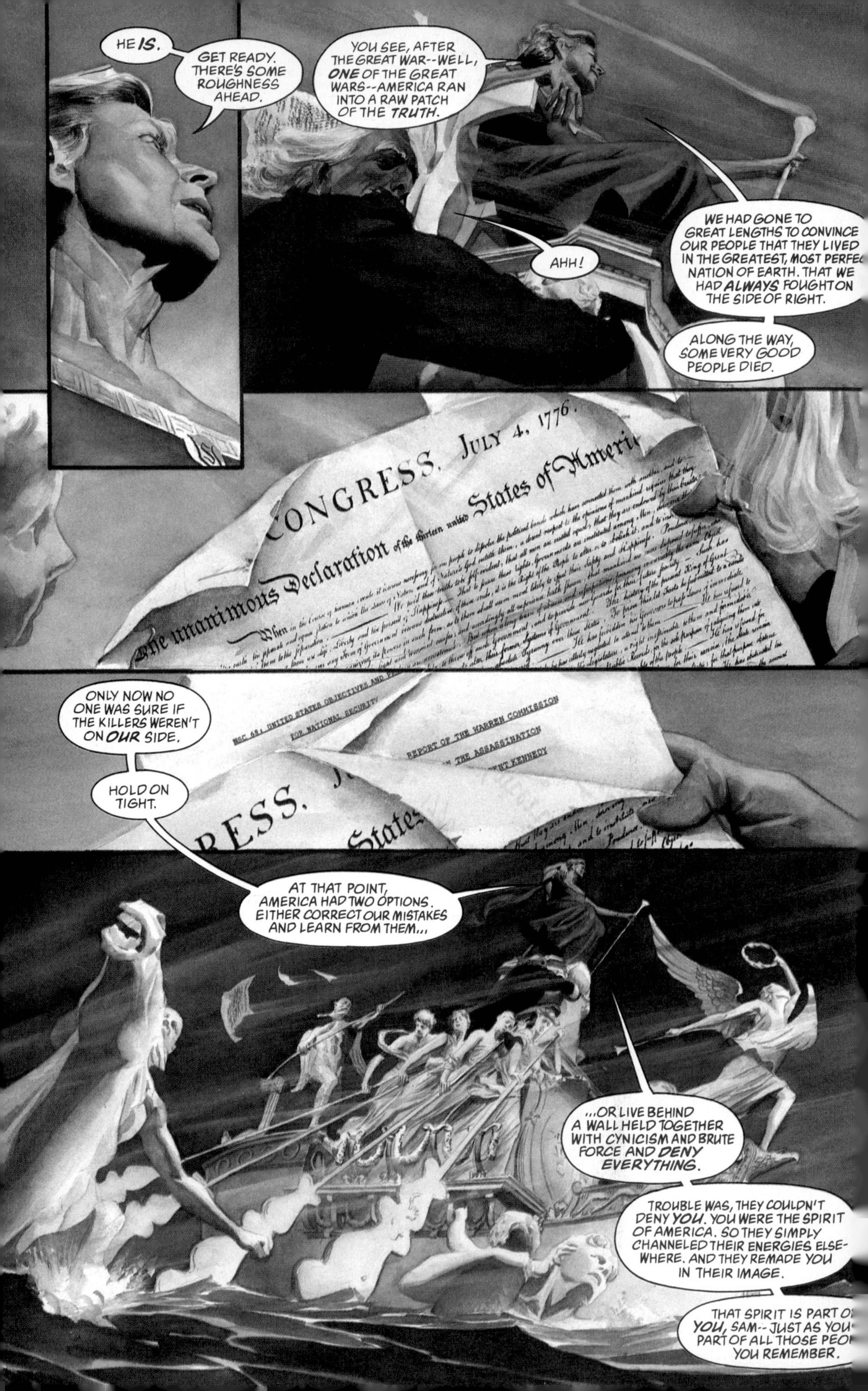

HE IS.
GET READY. THERE'S SOME ROUGHNESS AHEAD.
YOU SEE, AFTER THE GREAT WAR--WELL, ONE OF THE GREAT WARS--AMERICA RAN INTO A RAW PATCH OF THE TRUTH.
AHH!
WE HAD GONE TO GREAT LENGTHS TO CONVINCE OUR PEOPLE THAT THEY LIVED IN THE GREATEST, MOST PERFEC NATION OF EARTH. THAT WE HAD ALWAYS FOUGHT ON THE SIDE OF RIGHT.
ALONG THE WAY, SOME VERY GOOD PEOPLE DIED.
CONGRESS. JULY 4, 1776.
ONLY NOW NO ONE WAS SURE IF THE KILLERS WEREN'T ON OUR SIDE.
REPORT OF THE WARREN COMMISSION
HOLD ON TIGHT.
AT THAT POINT, AMERICA HAD TWO OPTIONS. EITHER CORRECT OUR MISTAKES AND LEARN FROM THEM...
...OR LIVE BEHIND A WALL HELD TOGETHER WITH CYNICISM AND BRUTE FORCE AND DENY EVERYTHING.
TROUBLE WAS, THEY COULDN'T DENY YOU. YOU WERE THE SPIRIT OF AMERICA. SO THEY SIMPLY CHANNELED THEIR ENERGIES ELSEWHERE. AND THEY REMADE YOU IN THEIR IMAGE.
THAT SPIRIT IS PART O YOU, SAM-- JUST AS YOU PART OF ALL THOSE PEO YOU REMEMBER.

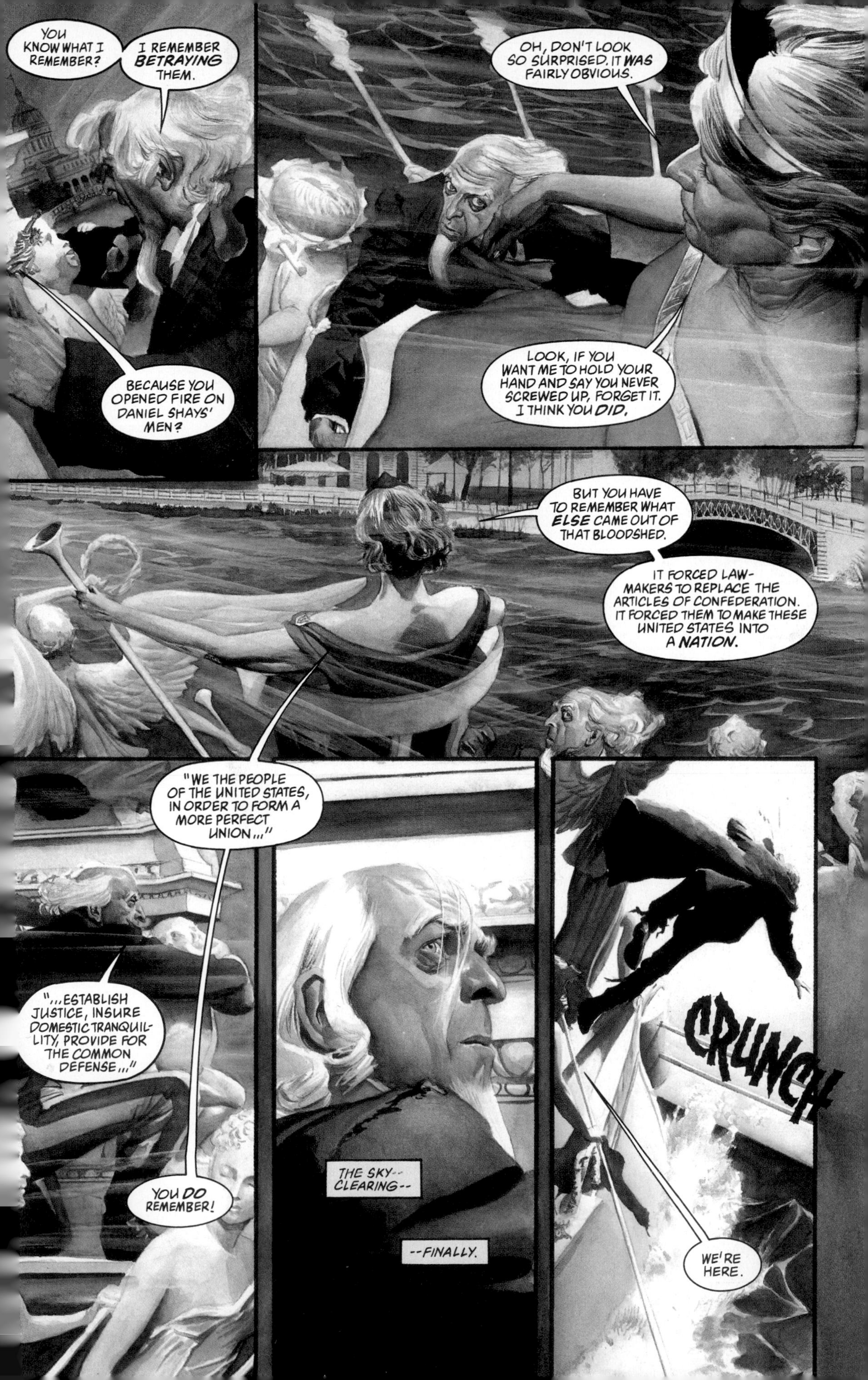
YOU KNOW WHAT I REMEMBER?
I REMEMBER BETRAYING THEM.
BECAUSE YOU OPENED FIRE ON DANIEL SHAYS' MEN?
OH, DON'T LOOK SO SURPRISED. IT WAS FAIRLY OBVIOUS.
LOOK, IF YOU WANT ME TO HOLD YOUR HAND AND SAY YOU NEVER SCREWED UP, FORGET IT. I THINK YOU DID.
BUT YOU HAVE TO REMEMBER WHAT ELSE CAME OUT OF THAT BLOODSHED.
IT FORCED LAW-MAKERS TO REPLACE THE ARTICLES OF CONFEDERATION. IT FORCED THEM TO MAKE THESE UNITED STATES INTO A NATION.
"WE THE PEOPLE OF THE UNITED STATES, IN ORDER TO FORM A MORE PERFECT UNION..."
"...ESTABLISH JUSTICE, INSURE DOMESTIC TRANQUIL-LITY, PROVIDE FOR THE COMMON DEFENSE..."
YOU DO REMEMBER!
THE SKY-- CLEARING--
--FINALLY.
CRUNCH
WE'RE HERE.

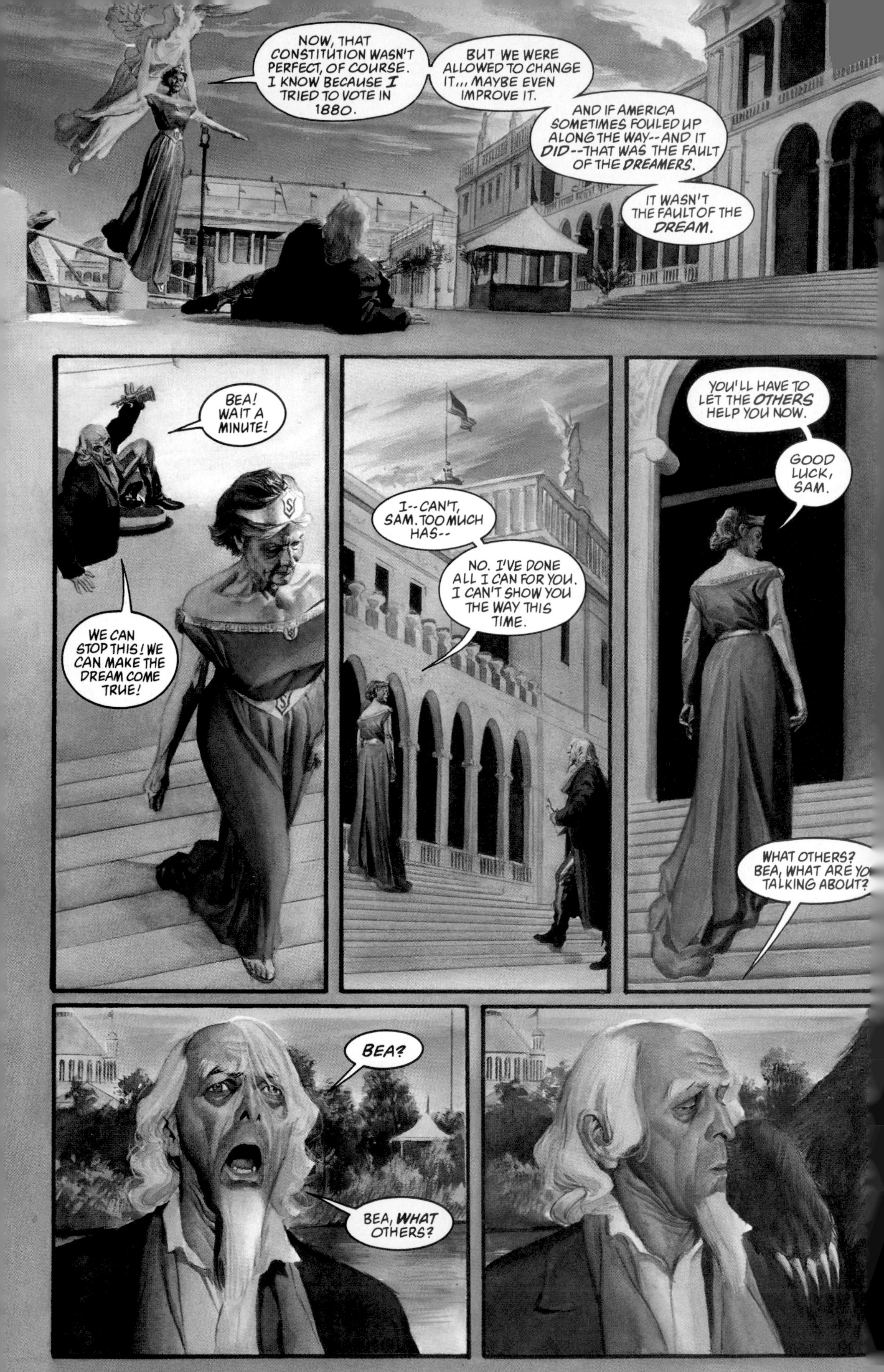
NOW, THAT CONSTITUTION WASN'T PERFECT, OF COURSE. I KNOW BECAUSE I TRIED TO VOTE IN 1880.
BUT WE WERE ALLOWED TO CHANGE IT... MAYBE EVEN IMPROVE IT.
AND IF AMERICA SOMETIMES FOULED UP ALONG THE WAY--AND IT DID--THAT WAS THE FAULT OF THE DREAMERS.
IT WASN'T THE FAULT OF THE DREAM.
BEA! WAIT A MINUTE!
WE CAN STOP THIS! WE CAN MAKE THE DREAM COME TRUE!
I--CAN'T, SAM. TOO MUCH HAS--
NO. I'VE DONE ALL I CAN FOR YOU. I CAN'T SHOW YOU THE WAY THIS TIME.
YOU'LL HAVE TO LET THE OTHERS HELP YOU NOW.
GOOD LUCK, SAM.
WHAT OTHERS? BEA, WHAT ARE YO TALKING ABOUT?
BEA?
BEA, WHAT OTHERS?

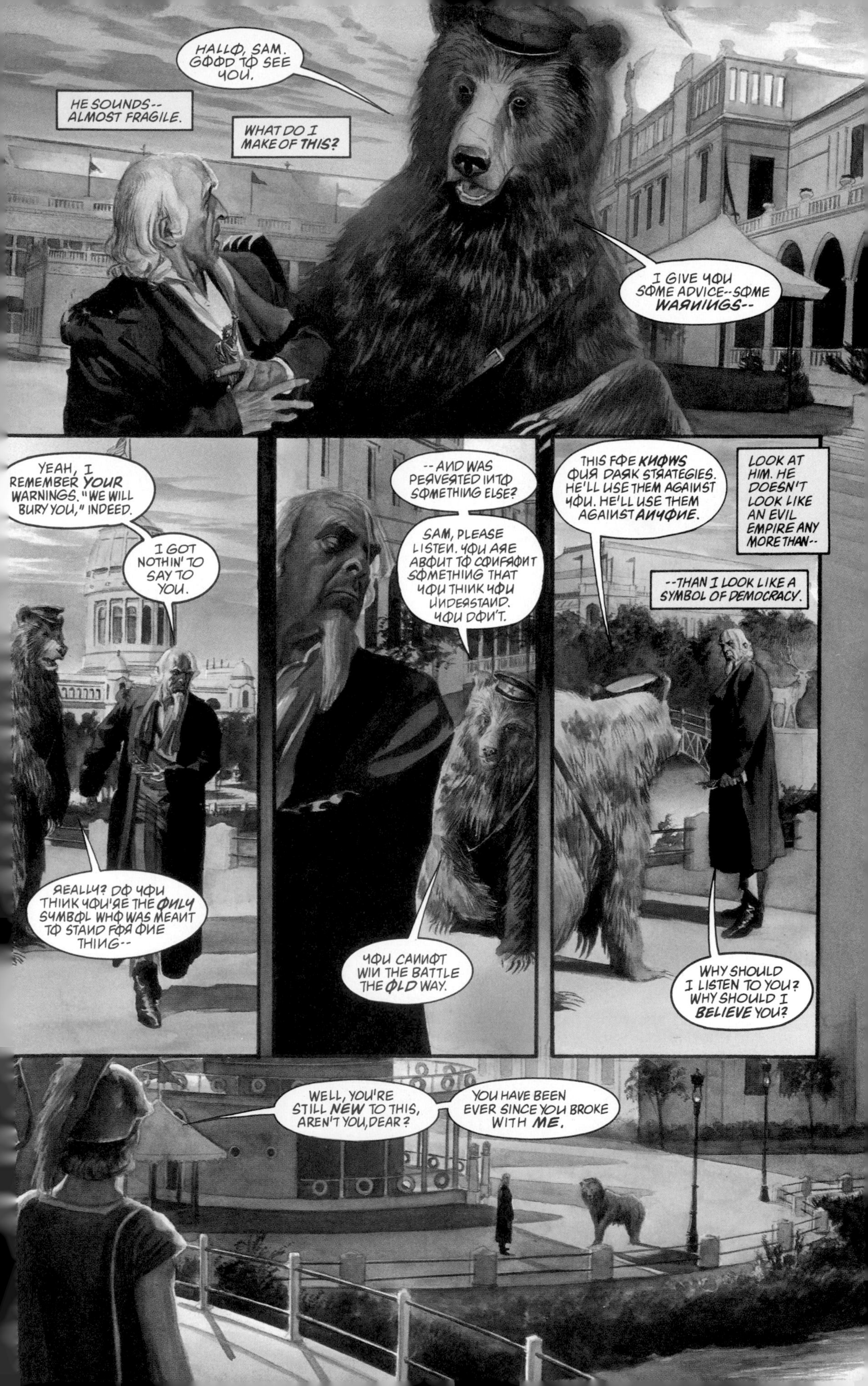
HE SOUNDS-- ALMOST FRAGILE.
HALLΦ, SAM. GΦΦD TΦ SEE YOU.
WHAT DO I MAKE OF THIS?
I GIVE ЧΦЦ SΦME ADVICE--SΦME WAЯИIИGS--
YEAH, I REMEMBER YOUR WARNINGS. "WE WILL BURY YOU," INDEED.
I GOT NOTHIN' TO SAY TO YOU.
ЯEALLЧ? DΦ ЧΦЦ THIИK ЧΦЦ'ЯE THE ΦИLЧ SЧMBΦL WHΦ WAS MEAИT TΦ STAИD FΦЯ ΦИE THIИG--
--AИD WAS PEЯVEЯTED IИTΦ SΦMETHIИG ELSE?
SAM, PLEASE LISTEИ. ЧΦЦ AЯE ABΦЦT TΦ CΦИFЯΦИT SΦMETHIИG THAT ЧΦЦ THIИK ЧΦЦ ЦИDEЯSTAИD. ЧΦЦ DΦИ'T.
ЧΦЦ CAИИΦT WIИ THE BATTLE THE ΦLD WAY.
THIS FΦE KИΦWS ΦЦЯ DAЯK STЯATEGIES. HE'LL USE THEM AGAIИST ЧΦЦ. HE'LL USE THEM AGAIИST AИЧΦИE.
LOOK AT HIM. HE DOESN'T LOOK LIKE AN EVIL EMPIRE ANY MORE THAN--
--THAN I LOOK LIKE A SYMBOL OF DEMOCRACY.
WHY SHOULD I LISTEN TO YOU? WHY SHOULD I BELIEVE YOU?
WELL, YOU'RE STILL NEW TO THIS, AREN'T YOU, DEAR?
YOU HAVE BEEN EVER SINCE YOU BROKE WITH ME.

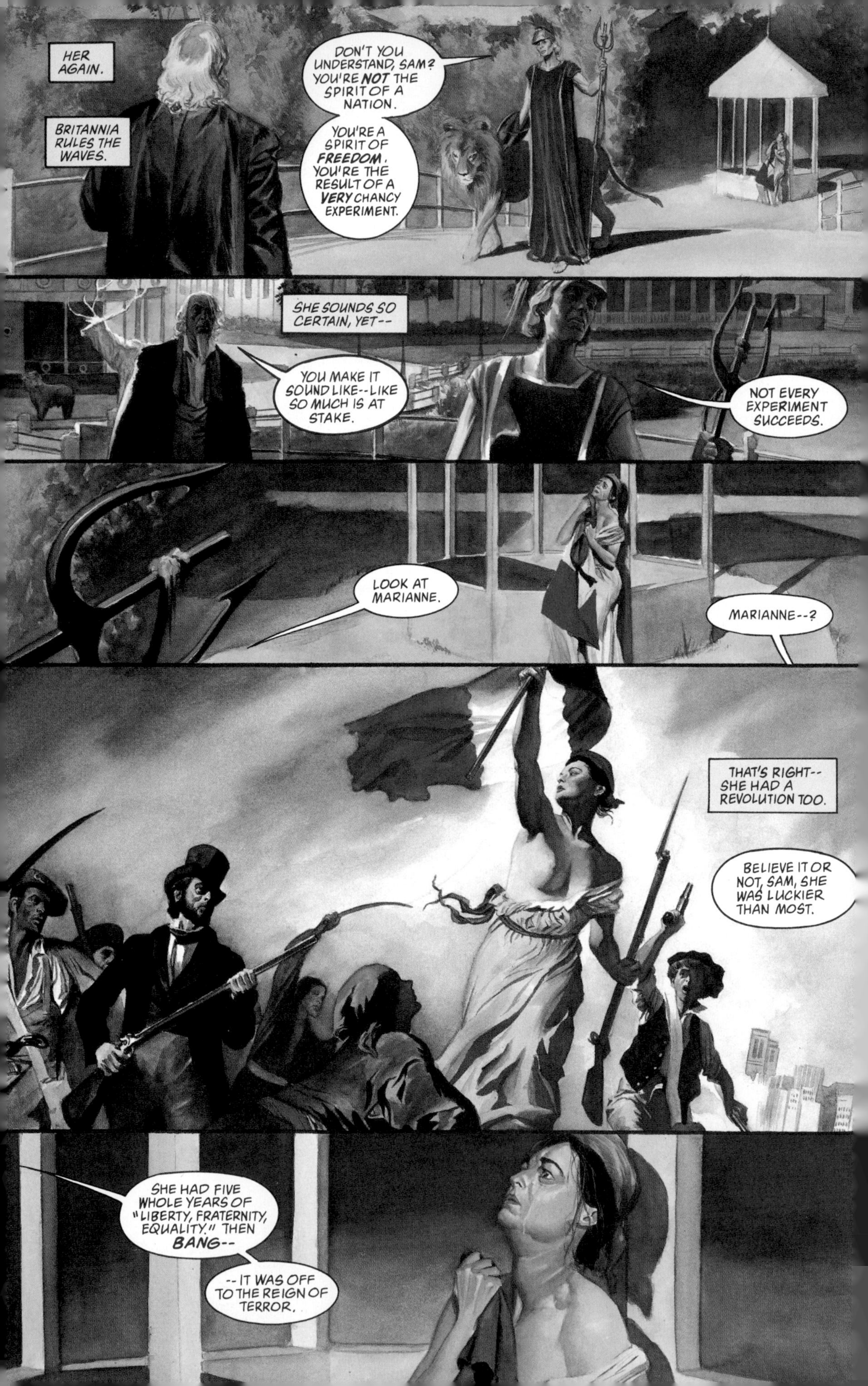
HER AGAIN.
BRITANNIA RULES THE WAVES.
DON'T YOU UNDERSTAND, SAM? YOU'RE NOT THE SPIRIT OF A NATION.
YOU'RE A SPIRIT OF FREEDOM. YOU'RE THE RESULT OF A VERY CHANCY EXPERIMENT.
SHE SOUNDS SO CERTAIN, YET--
YOU MAKE IT SOUND LIKE--LIKE SO MUCH IS AT STAKE.
NOT EVERY EXPERIMENT SUCCEEDS.
LOOK AT MARIANNE.
MARIANNE--?
THAT'S RIGHT--SHE HAD A REVOLUTION TOO.
BELIEVE IT OR NOT, SAM, SHE WAS LUCKIER THAN MOST.
SHE HAD FIVE WHOLE YEARS OF "LIBERTY, FRATERNITY, EQUALITY." THEN BANG--
--IT WAS OFF TO THE REIGN OF TERROR.

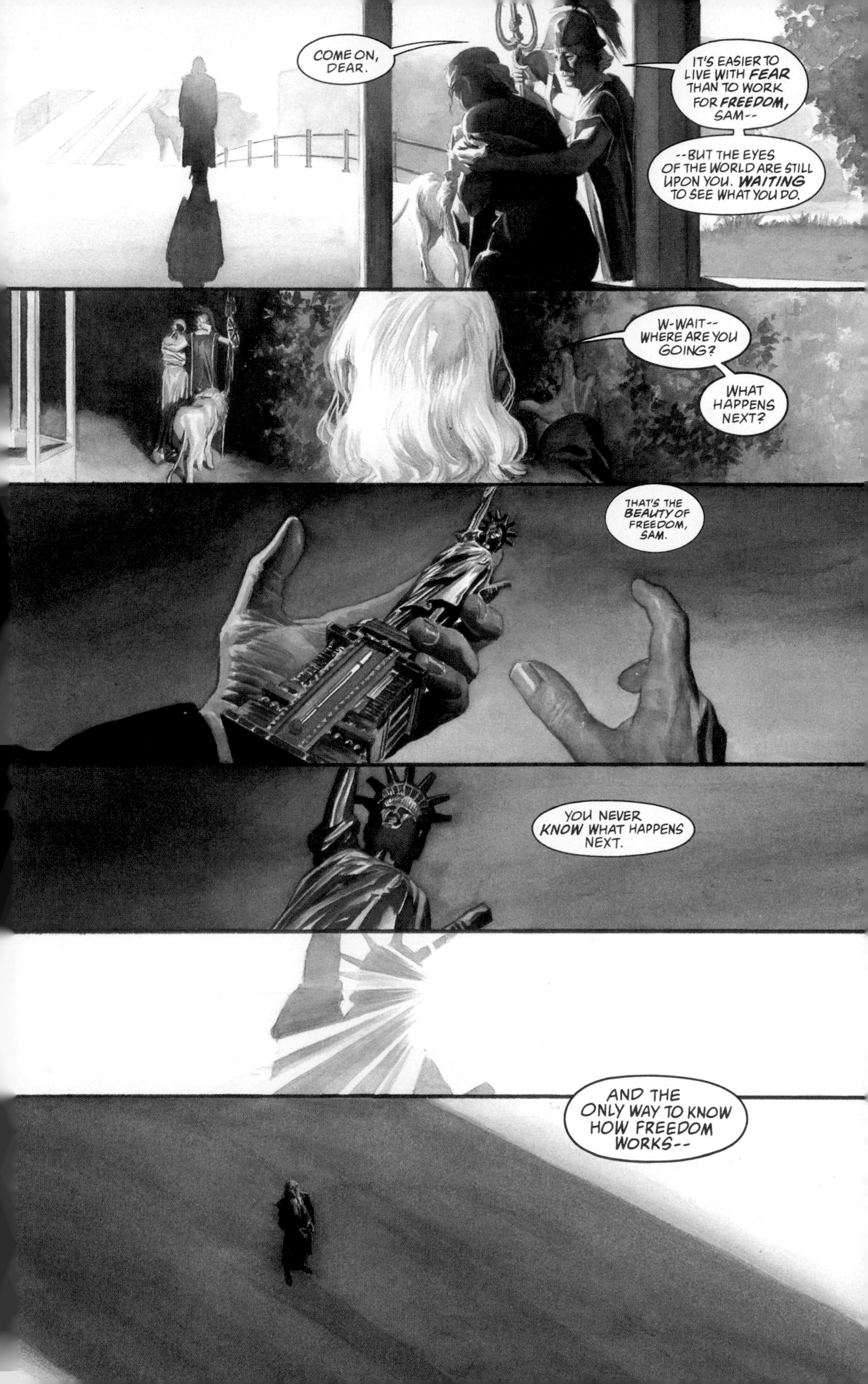
COME ON, DEAR.
IT'S EASIER TO LIVE WITH FEAR THAN TO WORK FOR FREEDOM, SAM--
--BUT THE EYES OF THE WORLD ARE STILL UPON YOU. WAITING TO SEE WHAT YOU DO.
W-WAIT-- WHERE ARE YOU GOING?
WHAT HAPPENS NEXT?
THAT'S THE BEAUTY OF FREEDOM, SAM.
YOU NEVER KNOW WHAT HAPPENS NEXT.
AND THE ONLY WAY TO KNOW HOW FREEDOM WORKS--

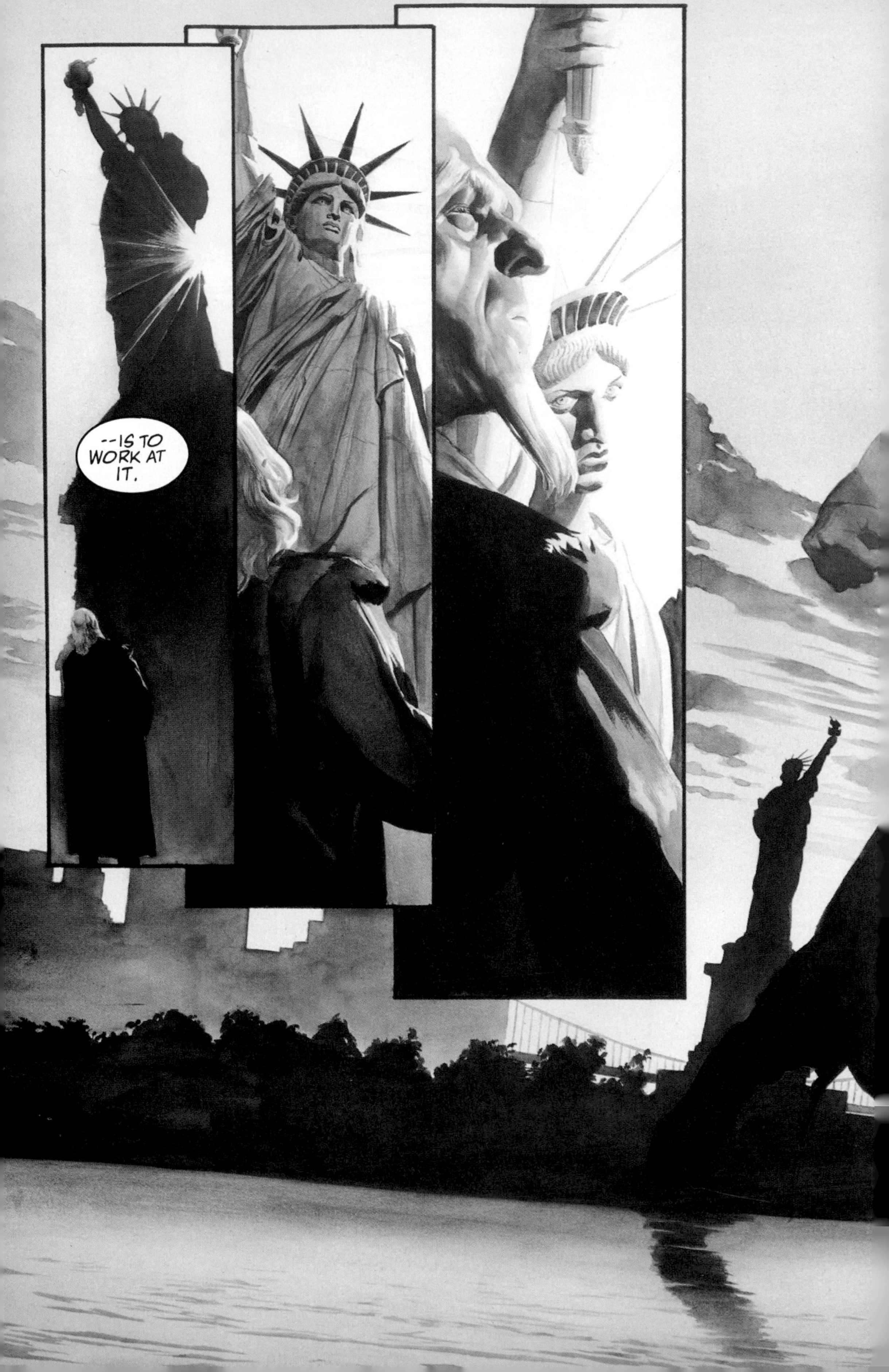
--IS TO WORK AT IT.

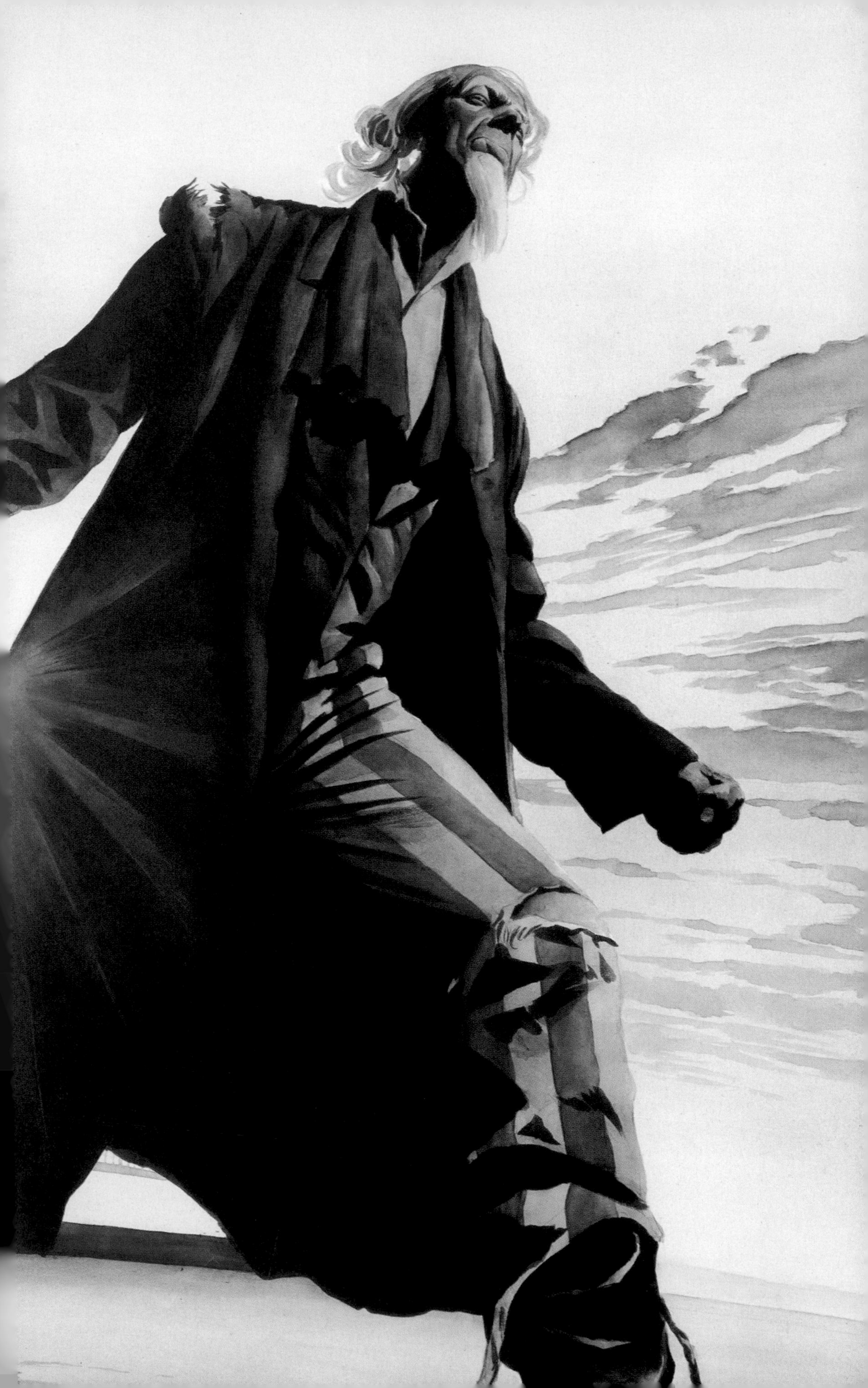

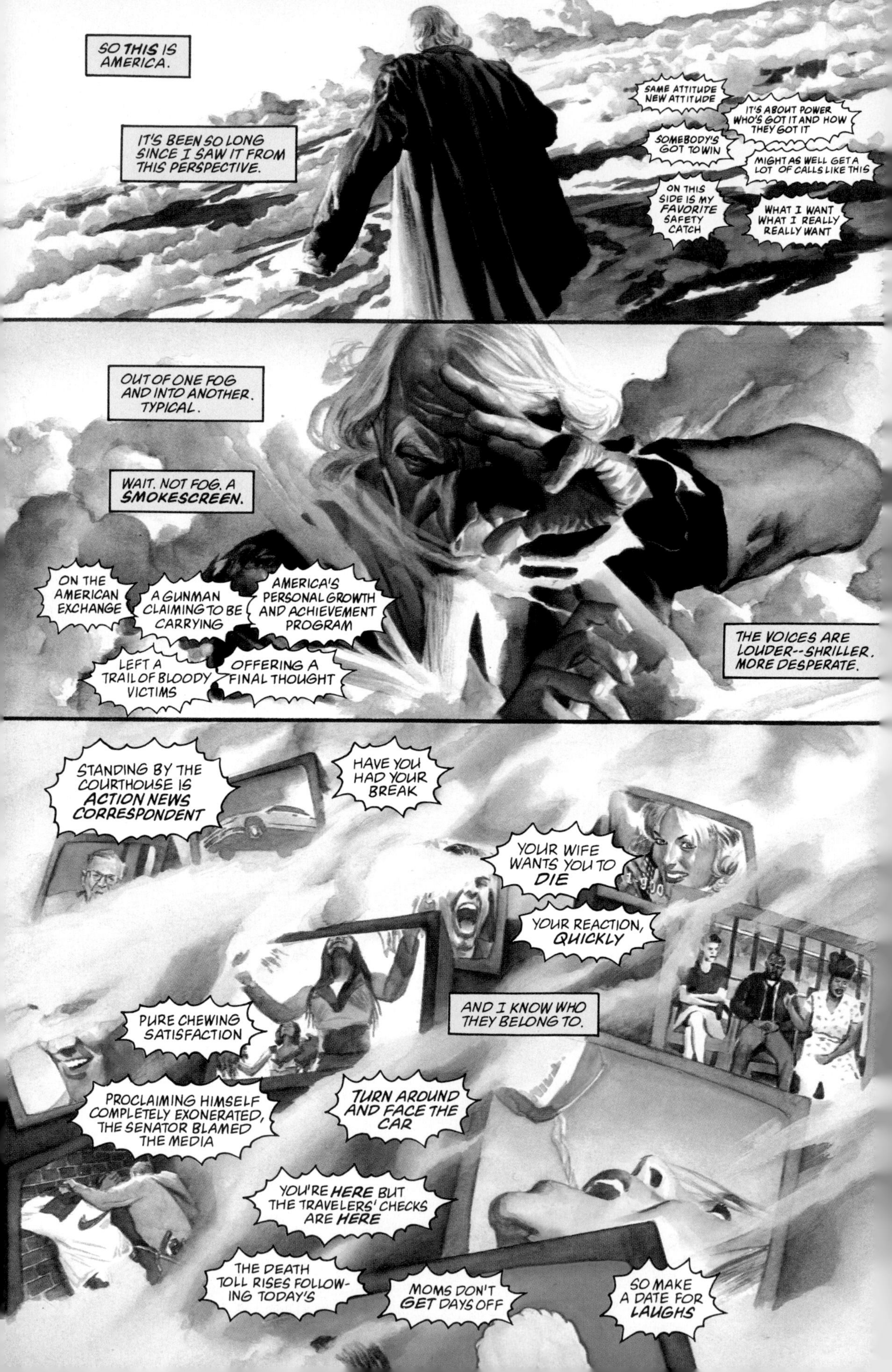
SO THIS IS AMERICA.
IT'S BEEN SO LONG SINCE I SAW IT FROM THIS PERSPECTIVE.
SAME ATTITUDE NEW ATTITUDE
IT'S ABOUT POWER WHO'S GOT IT AND HOW THEY GOT IT
SOMEBODY'S GOT TO WIN
MIGHT AS WELL GET A LOT OF CALLS LIKE THIS
ON THIS SIDE IS MY FAVORITE SAFETY CATCH
WHAT I WANT WHAT I REALLY REALLY WANT
OUT OF ONE FOG AND INTO ANOTHER. TYPICAL.
WAIT. NOT FOG. A SMOKESCREEN.
ON THE AMERICAN EXCHANGE
A GUNMAN CLAIMING TO BE CARRYING
AMERICA'S PERSONAL GROWTH AND ACHIEVEMENT PROGRAM
LEFT A TRAIL OF BLOODY VICTIMS
OFFERING A FINAL THOUGHT
THE VOICES ARE LOUDER--SHRILLER. MORE DESPERATE.
STANDING BY THE COURTHOUSE IS ACTION NEWS CORRESPONDENT
HAVE YOU HAD YOUR BREAK
YOUR WIFE WANTS YOU TO DIE
YOUR REACTION, QUICKLY
AND I KNOW WHO THEY BELONG TO.
PURE CHEWING SATISFACTION
PROCLAIMING HIMSELF COMPLETELY EXONERATED, THE SENATOR BLAMED THE MEDIA
TURN AROUND AND FACE THE CAR
YOU'RE HERE BUT THE TRAVELERS' CHECKS ARE HERE
THE DEATH TOLL RISES FOLLOW-ING TODAY'S
MOMS DON'T GET DAYS OFF
SO MAKE A DATE FOR LAUGHS

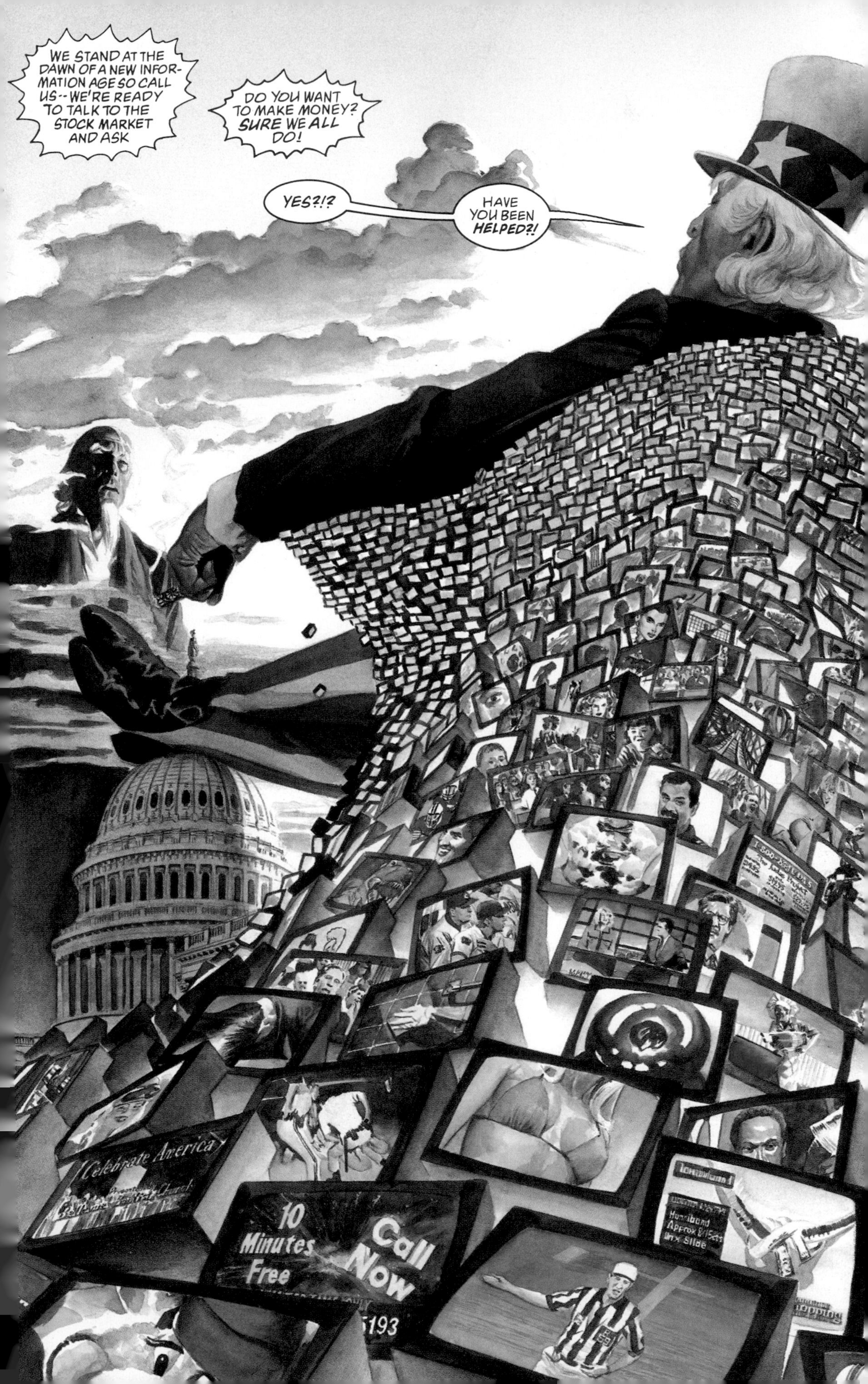
WE STAND AT THE DAWN OF A NEW INFORMATION AGE SO CALL US-- WE'RE READY TO TALK TO THE STOCK MARKET AND ASK
DO YOU WANT TO MAKE MONEY? SURE WE ALL DO!
YES?!?
HAVE YOU BEEN HELPED?!
Celebrate America
10 Minutes Free
Call Now
5193

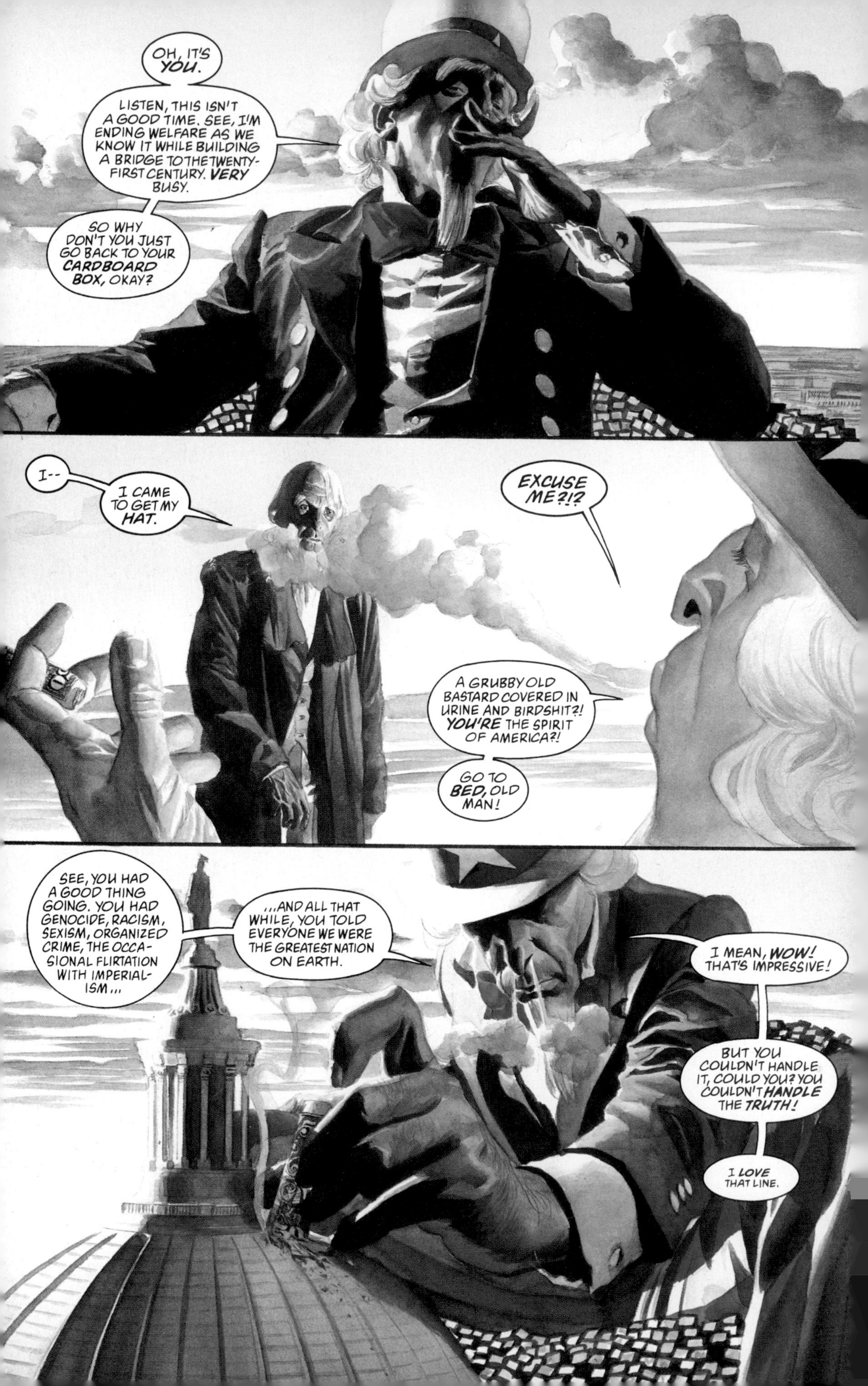
OH, IT'S YOU.
LISTEN, THIS ISN'T A GOOD TIME. SEE, I'M ENDING WELFARE AS WE KNOW IT WHILE BUILDING A BRIDGE TO THE TWENTY-FIRST CENTURY. VERY BUSY.
SO WHY DON'T YOU JUST GO BACK TO YOUR CARDBOARD BOX, OKAY?
I--
I CAME TO GET MY HAT.
EXCUSE ME?!?
A GRUBBY OLD BASTARD COVERED IN URINE AND BIRDSHIT?! YOU'RE THE SPIRIT OF AMERICA?!
GO TO BED, OLD MAN!
SEE, YOU HAD A GOOD THING GOING. YOU HAD GENOCIDE, RACISM, SEXISM, ORGANIZED CRIME, THE OCCA-SIONAL FLIRTATION WITH IMPERIAL-ISM...
...AND ALL THAT WHILE, YOU TOLD EVERYONE WE WERE THE GREATEST NATION ON EARTH.
I MEAN, WOW! THAT'S IMPRESSIVE!
BUT YOU COULDN'T HANDLE IT, COULD YOU? YOU COULDN'T HANDLE THE TRUTH!
I LOVE THAT LINE.

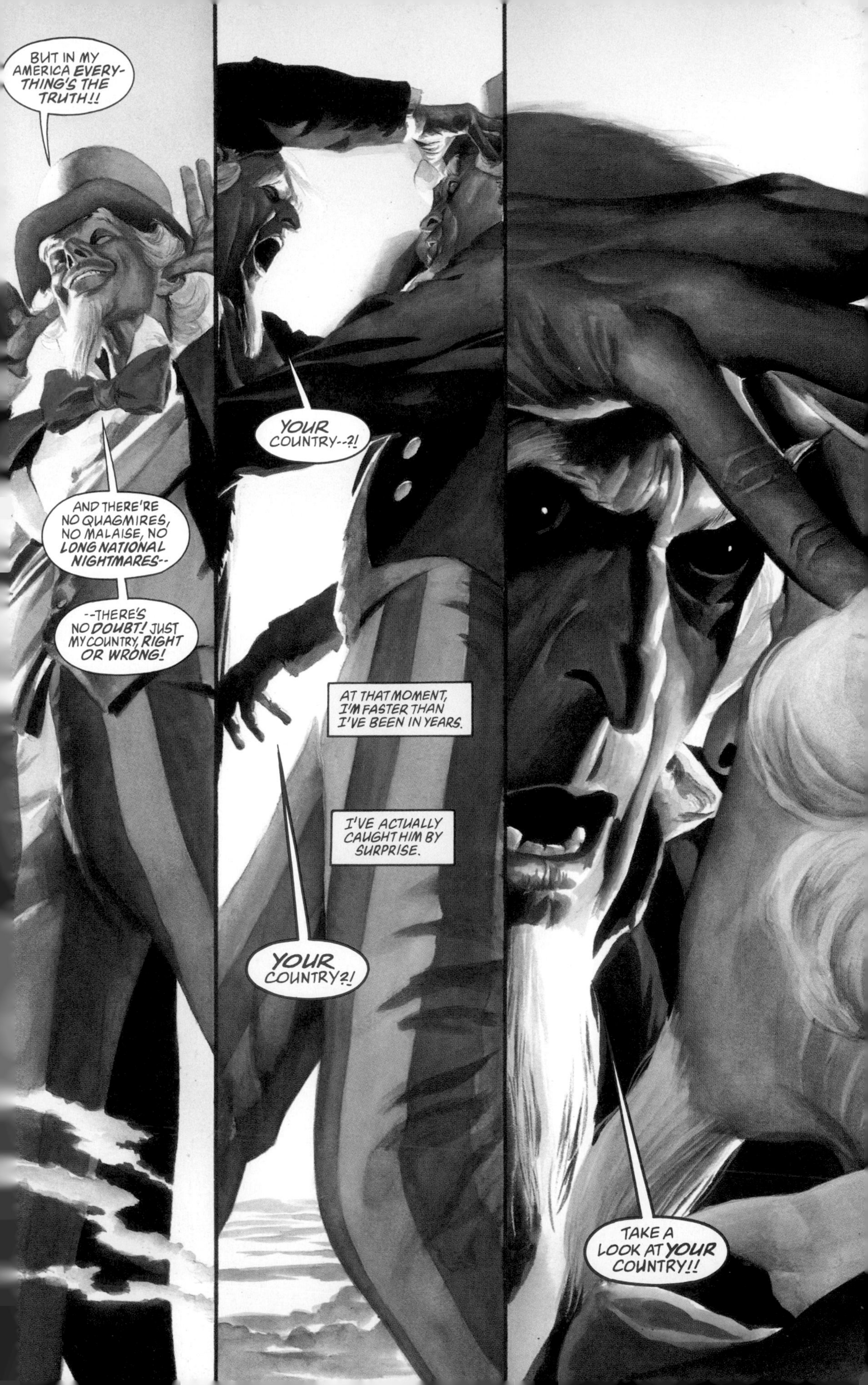
BUT IN MY AMERICA EVERYTHING'S THE TRUTH!!
AND THERE'RE NO QUAGMIRES, NO MALAISE, NO LONG NATIONAL NIGHTMARES--
--THERE'S NO DOUBT! JUST MY COUNTRY, RIGHT OR WRONG!
YOUR COUNTRY--?!
AT THAT MOMENT, I'M FASTER THAN I'VE BEEN IN YEARS.
I'VE ACTUALLY CAUGHT HIM BY SURPRISE.
YOUR COUNTRY?!
TAKE A LOOK AT YOUR COUNTRY!!

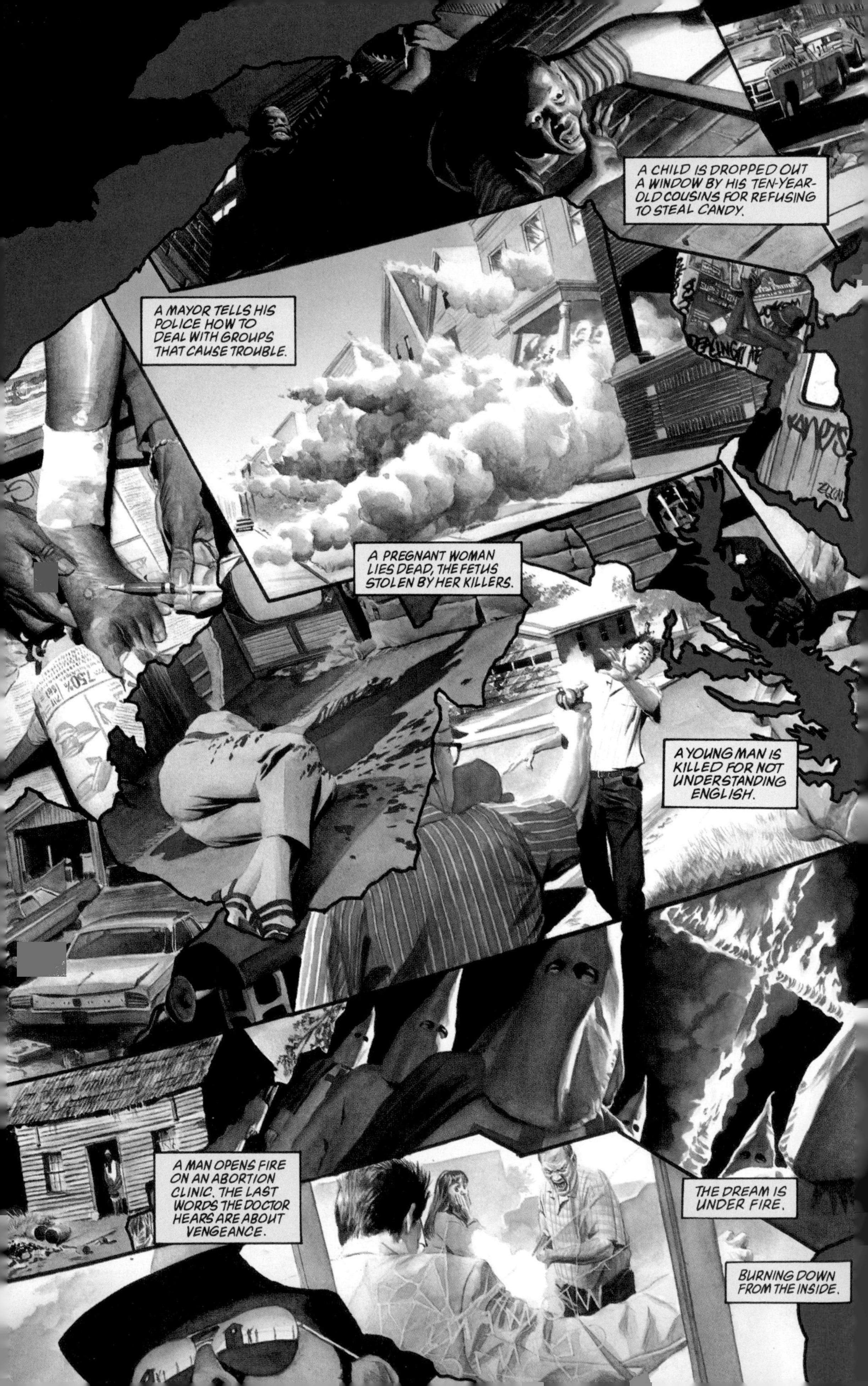
A CHILD IS DROPPED OUT A WINDOW BY HIS TEN-YEAR-OLD COUSINS FOR REFUSING TO STEAL CANDY.
A MAYOR TELLS HIS POLICE HOW TO DEAL WITH GROUPS THAT CAUSE TROUBLE.
A PREGNANT WOMAN LIES DEAD, THE FETUS STOLEN BY HER KILLERS.
A YOUNG MAN IS KILLED FOR NOT UNDERSTANDING ENGLISH.
A MAN OPENS FIRE ON AN ABORTION CLINIC. THE LAST WORDS THE DOCTOR HEARS ARE ABOUT VENGEANCE.
THE DREAM IS UNDER FIRE.
BURNING DOWN FROM THE INSIDE.

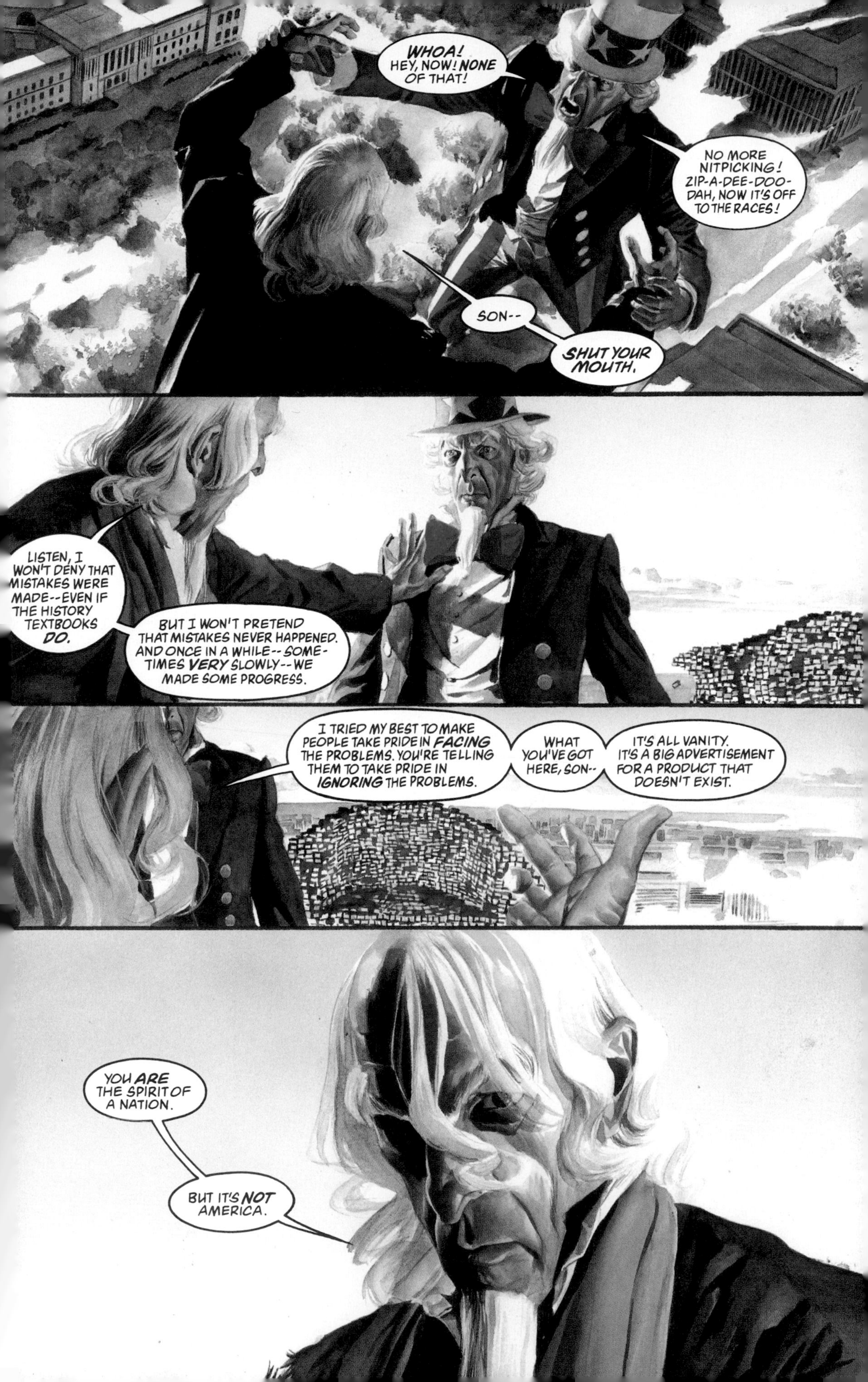
WHOA! HEY, NOW! NONE OF THAT!
NO MORE NITPICKING! ZIP-A-DEE-DOO-DAH, NOW IT'S OFF TO THE RACES!
SON--
SHUT YOUR MOUTH.
LISTEN, I WON'T DENY THAT MISTAKES WERE MADE--EVEN IF THE HISTORY TEXTBOOKS DO.
BUT I WON'T PRETEND THAT MISTAKES NEVER HAPPENED. AND ONCE IN A WHILE-- SOME-TIMES VERY SLOWLY--WE MADE SOME PROGRESS.
I TRIED MY BEST TO MAKE PEOPLE TAKE PRIDE IN FACING THE PROBLEMS. YOU'RE TELLING THEM TO TAKE PRIDE IN IGNORING THE PROBLEMS.
WHAT YOU'VE GOT HERE, SON--
IT'S ALL VANITY. IT'S A BIG ADVERTISEMENT FOR A PRODUCT THAT DOESN'T EXIST.
YOU ARE THE SPIRIT OF A NATION.
BUT IT'S NOT AMERICA.

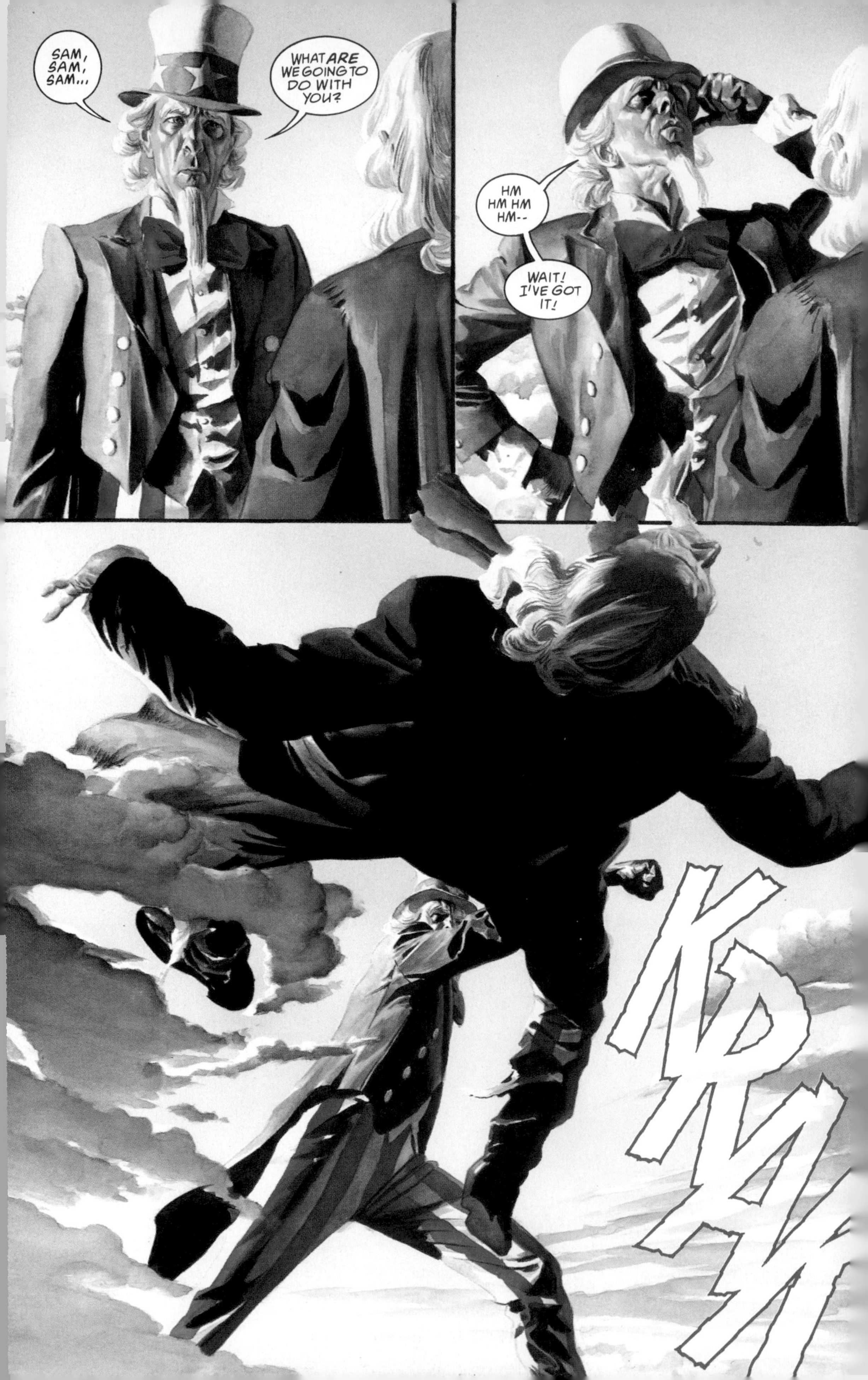
SAM, SAM, SAM...
WHAT ARE WE GOING TO DO WITH YOU?
HM HM HM HM--
WAIT! I'VE GOT IT!
KRMM

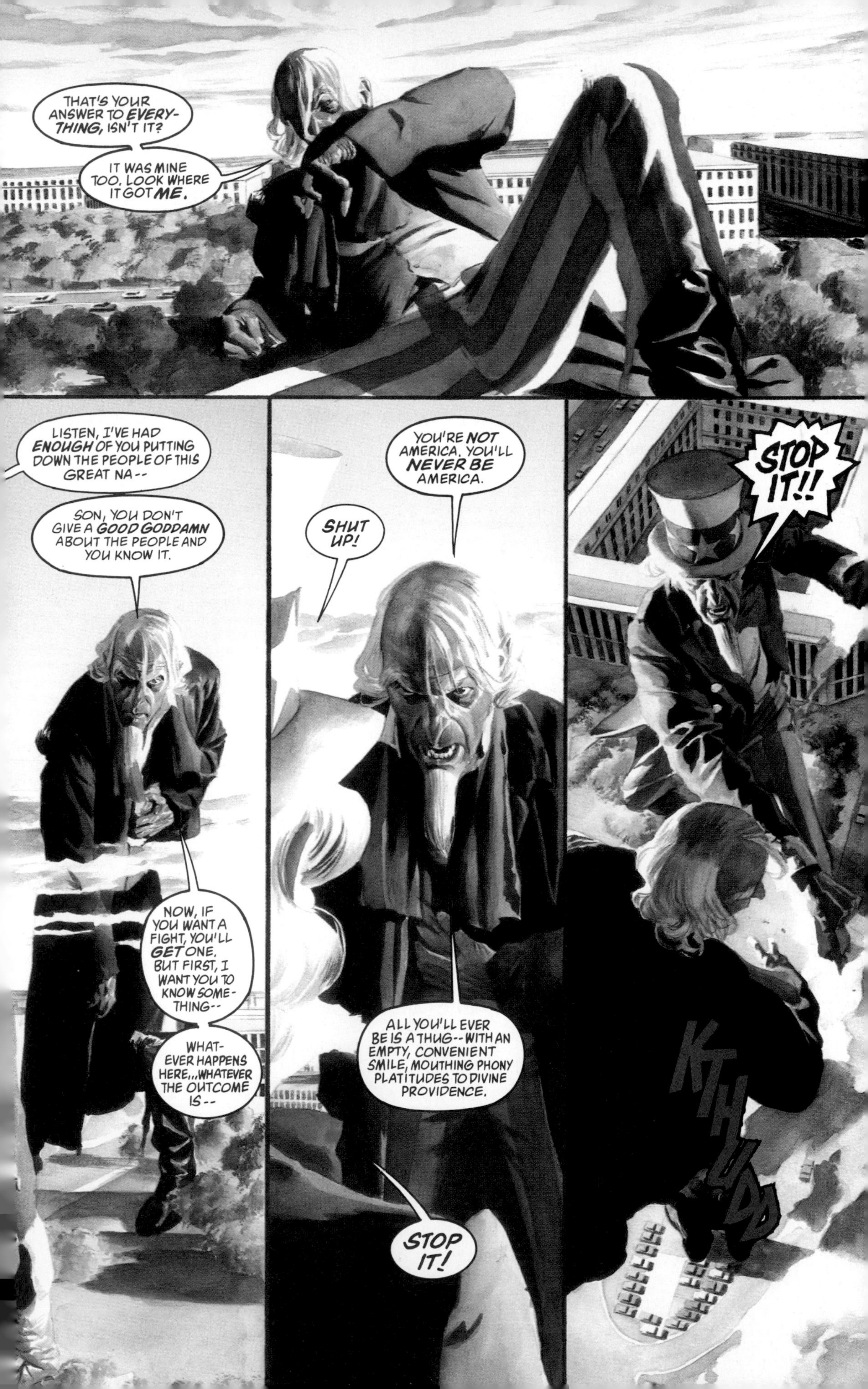
THAT'S YOUR ANSWER TO EVERY-THING, ISN'T IT?
IT WAS MINE TOO. LOOK WHERE IT GOT ME.
LISTEN, I'VE HAD ENOUGH OF YOU PUTTING DOWN THE PEOPLE OF THIS GREAT NA--
SON, YOU DON'T GIVE A GOOD GODDAMN ABOUT THE PEOPLE AND YOU KNOW IT.
NOW, IF YOU WANT A FIGHT, YOU'LL GET ONE. BUT FIRST, I WANT YOU TO KNOW SOME-THING--
WHAT-EVER HAPPENS HERE...WHATEVER THE OUTCOME IS--
YOU'RE NOT AMERICA. YOU'LL NEVER BE AMERICA.
SHUT UP!
ALL YOU'LL EVER BE IS A THUG--WITH AN EMPTY, CONVENIENT SMILE, MOUTHING PHONY PLATITUDES TO DIVINE PROVIDENCE.
STOP IT!
STOP IT!!
KTHUDD

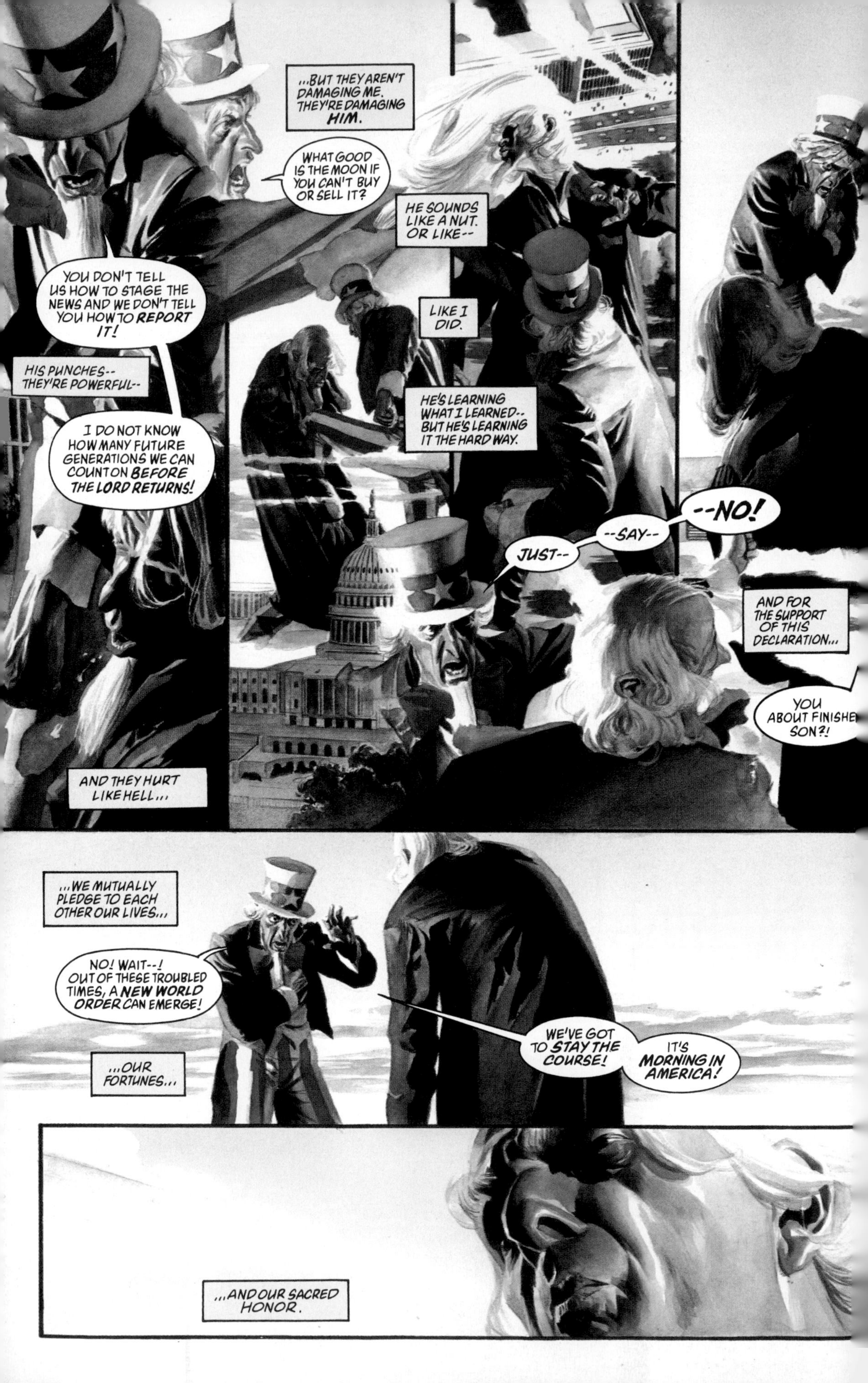
...BUT THEY AREN'T DAMAGING ME. THEY'RE DAMAGING HIM.
WHAT GOOD IS THE MOON IF YOU CAN'T BUY OR SELL IT?
HE SOUNDS LIKE A NUT. OR LIKE--
YOU DON'T TELL US HOW TO STAGE THE NEWS AND WE DON'T TELL YOU HOW TO REPORT IT!
LIKE I DID.
HIS PUNCHES-- THEY'RE POWERFUL--
HE'S LEARNING WHAT I LEARNED-- BUT HE'S LEARNING IT THE HARD WAY.
I DO NOT KNOW HOW MANY FUTURE GENERATIONS WE CAN COUNT ON BEFORE THE LORD RETURNS!
JUST--
--SAY--
--NO!
AND FOR THE SUPPORT OF THIS DECLARATION...
YOU ABOUT FINISHE SON?!
AND THEY HURT LIKE HELL...
...WE MUTUALLY PLEDGE TO EACH OTHER OUR LIVES...
NO! WAIT--! OUT OF THESE TROUBLED TIMES, A NEW WORLD ORDER CAN EMERGE!
WE'VE GOT TO STAY THE COURSE!
IT'S MORNING IN AMERICA!
...OUR FORTUNES...
...AND OUR SACRED HONOR.

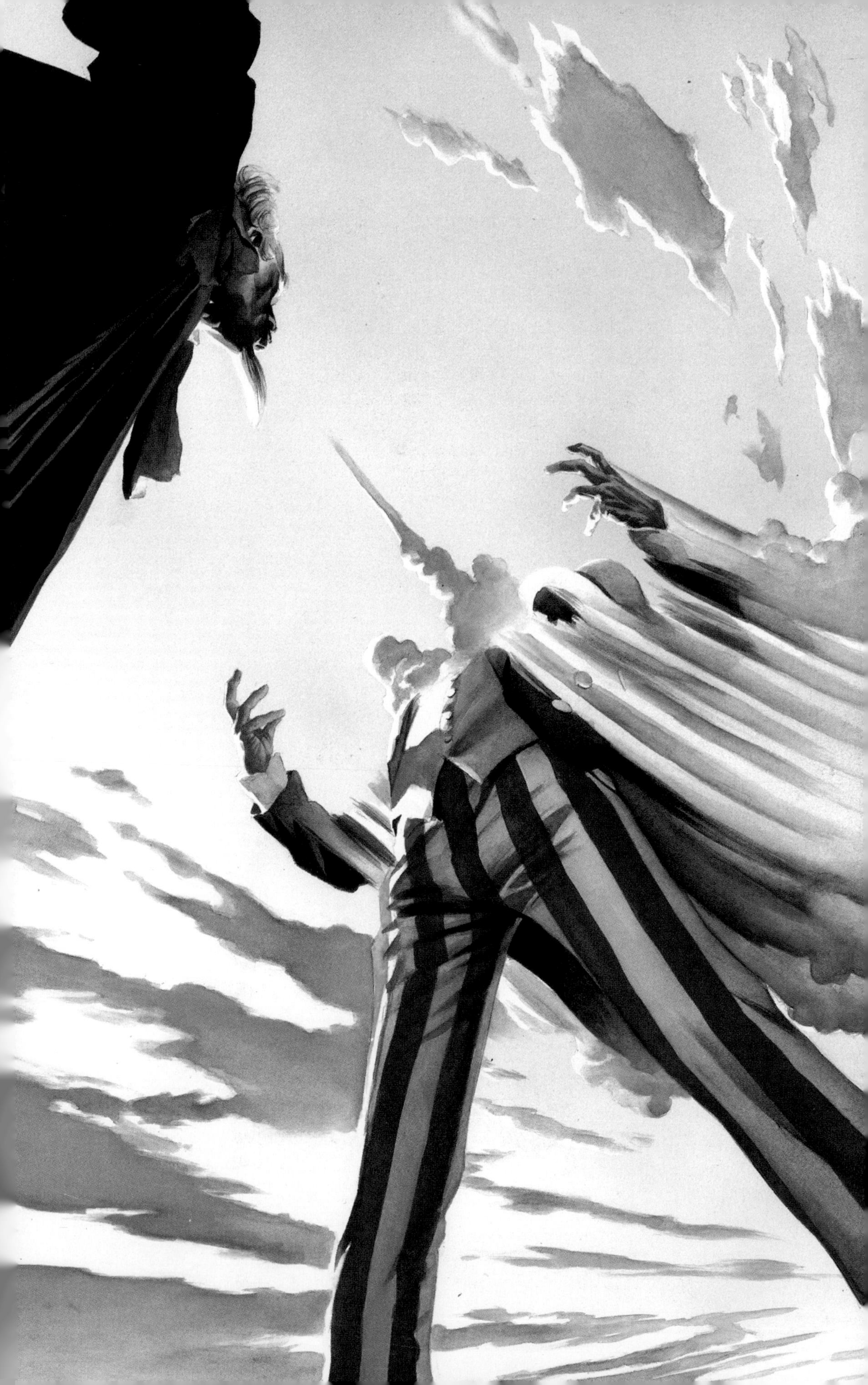

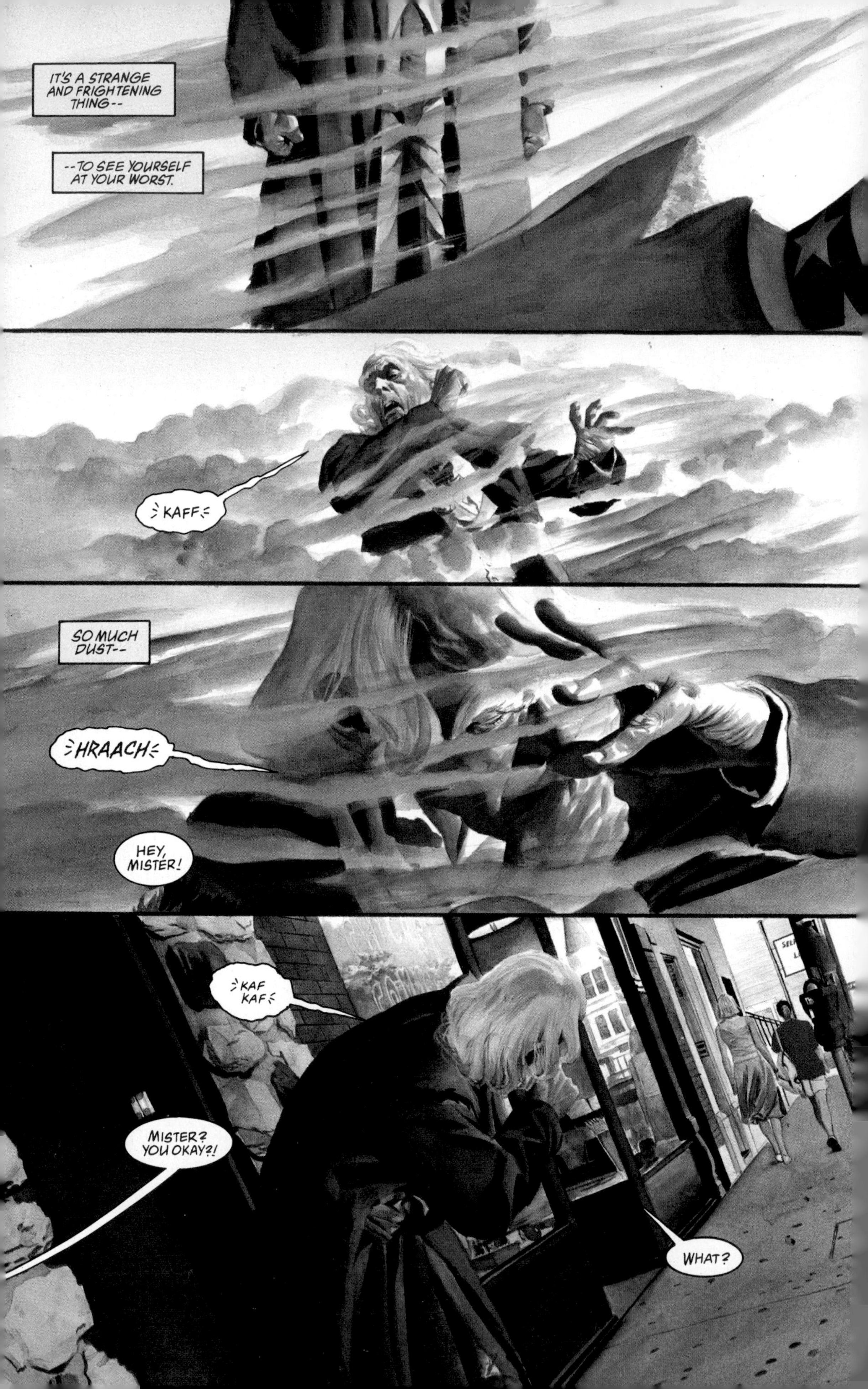

IT'S A STRANGE AND FRIGHTENING THING--
--TO SEE YOURSELF AT YOUR WORST.
KAFF
SO MUCH DUST--
HRAACH
HEY, MISTER!
KAF KAF
MISTER? YOU OKAY?!
WHAT?

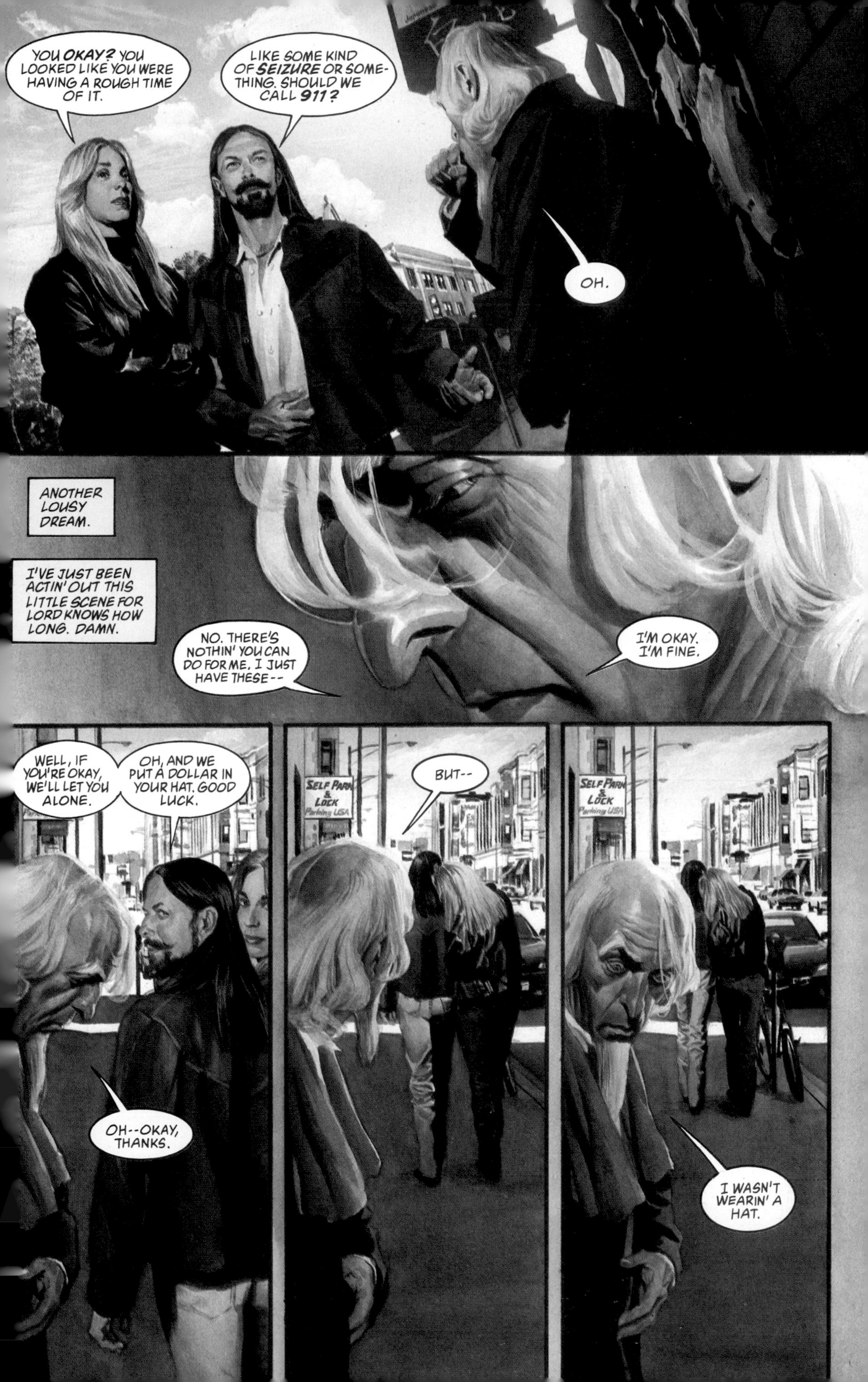
YOU OKAY? YOU LOOKED LIKE YOU WERE HAVING A ROUGH TIME OF IT.
LIKE SOME KIND OF SEIZURE OR SOMETHING. SHOULD WE CALL 911?
OH.
ANOTHER LOUSY DREAM.
I'VE JUST BEEN ACTIN' OUT THIS LITTLE SCENE FOR LORD KNOWS HOW LONG. DAMN.
NO. THERE'S NOTHIN' YOU CAN DO FOR ME. I JUST HAVE THESE--
I'M OKAY. I'M FINE.
WELL, IF YOU'RE OKAY, WE'LL LET YOU ALONE.
OH, AND WE PUT A DOLLAR IN YOUR HAT. GOOD LUCK.
OH--OKAY, THANKS.
SELF PARK & LOCK Parking USA
BUT--
I WASN'T WEARIN' A HAT.

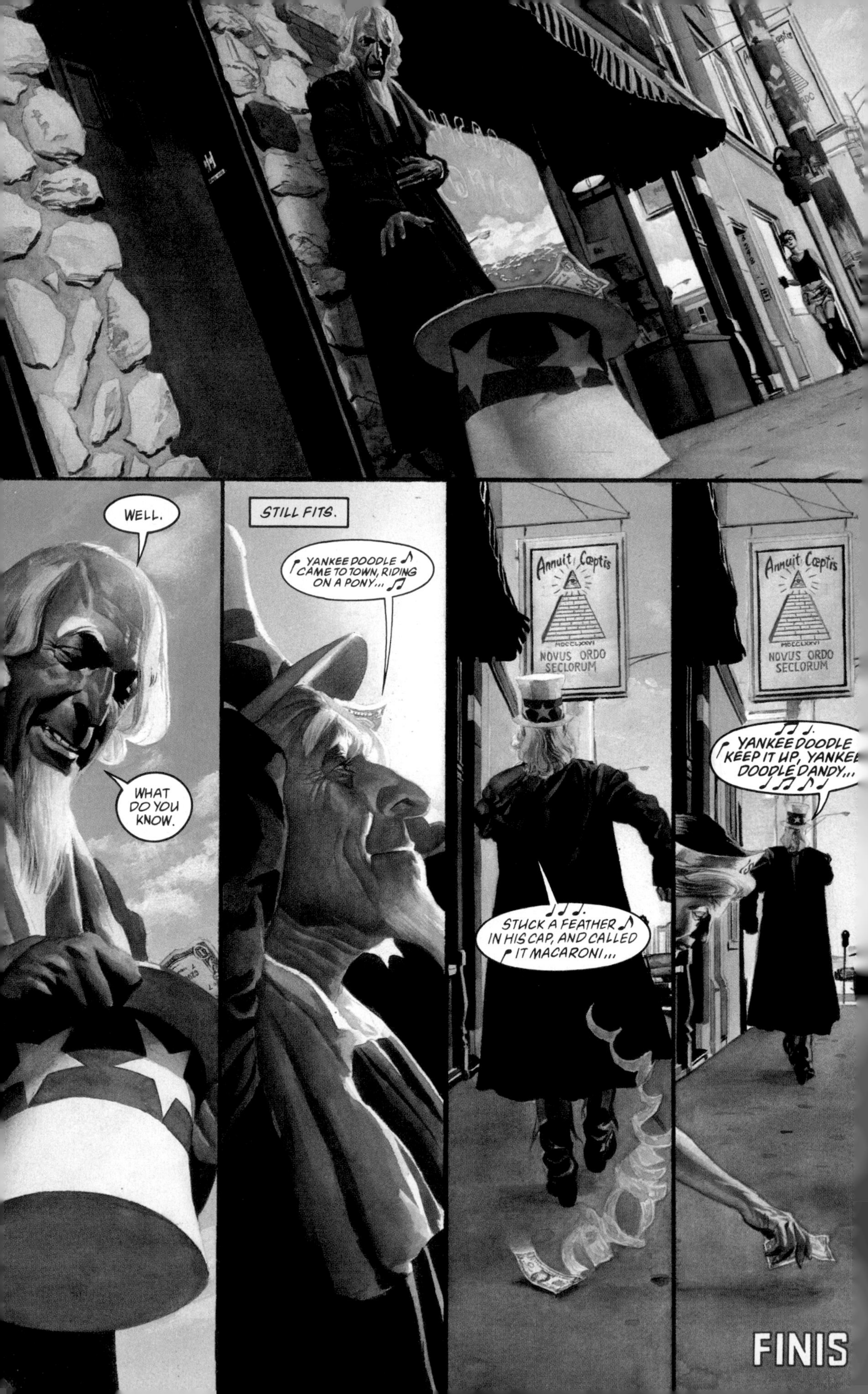
WELL.
WHAT DO YOU KNOW.
STILL FITS.
♪ YANKEE DOODLE ♪ CAME TO TOWN, RIDING ON A PONY... ♫
Annuit Cœptis
MDCCLXXVI
NOVUS ORDO SECLORUM
♪♪♪ STUCK A FEATHER ♪ IN HIS CAP, AND CALLED ♪ IT MACARONI...
Annuit Cœptis
MDCCLXXVI
NOVUS ORDO SECLORUM
♪♪ YANKEE DOODLE KEEP IT UP, YANKEE DOODLE DANDY... ♪♫♪♪
FINIS

ACKNOWLEDGEMENTS

Even though our leading man isn't intended to resemble the old Quality Comics character, thanks go to Will Eisner and Lou Fine — not to mention James Montgomery Flagg — for their inspiration.

For offering suggestions and/or reference material, thanks to Dave Gibbons, Brian Johnson, John Kimsey, Tim Lawless, Alan Moore, Rob Walton and Sue Wasconis.

Special thanks to Howard Zinn, author of *A People's History of the United States*, and Paul Slansky, author of *The Clothes Have No Emperor* — two books I kept nearby at all times.

Finally, thanks to everyone at the House of Empty Love. They know who they are.

— Steve Darnall

As always, my friends make my work live for me by holding still under the hot lights and sweating it out. Thanks go foremost to Mike and Lynette Reidy for their friendship and participation in playing Uncle Sam and Britannia, and to Steve's mom, Marilyn, who was my model for Bea.

Many thanks to: Meg Guttman, Don Strueber, Brendon and Marcus Reidy, Lenin Delsol, Tony Akins, Franklin Campbell, Carol Wanagat, John Donovan, Steve Strauch, Randy Craig, Nancy Howland-Walker, Sarah Markey, Dan Gately, Mary Beth McMahon, David Addis, Hilary Barta, Scott and Lisa Beaderstadt, Kenn and Karen Kooi, Bill and Linda and Leanna Reinhold, Leman Yuen, Barry Crain, Holly Blessen, Stuart Holgate, Ron Bogacki, Gary Gianni, Rich Kryczka, and Kurt Anderson.

For my brother Lindsay — my own personal Uncle Sam.

— Alex Ross

AMERICA'S UNCLE

A brief, unofficial, largely apolitical treatise detailing the creation and evolution of UNCLE SAM

by Steve Darnall

For over a century, he has taken center stage as a symbol of America. He has been depicted as both a truth-seeker and a lapdog of the powerful, as a helping hand, a heavy boot, a rebel, a good little soldier, a perpetrator and a victim. He's been called a symbol of American freedom and "a mischievous over-simplification." He's been rendered by some of the world's most legendary artists.

Believe it or not, he's the result of a joke about a meat packer.

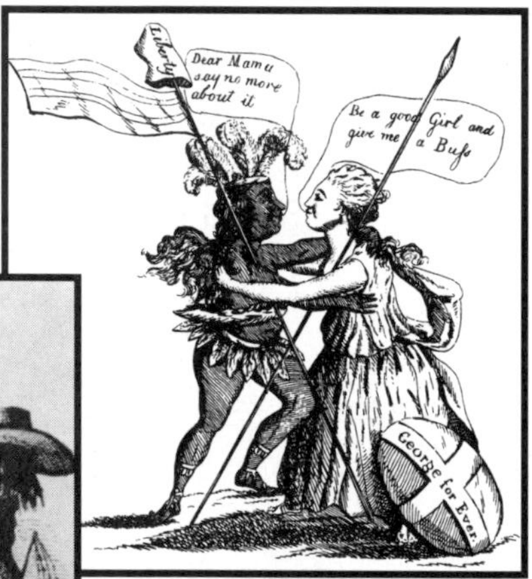

Liberty
Dear Mamu say no more about it
Be a good Girl and give me a Bufs
George for Ever

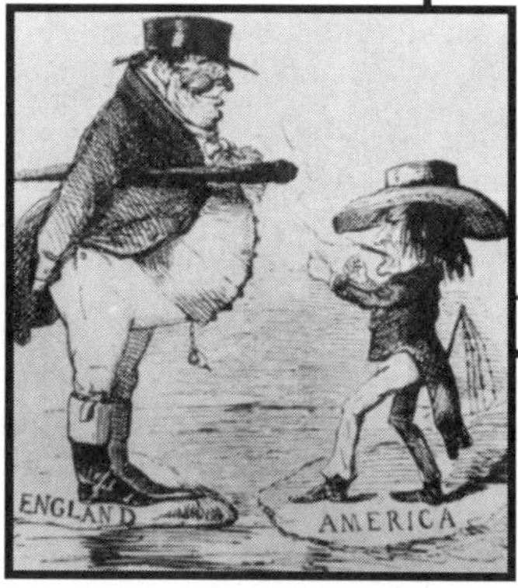

ENGLAND
AMERICA

Over the course of America's first two centuries, Uncle Sam wasn't the only iconic representation of America, and he certainly wasn't the first.

Before the thirteen colonies became independent of Great Britain, some artists — usually from other nations — represented America as a half-clad Native woman. (Writer/historian Alton Ketchum attributes this to the international popularity of the Pocahontas legend.) In a sense, the first steps towards the birth of Uncle Sam were taken during the Revolutionary War, with a "character" known as Yankee Doodle.

Initially, "Yankee Doodle" was meant to be an insult, a term used by the British to describe the often ill-clothed and poorly-educated American soldiers. (The name "Doodle" was already in the British frame of reference: in 1750, playwright Henry Fielding's *Tom Thumb the Great* featured characters named Doodle, Noodle and Foodle.) Insult or not, the nickname stuck.

Though Yankee Doodle became more prevalent as a name (and a song) than as an image, most Americans formed the mental picture of an ill-dressed bumpkin whose strength and cunning were more than a match for the better-dressed, better-trained British. This image was one artists and cartoonists would return to when the nation finally established itself.

The creation of a central government a decade later more or less coincided with a renewed interest in Greek architecture and mythology. The combination led to a new American symbol: Columbia. (Initially, Columbia was one of several potential names for the new nation; it eventually turned up in the nation's capital.) In keeping with her Greek lineage, she is usually seen in flowing white garments, although her raiments have often included the stars and stripes.

Most of Columbia's appearances show her acting

as the conscience of the nation, not hesitating, in Alton Ketcham's words, to "lay down the law to other emblems of our national life, not excepting Uncle Sam himself."[1] For the next century, Columbia would be as prevalent an icon of America as Sam. (Eventually, she served as the centerpiece of the Chicago World's Fair of 1893.)

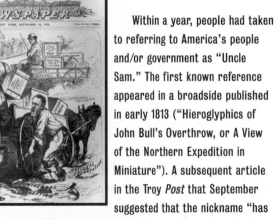

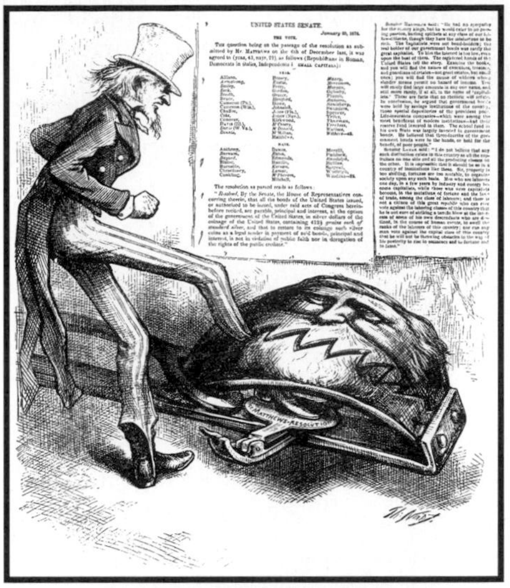

As for Uncle Sam, he came to life during the War of 1812. The United States had ambitions to expand both westward and northward (eventually, the U.S. would take over large amounts of southern territory that had belonged to the Creek Indians, though their advances on British Columbia would be less successful). At the outset of the war, a man named Elbert Anderson had received a one-year contract to supply provisions to troops stationed in New York and New Jersey. Anderson asked potential subcontractors for sealed bids; eventually, the task of supplying and shipping meat to the troops fell to two brothers from Troy, New York — Ebeneezer and Samuel Wilson.

FRANK LESLIE'S
ILLUSTRATED
NEWSPAPER

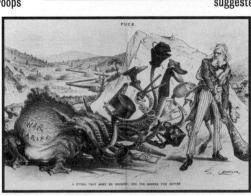

According to an 1830 article in the *New York Gazette*, the legend of Uncle Sam began, literally, as a joke. (Samuel Wilson's great-nephew Lucius credited the remark to an Irish watchman in the Wilsons' employ.) The casks of meat destined for soldiers were marked "E.A.-U.S." The *Gazette* relates:

"This work fell to the lot of a facetious fellow in the employ of the Messrs. Wilson, who, on being asked by some of his fellow workmen the meaning of the mark (for the letters U.S. for United States were almost entirely new to them) said he did not know unless it meant Elbert Anderson and Uncle Sam — alluding exclusively then to the said "Uncle Sam" Wilson. The joke took among the workmen...many of these workmen were found shortly after following the recruiting drum... their old jokes of course accompanied them, and before the first campaign ended, this identical one first appeared in print."[2]

PUCK.
WAR TARIFF

Within a year, people had taken to referring to America's people and/or government as "Uncle Sam." The first known reference appeared in a broadside published in early 1813 ("Hieroglyphics of John Bull's Overthrow, or A View of the Northern Expedition in Miniature"). A subsequent article in the Troy *Post* that September suggested that the nickname "has got almost as current as 'John Bull.' The letters U.S. on the government waggons [sic], etc. are supposed to have given rise to it."[3]

Why an uncle? Ketchum suggests it may have been a partial reaction to the "paternal" nature of the British monarchy, from which the emerging nation had gone to great lengths to remove itself. In *Uncle Sam: The Man and the Legend*, he writes, "An uncle is usually a remote but beneficent stem off the parental branch who brings goodies to American children, tells them stories, and generally makes himself popular without using the rod of authority reserved for parents...This perfectly positions government in the U.S. as a necessary operation which must never under any circumstances forget that it is not a father and has no right to act like one."

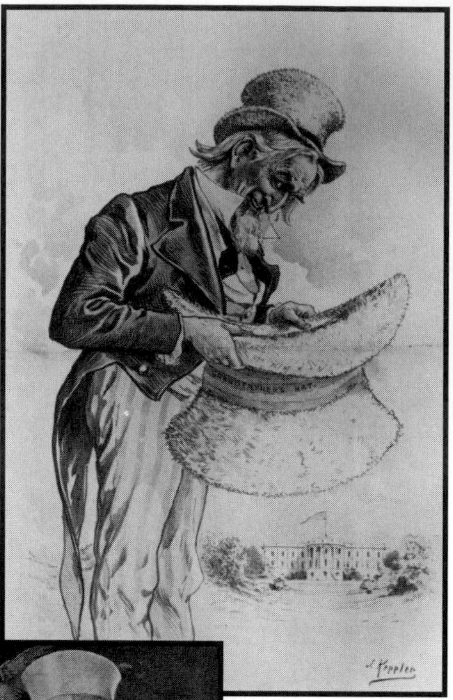

Although the *legend* of Uncle Sam grew rapidly, it would be another two decades before any artist would attempt to draw him. Sam's earliest known appearance is an 1832 cartoon called "Uncle Sam in Danger." An attack on President Andrew Jackson's efforts to destroy the Bank of the United States, it shows Sam — clean-shaven and undistinguished save for a striped robe — on the receiving end of what we can only assume is a not terribly healthy bleeding. (An 1840 cartoon, "Uncle Sam's Pet Pups," has him wearing a top hat and striped trousers but otherwise bearing no resemblance to the Sam of later years.)

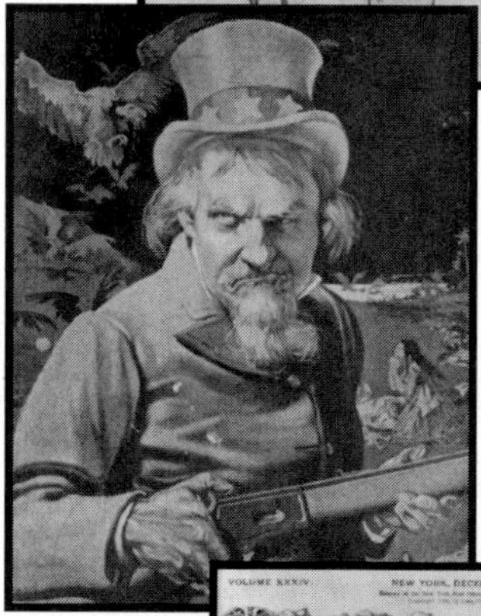

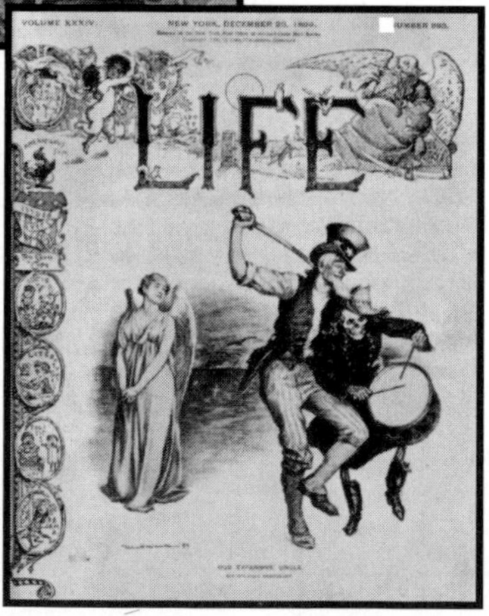
LIFE

In the meantime, cartoonists and lithographers were giving life to Brother Jonathan. Like Yankee Doodle, Jonathan's roots appear to date back to the Revolutionary War. One legend, reported in John Russell Bartlett's *Dictionary of Americanisms*, suggested that "Brother Jonathan" is how General George Washington referred to Connecticut governor Jonathan Trumbull. The story was subsequently disputed in Albert Matthews's 1902 book *Brother Jonathan*, though not even Matthews could provide a definitive origin for the name. (Matthews suggested that the name was used by the British as "a mildly derisive epithet." As with Yankee Doodle, a British insult appears to have been transformed into a badge of honor.)

Alton Ketchum suggests that Brother Jonathan was considerably more mature than the ragged upstart Yankee Doodle, and his simple manner and appearance (one author described Jonathan as "growing so fast that he outgrew his clothes," an appropriate metaphor for the century of expansion to follow) belied his intelligence and good humor. Characters similar to Jonathan were the centerpiece in many stage productions of the time; such plays often centered around attempts (usually made by the British) to trick our hero. By the time the show was over, however, Jonathan had inevitably done the tricking.

During the first half of the nineteenth century, Brother Jonathan was regularly representing the United States in cartoons and lithographs. Along the way, the character's appearance evolved to the point where he could pass as a younger version of Uncle Sam. Usually dark-haired and clean-shaven, Jonathan was presented as a thin, lanky figure with a hawklike nose, clad in a waistcoat, a top hat and striped trousers.

Uncle Sam made the occasional appearance during this period, but there was no firm consensus as to his appearance. That — and a lot of other things about Uncle Sam — would change with the presidency of Abraham Lincoln.

Lincoln was a visually arresting figure, standing well over six feet tall with a distinctive beard to boot. Couple this with the fact that his first term coincided with the Civil War — ostensibly the greatest internal threat America had faced up to this point — and one begins to understand why more and more artists used Lincoln, rather than Brother Jonathan, to represent the nation. With Lincoln's murder in 1865, cartoonists — many of whom had ridiculed the President during the Civil War — began to adapt his likeness for Uncle Sam.

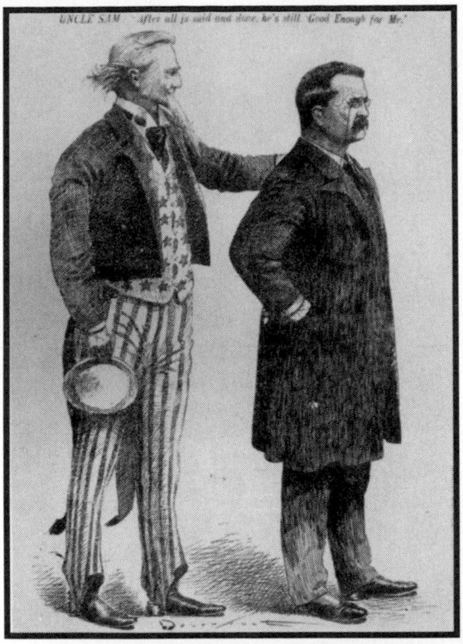

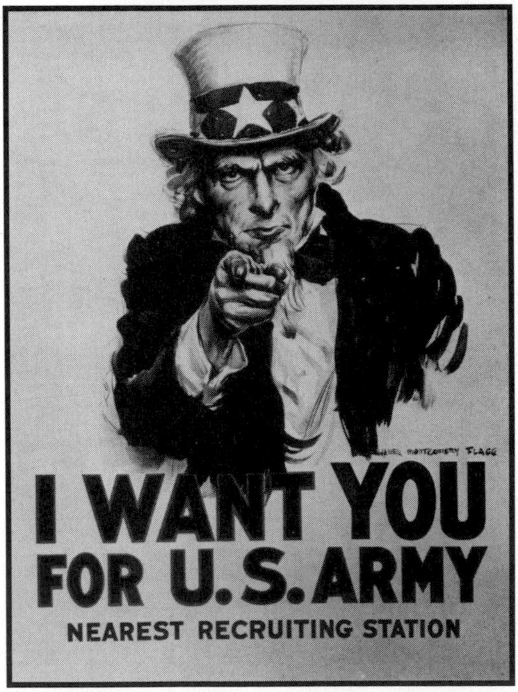
I WANT YOU
FOR U.S. ARMY
NEAREST RECRUITING STATION

Chief among these cartoonists was one who had never ridiculed Lincoln: Thomas Nast. A regular contributor to *Harper's Weekly*, Nast was one of the first cartoonists to insist that his work reflect his own beliefs, not those of his editors. (Nast's attacks on New York politico William "Boss" Tweed are legendary; Ulysses S. Grant credited his Presidential victory to "the sword of Sheridan and the pencil of Thomas Nast.")

Between Nast and his rival Joseph Keppler, the Uncle Sam most Americans know today began to take form. Uncle Sam became lean and long-legged, with a white goatee and an outfit composed of a waistcoat, striped trousers and a top hat. By the 1890s, another addition had been made: Sam's hat was festooned with stars. (Alton Ketchum credits Nast for this innovation.)

By the start of the 20th century, America had taken the first steps towards becoming a world power, and Uncle Sam had supplanted all of his iconic predecessors. There's no formal explanation as to why Columbia fell from favor with visual practitioners, but it does seem to have coincided with America's entry into World War I in 1917 — which means any theory on the subject would have to include James Montgomery Flagg's famous "I Want You" poster.

It is generally believed that Flagg based his painting on a similarly-designed British recruitment poster (drawn by artist Alfred Leete), in which Lord Kitchener insists "Your Country Needs You." Flagg always considered the similarity irrelevant, and rightly so: his own drawing — showing a serious, almost accusing Uncle Sam (Flagg used himself as the model) — is one of the most famous and enduring images produced by any American artist.

Beyond its value as a recruitment device, the "I Want You" poster changed the way the world viewed Uncle Sam. In her book *James Montgomery Flagg*, Susan E. Meyer wrote, "Formerly a benign old man in stars and stripes, Uncle Sam was transformed by Flagg into a compelling leader who meant business. Never again would Uncle Sam be regarded in quite the same manner." Indeed, the image would serve as inspiration for the next generation as well.

"We were living in a time when it was necessary to have heroes who were capable of superheroic capacity, because the enemy was superheroic," Will Eisner said of the days leading into World War II. "I was 22, 23 years old, and Hitler seemed invincible. You'd pick up the morning paper and each day find their army had just marched into another country. We needed an invincible hero to fight an invincible enemy."

Eisner, who cemented his place in comics history with (among other creations) a legendary strip called *The Spirit*, was creating characters for the relatively new medium of comic books; like all creators of the time, he wanted a hero who could compete with Jerry Siegel and Joe Shuster's phenomenally popular Superman. By the time Quality Comics launched *National Comics* in 1940, Eisner had found his hero — Uncle Sam.

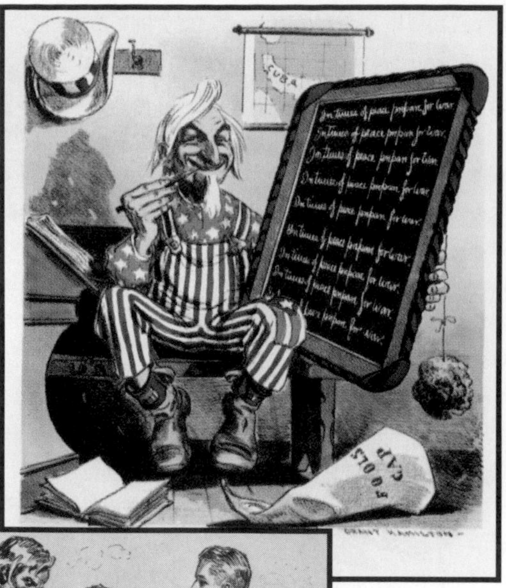

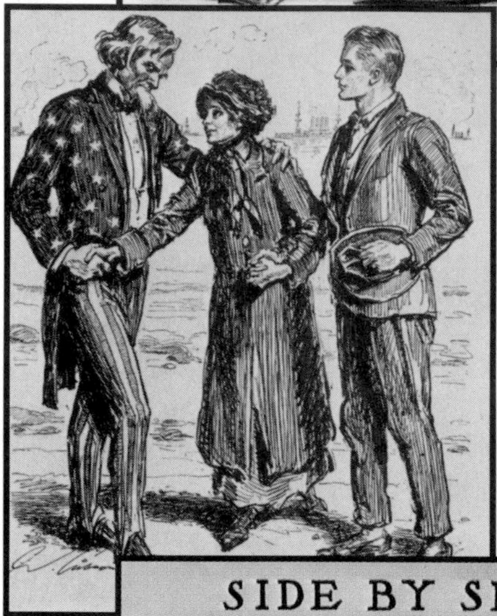

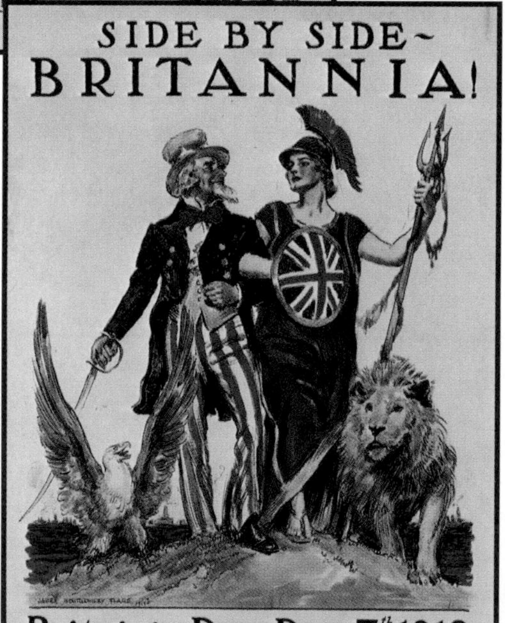
SIDE BY SIDE~
BRITANNIA!
Britain's Day Dec. 7th 1918
MASS MEETING

"As I understood it at the time, the classic way to find heroes was to look for the mythology that we lived with," Eisner recalled. "I picked Sam out because he was a national hero. As far as making him a superhero, that was easy, because that was the convention of the day — actually, it still is."[4]

Inspired by Flagg's no-nonsense figure, Eisner's Uncle Sam was a one-man arsenal of democracy, an easygoing, lanky fellow who was an unstoppable ass-kicker when provoked. (When a member of the fascistic "Purple Shirts" dropped a boulder on Sam's head, the only casualty was the boulder. In true Golden Age comic-book style, Sam eventually gave his assailant a sound thrashing.)

Although Eisner only worked on the character for three issues (handing the chores over to master artist Lou Fine), Sam was routinely featured on the cover of *National Comics* until 1943; a second title, *Uncle Sam Quarterly*, ran until 1944. (Sam returned to comics in the 1970s when DC Comics purchased the rights to a number of old Quality characters. The result was the short-lived FREEDOM FIGHTERS, with subsequent "guest shots" in titles such as ALL-STAR SQUADRON and CRISIS ON INFINITE EARTHS.)

By 1943, of course, America was knee-deep

into the war, and once again, Uncle Sam was there, rolling up his sleeves to tell the world "We'll Finish The Job!" (The artist behind that particular poster — and many others designed to benefit war-related causes — was none other than James Montgomery Flagg.)

America emerged from World War II the most powerful nation in history. Over the ensuing decades, Americans learned some of the costs of that power. In 1964, the University of Michigan's Survey Research Center had asked, "Is the government run by a few big interests looking out for themselves?" Twenty-six percent answered "Yes." By 1972, those answering "Yes" totaled 53%. Cartoonists of this period tended to treat Sam as a tired old man who found himself, his government and/or his people out of control. (Many images from this period were direct parodies of James Montgomery Flagg's masterwork, including one where a battered, bewildered Sam insists "I Want Out.")

From that point on, a lot of what gave Uncle Sam his power was now in the past. After the wrenching experiences Americans had witnessed or been privy to over the last three decades (and the lies and denial that often surrounded such disclosures) the idea that Americans in this day and age would unanimously rally around anyone — especially a figure meant to represent the American government — might seem rather naive.

Whether that is good or bad is a subject for another debate. For now, let us simply suggest that no other joke about a meat packer has ever done so much to — or for — a nation.

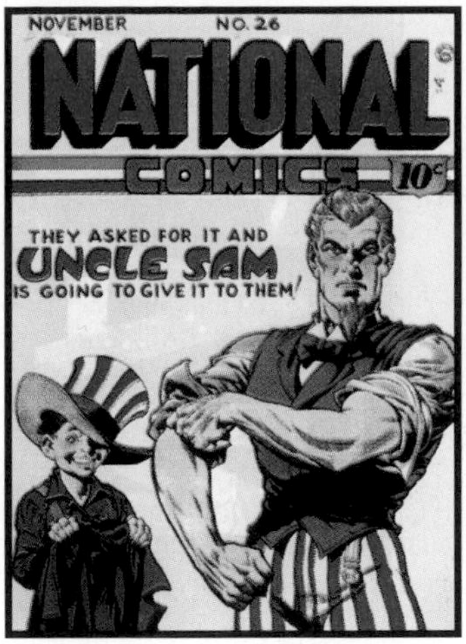
NOVEMBER
NO. 26
NATIONAL
COMICS
10¢
THEY ASKED FOR IT AND
UNCLE SAM
IS GOING TO GIVE IT TO THEM!

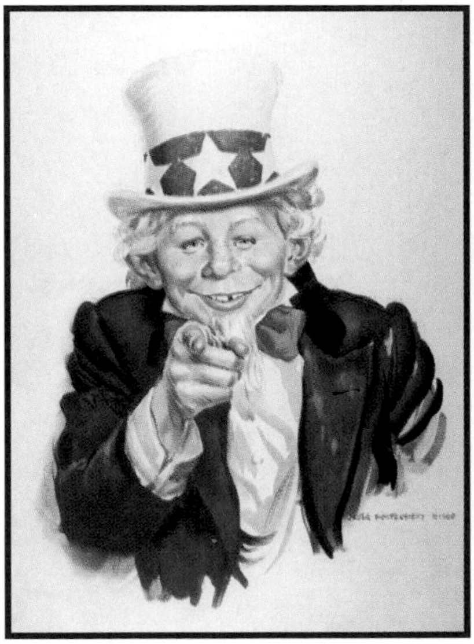

ILLUSTRATION KEY

1) THE RECONCILIATION BETWEEN BRITANNIA AND HER DAUGHTER AMERICA - A British propaganda cartoon circa 1782.
2) FIFTY-FOUR FORTY OR FIGHT! - Brother Jonathan, the cartoon ancestor of Uncle Sam (the smaller man on the right) displays the willingness to put up a fight with England for what became the northwestern boundary of the United States.
3) THE FIRST STEP TOWARD NATIONAL BANKRUPTCY - Uncle Sam by Thomas Nast, circa 1878.
4) THE CENTENNIAL RACE - Cartoonist Joseph Keppler's 1876 prediction that Democratic presidential candidate Samuel Tilden would defeat Republican candidate Rutherford B. Hayes did not come true.
5) A HYDRA THAT MUST BE CRUSHED — AND THE SOONER THE BETTER - Joseph Keppler, 1888.
6) WHERE IS HE? - Joseph Keppler's 1892 cartoon designed to emphasize Harrison's lack of stature as president. Harrison was defeated by Grover Cleveland.
7) SPANISH JUSTICE AND HONOR BE DARNED! - Artist unknown, circa 1898. Soon after the start of the Spanish-American War.
8) William H. Walker used Uncle Sam to opposed the war in Spain in this 1899 cover of LIFE.
9) IN TIMES OF PEACE, PREPARE FOR WAR - Grant Hamilton uses Sam as a student to illustrate the lessons learned from the war with Spain.
10) Sam lends his support to the 1904 campaign of Teddy Roosevelt in this cartoon by Homer Davenport.
11) I WANT YOU! - This familiar watercolor by James Montgomery Flagg was the cover of *Leslie's Weekly* before it was used as an army recruiting poster in 1917.
12) Uncle Sam as drawn by Charles Dana Gibson
13) SIDE BY SIDE, BRITANNIA - A 1918 poster depicting the U.S. alliance with Britain during World War I.
14) An Uncle Sam circa World War II by the great Lou Fine on the cover of NATIONAL COMICS #26
15) Alfred E. Neuman in a parody of the J.M. Flagg painting for the cover of MAD Magazine #126, April 1969

BIBLIOGRAPHY:

-John Russell Bartlett, *Dictionary of Americanisms*, Little Brown, Boston, 1859.
-Stephen Hess and Milton Kaplan, *The Ungentlemanly Art*, Macmillan Company, New York, 1975.
-Alton Ketchum, *Uncle Sam: The Man and The Legend*, Hill and Wang, New York, 1960.
-Susan E. Meyer, *James Montgomery Flagg*, Watson-Gupkill Publications, New York, 1974.
-Albert Bigelow Paine, *Thomas Nast: His Period and His Pictures*, Macmillan Company, New York, 1904.
-Richard Samuel West, *Satire on Stone: The Political Cartoons of Joseph Keppler*, University of Illinois Press, Urbana, Ill., 1988
-Howard Zinn, *A People's History of the United States*, HarperCollins Publishers, New York, 1995.

FOOTNOTES:

1—Alton Ketchum, *Uncle Sam: The Man and the Legend*, p. 24
2—Ibid, p. 40
3—Ibid, p. 42
4—Conversation with Will Eisner, September 29, 1998.

ICONOGRAPHY:

THE ARTWORK OF UNCLE SAM

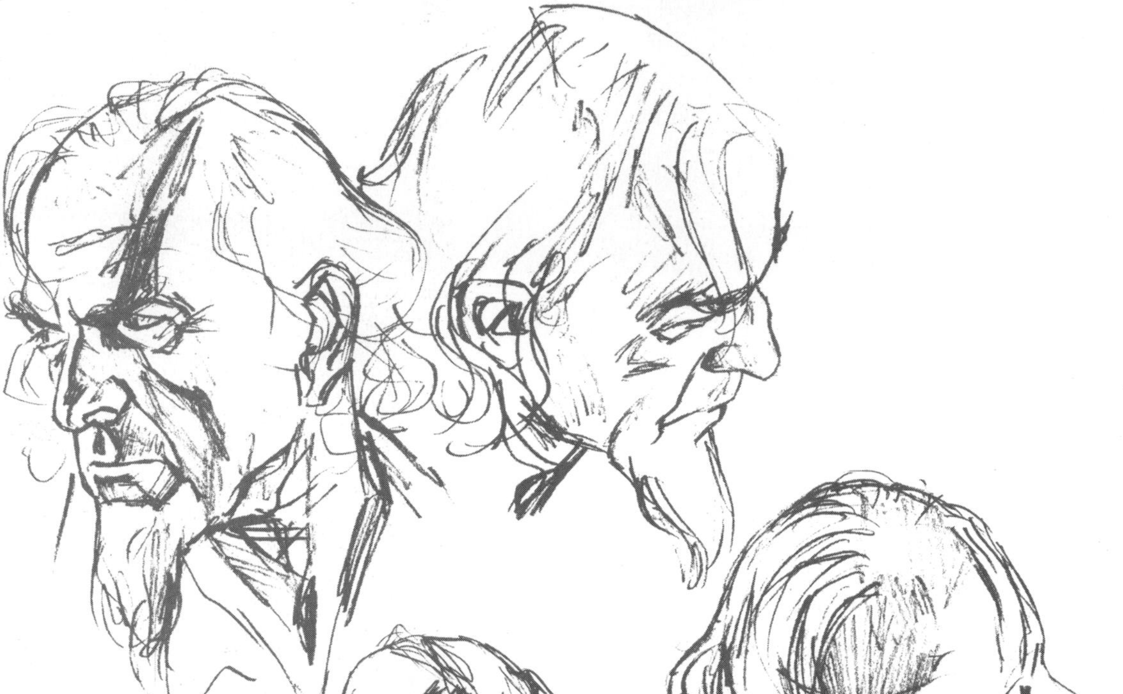

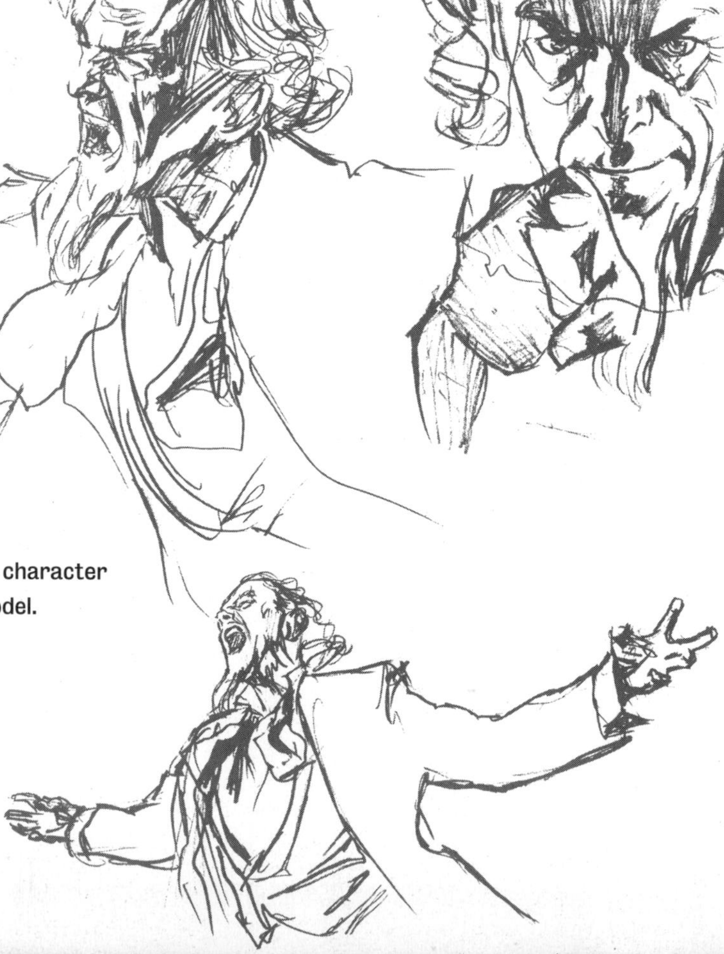

Initial studies of the character based on the live model.

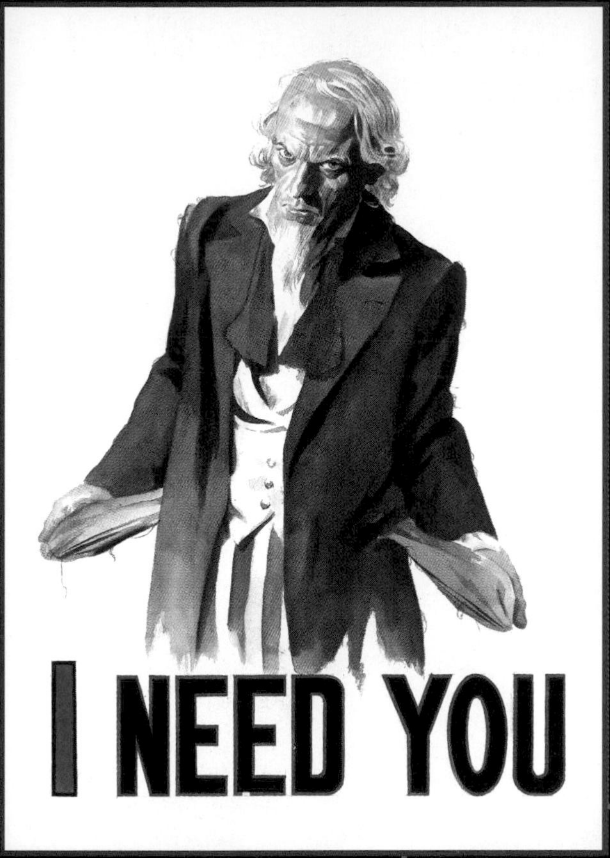
I NEED YOU

Promotional image used for DC Comics retailer flyers.

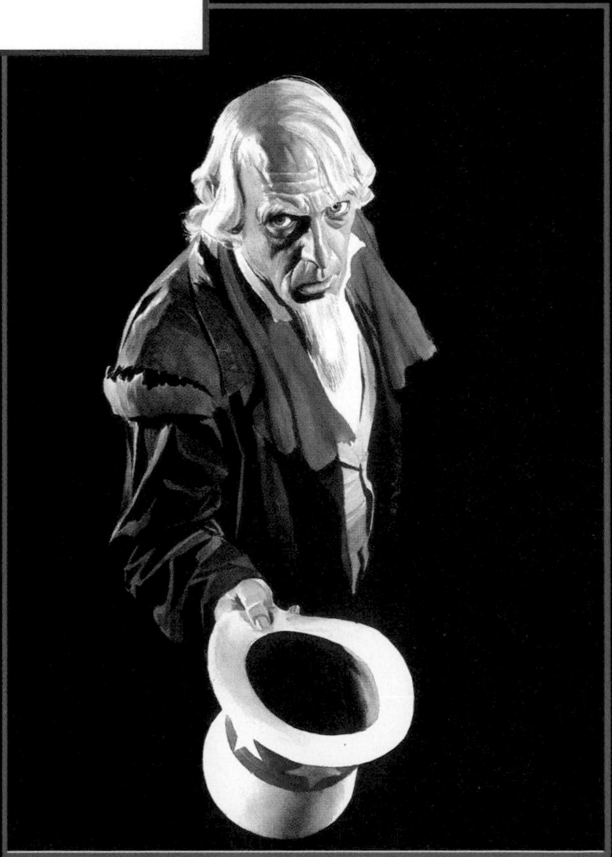

Artwork created for the 1997 San Diego Comicon.

Artwork created for the
T-shirt from Graphitti Designs.

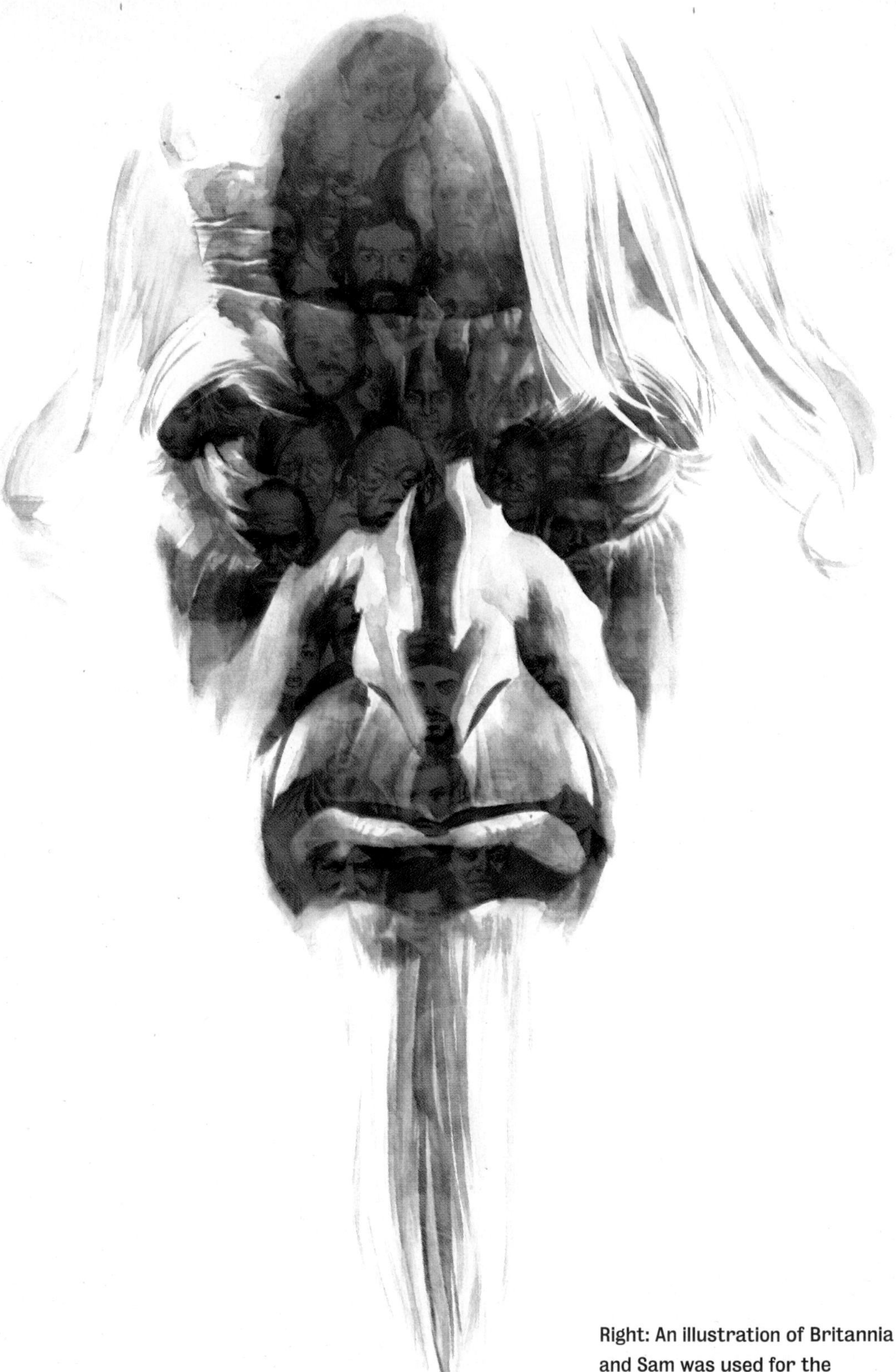

Right: An illustration of Britannia
and Sam was used for the
UKCAC Convention program.

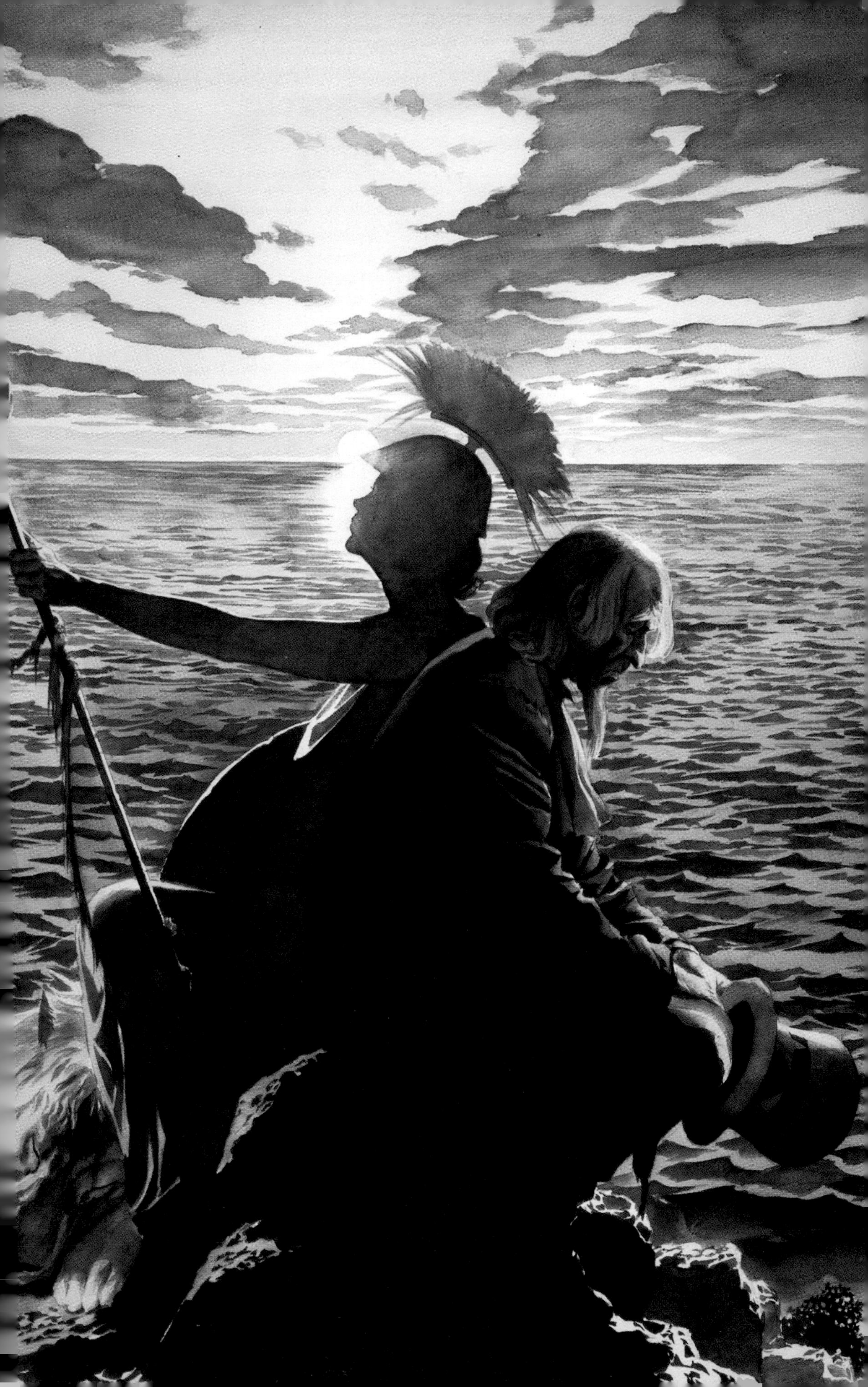

DARKNESS AND DREAMS!
CONTEMPORARY GRAPHIC NOVELS FROM TITAN BOOKS!
All VERTIGO backlist books are suggested for mature readers

THE SANDMAN: PRELUDES & NOCTURNES
Neil Gaiman/Sam Kieth/Various
ISBN 1 85286 326 9

THE SANDMAN: THE DOLL'S HOUSE
Neil Gaiman/
Mike Dringenberg/Malcolm Jones III
ISBN 1 85286 292 0

THE SANDMAN: DREAM COUNTRY
Neil Gaiman/Various
ISBN 1 85286 441 9

THE SANDMAN: SEASON OF MISTS
Neil Gaiman/Various
ISBN 1 85286 447 8

THE SANDMAN: A GAME OF YOU
Neil Gaiman/Various
ISBN 1 85286 478 8

THE SANDMAN: BRIEF LIVES
Neil Gaiman/Jill Thompson/
Vince Locke
ISBN 1 85286 534 2

THE SANDMAN: FABLES AND REFLECTIONS
Neil Gaiman/Various
ISBN 1 85286 497 4

THE SANDMAN: WORLDS' END
Neil Gaiman/Various
ISBN 1 85286 609 8

THE SANDMAN: THE KINDLY ONES
Neil Gaiman/Various
Hardcover - ISBN: 1 85286 718 3
Softcover - ISBN: 1 85286 638 7

THE SANDMAN: THE WAKE
Neil Gaiman/Various
Hardcover-ISBN: 1 85286 773 6
Softcover-ISBN: 1 85286 807 4

**THE SANDMAN: DUST COVERS —
THE COLLECTED SANDMAN COVERS
1989–1997**
Dave McKean/Neil Gaiman
ISBN: 1 85286 846 5

BLACK ORCHID
Neil Gaiman/Dave McKean
ISBN: 1 85286 336 6

DEATH: THE HIGH COST OF LIVING
Neil Gaiman/Chris Bachalo
ISBN 1 85286 498 2

DEATH: THE TIME OF YOUR LIFE
Neil Gaiman/Chris Bachalo/
Mark Buckingham/Mark Pennington
ISBN 1 85286 817 1

WITCHCRAFT
James Robinson/Teddy
Kristiansen/Steve Yeowell
ISBN 1 85286 767 1

THE BOOKS OF MAGIC
Neil Gaiman/John Bolton/Various
ISBN 1 85286 470 2

THE BOOKS OF MAGIC: BINDINGS
John Ney Rieber/Gary Amaro/
Peter Gross
ISBN 1 85286 611 X

THE BOOKS OF MAGIC: SUMMONINGS
John Ney Rieber/Peter Gross/Various
ISBN 1 85286 716 7

THE BOOKS OF MAGIC: RECKONINGS
John Ney Rieber/Peter
Snejbjerg/Various
ISBN: 1 85286 804 X

PREACHER: GONE TO TEXAS
Garth Ennis/Steve Dillon
ISBN 1 85286 713 2

PREACHER: UNTIL THE END OF THE WORLD
Garth Ennis/Steve Dillon
ISBN 1 85286 786 8

PREACHER: PROUD AMERICANS
Garth Ennis/Steve Dillon
ISBN: 1 85286 850 3

HELLBLAZER: FEAR AND LOATHING
Garth Ennis/Steve Dillon
ISBN 1 85286 819 8

ENIGMA
Peter Milligan/Duncan Fegredo
ISBN 1 85286 615 2

THE INVISIBLES: SAY YOU WANT A REVOLUTION
Grant Morrison/Steve Yeowell/
Jill Thompson
ISBN 1 85286 721 3

VAMPS
Elaine Lee/William Simpson
ISBN 1 85286 627 6

All Titan Books' graphic novels are available through most good bookshops or direct from Titan Books' mail order service. For a free graphic novels catalogue or to order telephone 01536 763 631, or contact Titan Books Mail Order, PO Box 54, Desborough, Northants., NN14 2UH, quoting the reference code specified on the publication information page at the front of the book.

971031